Identity Matters

Communication-Based Explorations and Explanations

edited by

Hartmut B. Mokros

Rutgers University

HAMPTON PRESS, INC.
CRESSKILL, NEW JERSEY

Printed in the United States of America

Library of Congress Cataloging-in-Publication Data

Identity matters : communication-based explorations and explanations / edited by Hartmut B. Mokros
     p. cm.
  Includes bibliographical references and index.
  ISBN 1-57273-409-4 (cl) -- ISBN 1-57273-410-8 (ppb)
    1. Identity (Psychology)--Social aspects. 2. Interpersonal communication.
I. Mokros, Hartmut B., 1949

BF697.5.S65 I33 2003
153.6--dc21

                           2002038803

Hampton Press, Inc.
23 Broadway
Cresskill, NJ 07626

Contents

Preface

Identity matters! This is the argument of this book and also its subject. How identity comes to matter and why it matters is inseparable from communication and it is communication, its investigation, generativity, and explanatory power, that identifies what this book is about as well.

The contributions to this book examine how, when and with what consequence identity is materialized in and through communication practices. Included are studies that target identity from a variety of familiar vantage points that collectively illuminate the relevance of identity for making sense of everyday experience and practice—communicationally. *Age, authority, culture, design, gender, otherness, play, signs* and *support* represent the range of concerns with identity, the types of matters that orient the discussion in the nine communication explorations that follow the first, introductory chapter. They are organized into sections according to three types of communicative engagements: with products and tools of communication (e.g., advertising, architecture, and signs); with distant others through computer-mediated interaction in virtual spaces; and, with physically present others through face-to-face encounter in real-world settings. This approach to the organization of chapters groups together those studies that share comparable methodological issues of data collection, reduction and analysis. Multiple alternative ways are not only possible but sensible and productive for organizing the chapters and the reader should certainly feel free to read along whatever path may suggest itself and not feel constrained by the grouping and sequencing presented.

The eight chapters that follow the introduction are products of doctoral research that each contributor conducted under my supervision, with the first completed in 1996 and the last in 2001. All eight contributors were students in the multidisciplinary Communication, Information and Library Studies PhD program at Rutgers University. These dissertations involved unique and mostly independent programs of research, developed in relative isolation and involved study of quite distinct situations and research questions. Indeed, many of the contributors were unfamiliar with each other's work prior to this book's completion. Yet, I claim in the introduction that the contributions are products of a common program of research, with *Identity Matters*, from this perspective, much more a monograph than an edited volume. The final chapter draws on research I conducted as a doctoral student more than 20 years earlier wherein I began to formulate ideas that subsequently guided my teaching and thinking while working with these individuals. The book's epilogue examines this claim of a common program of research based on an online discussion among its contributors that followed completion of the manuscript.

Even though the phenomena studied and questions of interest vary considerably across contributions, each involves a commitment to the development of communication scholarship through the analysis and interpretation of real-world communication practices. Each study is, to some degree, grounded in a constitutive view that guided my thinking and teaching, a view that regards communication as the crucible of human experience, the source and site of meaning in the world, and the context within and process by which persons are shaped as social and psychological beings. This constitutive view suspends everyday and scholarly assumptions of what communication is, particularly those assumptions that limit communication to manifest messages, felicitous processes or desired message effects. Silence, unemployed possibilities, ambiguity, missteps and insult are as much aspects of communication from this constitutive perspective in addition to those practices characterized as effective, persuasive, or good. Indeed, occasions of silence, unemployed possibilities, ambiguity, missteps and insult, often viewed as failures of communication are argued to be moments when identity becomes relevant to interactants and visible to analytic inquiry. It is only by suspending assumptions about what communication is at the outset that researchers may indeed appreciate its centrality and begin to envision communication-based explanations of phenomena, like identity, typically accounted for through individual-based or system-oriented perspectives.

A constitutive view attempts to move past strategic, outcome-oriented and informational senses of communication so as to consider how the doing of communication invariably produces and engenders social spaces within which issues of who we are, and how who we are, matter. Such activ-

ities shape and reconfigure local renditions of social order, based in enduring systems of cultural value. These systems of cultural value and expressive
possibility are themselves viewed as products of communication practice
even as they vitalize moments of interaction. And such activities exhibit
interactionally, and stimulate through reflection, experiences of confirmation
and disconfirmation, senses of self and other, and thereby the very sense
and quality of being in the world. Issues or questions of identity, questions
about how we come to represent the things of this world, and how we come
to represent ourselves to ourselves and experience ourselves represented by
others are inescapable tensions of everyday being.

Within this constitutive perspective questions of identity constantly
matter, for the social cultural spaces created by communication invariably
reference the psychosocial value of the participants within them. Identity
may thereby be treated as a product (and more often than not a byproduct)
of communication, constituted through the interface of potential practices
(i.e., discursive resources or possibilities), those practices actually instantiated within relational activities, and reflections on the relationship between
potential practices and observable relational activities. Identity from this
perspective represents an ever-present dimension, indeed an unavoidable
indexicality of lived experience with identity then a matter that is thoroughly communicational.

Each contribution explores identity by attending to communication
processes and practices within a clearly focused and meaningful real-world
setting. Each grapples with identifying methods of data collection and analysis appropriate to the implications of a constitutive perspective and sensitive
to the nature of the phenomenon being investigated. What is common
across these studies is best described as a marriage of descriptive methods
and interpretive/critical theorizing. The approach involves movement
through three general stages of inquiry: systematic description of a communicative event or phenomenon being studied that produces a map of this
event or phenomenon; analysis of the contours, features, and terrain of this
map; and, critical interrogation and interpretation of the descriptive and
analytic accounts produced.

Apparent across contributions to this book, in what their explorations reveal, is the inescapable relevance of identity in human relationships, be it to physically present others or to how aspects of human product
design convey senses of possible or expected models of identity to those
who engage them. What is equally apparent is the roughness, contradiction
and expansiveness that seemingly simple, innocent and no doubt well-
intentioned acts of communication engender. This is why identity matters
and why its exploration within and explanation through communication
appears so productively interesting.

Acknowledgments

Many individuals merit acknowledgement for their contributions to the production of this book. First and foremost are the former doctoral students whose work is contained in this volume. Without their agreement to contribute to this project there would be no book. And without their willingness to engage with my ideas and trust me as their dissertation supervisor during a hectic, at times chaotic and rather all consuming 5-year period during which I chaired my department, there would have been no research program and no clear record of my scholarly thinking through empirical study of identity matters. This book is most certainly a gesture of appreciation for their significant contribution; the creation of a space in my life devoted to scholarship. I especially thank Christine Lemesianou for writing the epilogue and Hester Coan for assistance with the index and the much more that both contributed throughout.

The influence of my teachers is apparent throughout the pages of this volume. Norman McQuown set me in a direction of scholarship I had never envisioned prior to arriving at the University of Chicago as a graduate student. He introduced me to microanalysis and the pioneering work of Gregory Bateson and those significant others who collaborated in this pioneering multidisciplinary approach that sought to develop a natural history of communication. McQuown also introduced me to Starkey Duncan, Jr., whose research program advanced a systematic approach to the study of interaction structure and strategy developed from the work conducted by Bateson and his colleagues. Duncan guided my dissertation and most certainly his teaching and support of my thinking have made this book possible. Donald Fiske, David McNeill, Michael Silverstein, Gerry Suttles and Stephen Toulmin were other teachers at Chicago that also really mattered.

My colleagues since joining the department of communication at Rutgers University, along with colleagues at SCILS provided grounding, support and challenge within which to develop my ideas. Brent Ruben has consistently provided me a space to share and explore ideas. Mark Aakhus, Getinet Belay, Nick Belkin, Dave Gibson, Radha Hegde, Jim Katz, Bob Kubey, Carol Kuhlthau, Linda Lederman, Lea Lievrouw, Jenny Mandelbaum, Tefko Saracevic, Jorge Schement, and Lea Stewart have been helpful and supportive in multiple ways. My former colleague, Stan Deetz stands alone in his influence on my thinking and support of the ideas I wished to express and work out.

Multiple colleagues across disciplines have commented on and influenced my thinking in the development of this book with special thanks to Donal Carbaugh and Robert Craig for their helpful comments at the 2001 ICA conference in response to presentations of drafts of most of the chapters included in this book. Tom Scheff has been a source of influence for more than a decade and most certainly was more a teacher than colleague in the development of my thinking generally. And Margaret Carr and Jan Levinsohn Milner provided useful reads that assisted me in bringing closure to the manuscript.

This book was developed while on sabbatical after a five-year tour of duty as department chair. I appreciate the support and encouragement of Dean Gus Friedrich in making this possible. The idea for this book emerged in spring 2000 as I approached my sabbatical leave, with a formal prospectus circulated among colleagues and publishers that October. The decision to publish with Hampton Press in the last days of that year would not have occurred without Ron Rice's assistance. I was, at the time, trying to decide between two publishers and had sought the advice of my colleagues. Ron complicated my ability to choose, suggesting that I consider Hampton Press as a potential publisher and placed me in touch with Barbara Bernstein. Ron's review of the prospectus was supportive and more importantly productive as he urged me to expand the proposed introduction. Don Cegala, as the series editor for Hampton Press, reviewed the prospectus and endorsed the project and ultimately convinced me that Hampton Press was the right publisher. His comments on the completed manuscript improved its quality and also resulted in the addition of the epilogue. Barbara Bernstein interrupted her busy life to quickly turn around a contract offer so that I indeed might be able to include Hampton as a choice among publishers. Indeed, Barbara has been an absolute pleasure to work with. Her efforts on behalf of scholars within the field of communication has been impressive to say the least. Many thanks indeed to Ron, Don and Barbara.

Finally, there are two groups of individuals who merit acknowledgment and sincere appreciation. First among these are the many people who allowed us access to the sacred world of their everyday activities in all its complexity. Second, there is my family; the one that gave me origins, and the one that I have made as it places me in a context of personal meaning and connection. My parents and brother, through their struggles to quite literally survive and live on, and their will to place me in a context where such struggles would not again occur have grounded my career choices and what I have came to see as enduring interests: what exactly identity is and how communication works. My children assisted with editing references, proofreading at various stages, and ideas for a book cover. As their father, this is a source of great pride to be sure. But it is not just assistance and resulting pride that I appreciate. It is indeed the meaningful co-presence they provide and the hopes they inspire that is most certainly not only a bedrock for who I am but also quite clearly apparent in how I have come to articulate the feeling that underlies answers to this question.

Princeton, New Jersey

October 3, 2002

I

INTRODUCTION

1

A Constitutive Approach
to Identity

Hartmut B. Mokros

My aim in this chapter is to contextualize a program of research and approach to inquiry that guided the development of contributions to *Identity Matters*. This research examines identity from a communicational perspective (cf. Hecht, 1993; Pearce, 1989) approached in the studies contained in this book through the analysis of *communication products* (e.g., architecture, print advertising, online databases) and *permanent recordings* (e.g., audiotapes, computer logs, videotapes) of meaningful events obtained from real-world contexts. Such events involve the engagement of individuals with products, systems, or social others and may be described as natural histories or everyday units of communication that are treated as psychologically and socially meaningful in the social world. Recordings of such events are "entextualized" (Silverstein & Urban, 1996) from everyday contexts where they are but moments within a continuous natural history of meaningful worldly activities. For this reason, *contextual familiarity* developed through participant-observation anchors the selection and entextualization of specific products or recordings extracted or removed from these contexts within this research program. These records are first studied descriptively through *microanalysis*. Interpretive and critical inquiry is systematically grounded in *descriptive mappings of the natural history of the recorded event* as developed through the initial stages of microanalytic inquiry. A key goal of these efforts is the development of *communication explanations* of identity (Deetz, 1994). The look of such explanations oriented my work with the eight former doctoral students who contribute chapters to this book.

IDENTITY MATTERS: AN OVERVIEW

A constitutive view of communication (Mokros, 1996; Mokros & Deetz, 1996; Mokros, Mullins, & Saracevic, 1995) has guided the development of this research. It is a view that takes seriously the centrality of communication for making sense of personal and social being generally, in the sense that this has been articulated by a number of significant 20th-century scholars (e.g., Bateson, 1996; Goffman, 1967; Jakobson, 1990; Mead, 1934; Sapir, 1949; Vygotsky, 1978). By extension, it encourages the researcher to envision communication as a mode of explanation (Deetz, 1994) for personal and social being, not just a site, phenomenon, or process.

Direct study of communication as a phenomenon, nevertheless, represents a first step for developing communication explanations and this aims to achieve two things. First, it aims to expose to exploration the researcher's implicit assumptions about communication, based in native or everyday understandings and scholarly or privileged accounts (Mokros, 1993), and thereby seeks to encourage, generally, an attitude of skepticism as foundational to the research act. Second, this challenging of one's implicit explanatory assumptions of what communication or identity is (e.g., Carbaugh, 1996), aims to enhance appreciation of the complexity of communication. This then presents the researcher a quite daunting task, of how one might systematically or methodically approach communication in the context of some specific interest or problem.

Although method issues represent important considerations, as discussed in more detail later, and as notable in each of the chapters included in this book, method is only of interest in so far as it contributes to the possibilities of developing communication explanations. As hinted at earlier, implicitly held assumptions about communication, for example, as either an outcome—as effective, good, informative, persuasive, or productive—or as a phenomenon—as messages or processes of message exchange—preclude the possibilities of such explanations. These types of communication orientations, by and large, offer cognitive or macro-system explanations. Cognitive explanations prioritize the individual and thereby treat communication as a tool employed by cognitive beings to achieve individually and internally based goals and purposes. System explanations, as for example appeals to culture, prioritize the system and thereby treat communication as symbolic or ritual activity through which cultural values and ideals are expressed in everyday activities as the "native's point of view" (Geertz, 1976). A constitutive view envisions explanations that are neither grounded in the individual nor the system as the unit of analysis. It imagines explanations of individuals and systems from the perspective of communication. This then assumes that communication produces and reproduces systems of order and meaning through the everyday practices of individuals in interaction, in moments of communicational engagement. It is the aim of this research to offer first approximations of communication explanations in the context of identity. Assuming that identity may be usefully conceptualized as produced communicationally, it is then the goal of this research to study how communication positions identity as practically relevant, in context.

The practical relevance of identity may be understood in terms of the types of problems contributors to this book sought to address in their research programs. These include considerations of identity within face-to-face, mediated, and idealized contexts, such as globalization and semiotic spaces; within encounters with communication or media products; within unfocused, playful, and work-related activities; and, within contexts defined by the motivated efforts of individuals to seek and deliver task-related assistance or service, develop skills and provide instruction, make collective decisions, deal with life-threatening illness, and resolve contextually based relational crises.

Each of these lines of inquiry was organized by one or more of these problems or considerations. Concern with how "identity matters," as an issue of contextual production and contextual relevance, defines the common motive across the range of problems that focus the interests of these researchers.

IDENTITY IN CONTEXT

The contributions to, and general spirit of this line of research is but one development within the context of a broad rethinking of identity, be it the identity of the individual, group, or things generally. This rethinking has raised fundamental questions about the common everyday and scholarly definitional sense of identity as an essential or given property of, for example, a person as a gendered being or a word as merely a referring term that points to some real-world object.

Identity as the Definition of Things

Considerations of identity are quite commonly thought of as philosophical concerns related to questions about the nature of the world and the nature of being and existence generally. From a philosophical perspective, questions of identity involve questions about the things that make up this world. Is the world to be thought of as composed of objects and forces or is it to be thought of in terms of interactive systems or processes with objects in a sense byproducts of these processes? This question is, of course, inseparable from consideration of how we can possibly know about such matters.

The Western tradition has tended to favor an "objects and forces" view of the world, as composed of things that are affected by forces that potentially act on these things. Within this tradition, identity represents a statement about the essential properties of a thing or force (as a thing). This is reflected in dictionary definitions wherein identity is "the condition or fact of being the same in all qualities under consideration; sameness; oneness" (*Webster's New World Dictionary*). This definition presupposes a world independent of our thinking about it, independent of how we might come to know it: one composed of things and forces. That is to say, it assumes a reality independent of our characterizations of it, a reality that can be captured and described.

The invention of the dictionary and such similar repositories of knowledge, such as the encyclopedia, and, more recently, the textbook (and maybe even method and theory courses) presuppose such a reality. These developments date from the Enlightenment, particularly the efforts of 18th-century French *Philosophes* (e.g., Diderot, Montesquieu, Voltaire) who sought to package facts that would guard and deliver individuals from systems of oppression (i.e., the church, nature, and nobility) and everyday superstition (see Becker, 1932). Packaged, factual knowledge places tools at the hands of, and indeed "in" individuals through popular education, enabling them thereby to modernize the world by mitigating its power to dominate humankind.

The dictionary is approached and treated on an everyday basis as a catalogue of labels (words) that represent features of reality that may be said to have an identity. Words are treated as labels of things in the world with definitions providing descriptive statements or accounts of the reality of these things. The dictionary invites us to think of words as representations of reality that are captured through observation and "inscription" (cf. Geertz, 1973; Ricoeur, 1981; Silverstein & Urban, 1996), a writing down of what *is*. Observation captures how reality is reflected or mirrored, whose inscription language and language-like systems (e.g., iconography) make possible.

Within this view, whether we sufficiently and accurately account for reality is a matter of observational limitations or the inadequate application of the tools of inscription.

The dictionary's representational bias creates the illusion that limits on inscription are minor once human observational difficulties are resolved through discovery of a phenomenon or the invention of new observational tools. Thus, words are invented, from this perspective, to label things in the world, to label features of reality that had not previously been observed clearly. Most dictionaries reveal this invention process by tracing the history of the word—its etymology. The *Oxford English Dictionary* (*OED*) entry for *identity* speculates its invention as follows: "Need was evidently felt of a noun of condition or quality . . . to express the notion of 'sameness,' side by side with those of 'likeness' and 'oneness'. . . ." Once invented, descriptive definition follows. The invention addresses a need to support inscription based on observation that definition ultimately resolves by stating what kind of "thing" identity is. The OED definition parallels *Webster's*: "the quality or condition of being the same in substance, composition, nature, properties, or in particular qualities under consideration; absolute or essential sameness; oneness."

Dictionaries are not just places where one looks up what a word means and how it might be used. Much more fundamentally, the dictionary conditions a view that words present an account of our knowledge of the world as it has been inscribed through linguistic inventions. What this suggests is that dictionaries do not merely tell us about the world but also encourage a particular way of thinking about knowledge and its production. This privileges the existence of a reality independent of human engagement in the world. It privileges an account of reality based on observation, and not just this, but an orientation to observation that assumes observation to be a direct relationship between the observer and the observed. It privileges a view of language as a tool for labeling those things observed, with what is observed and labeled, merely a reflection of reality (e.g., Stewart, 1996).

If the dictionary encourages a particular way of thinking about knowledge, then it is important to consider the consequences of this for conceptualizing "being in the world." This is meant to invite consideration as to whether words are merely tools for knowledge production or whether they also influence or shape thinking to some degree (e.g., Vygotsky, 1962; Wittgenstein, 1958), including thinking about such things as identity. This line of argument was developed in the early decades of the 20th century by the linguistic anthropologist Edward Sapir (1949) and elaborated by his student and colleague Benjamin Lee Whorf (1956) in a way that deserves a closer look among those who are interested in the possibility of offering communication explanations. Sapir asserted: "The fact of the matter is that the 'real world' is to a large extent unconsciously built up on the language habits of the group. . . . We see and hear and otherwise experience very largely as we do because the language habits of our community predispose certain choices of interpretation" (cited in Whorf, 1956, p. 134).

Sapir here anticipated interest in constitutivity as an explanatory term and concept within a broad-based view of human reality as socially constructed (cf. Berger & Luckmann, 1966) within contemporary scholarship of the human sciences.

A Constitutive (re)View(ing) of Identity

The appeal of *constitutivity* is apparent across the disparate yet interrelated literatures that have come to fall under the rubric of social theory and postmodernism (e.g., Faubion, 1995b). Within these literatures, identity is positioned in relationship to assumptions about language, knowledge and its production, social organization, and individuals as key aspects of a fundamental critique of the social world produced (invisibly) through the particular profile of modernist assumptions about these things.

These literatures view lives as positioned—positioned as identities, not persons with identities. Identities are defined socially, through politicized semiotic distinctions, such as gender, race, or other social statuses and the hierarchy of significations these distinctions invite and appropriate within the social world. Such apparently biologically based distinctions as gender and race, are argued to be historical developments that have much more to do with enduring patterns of domination and subordination than evolutionary differentiation. Patterns of domination and subordination are most certainly apparent in the relationship of elites to marginalized minorities (or majorities) historically. And, it is indeed the case that historical patterns of marginalization, by gender (e.g., Ortner, 1996), race (e.g., West, 1994), and colonial domination (e.g., Said, 1979), for example, have shaped the trajectory of these literatures and their concerns over identity. Such perpetuating patterns of marginalization have led to widespread struggles to undo the fixity of associations that accompany being Black, being woman, or being "exotic" and the costs that these fixed associations impose on the ability to participate freely within and across societies.

Nevertheless, the employment of the term *constitutive*, and thereby its appeal and appropriation, may also be understood in relation to an enduring problem for the human sciences that may be thought of as a conversation with the Enlightenment, with Kant in particular (see Faubion, 1995a). That problem is how to account for the relationship between the micro and the macro (e.g., Mokros, 1995), the individual and society (e.g.,

Elias, 1991), or agency and structure (e.g., Giddens, 1979) without appealing to a transcendental subject and a world of ideas as separable from phenomena. In these contexts, constitutivity captures the recursive or dialectic tension between these levels, rather than treating them as analytically independent. This is expressed as interest in the constitution of the subject, the constitution of society, the constitution of knowledge, and the constitution of subject practices in the social world, for example.

The social world is thought of as a semiotic world, a world organized by meaning that guides the subject's actions and perceptions, generatively. This is a world of multiple and competing discourses, or organized systems of meaning that impose an order of things and structure thought and action, namely practices in the world, such that systems of meaning are reproduced through everyday practices. The generativity of discourse enables the very possibility of meaning, the very idea of everyday practices, and shapes everyday engagements within the world, in habitual or routinized ways. The notion that the world is made of things is an example, as is, by extension, the concept of the individual as an autonomous rational agent. These discursive orientations are apparent in wordly practices especially in metapragmatic accounts of practice, namely, discourses about practice that presuppose a given, common sense world. In this sense discourses may be thought of as constituting space, that of the social world in its population, a semiotic surround within which the subject practices.

Structuration theory (e.g., Giddens, 1984) represents but one of the seminal privileged discourses that attempt to reconcile the relationship between structural systems and everyday practices (cf. Bourdieu, 1977; Foucault, 1972; Habermas, 1987), and thereby aims to account for the reproduction and production of (and in) lived experience generally. Reproduction references concerns with continuity over time as exhibited in time. In other words, everyday practices by individuals reproduce a variety of often competing discourses that define macro-systems. In contrast, production is a concern with change in the disciplining discourses that organize the subject's everyday practices. The problem here is to make sensible how shifts in disciplining discourses may be understood as "inventions" produced in the context of habitual everyday practices, particularly those that become socially appropriated as new discourses or as amendments to existing discursive formations (see Giddens, 1992).

Considerations of identity have been prominent in these literatures, especially cultural studies, feminism, and social constructionism. These literatures are quite consistent in their approach to identity, in their formulation of the "nature" and condition of the human "subject." Identity is to be viewed not as fixed but malleable. Identity is not of the person, or of a culture or society. Tendencies to personify macro-systems (e.g., Benedict, 1959) are wholly rejected. Instead, the subject is viewed as historically and structurally situated and conditioned but not in a holistic sense. For, as previously suggested, these efforts seek to understand the relationship between the micro and macro as an ongoing dynamic process and to thereby make consistency through time, and historical transformations, or changes, sensible. Common across these literatures is an emphasis on language and power as generative systems that produce identity, both in terms of how we conceptualize it and how it functions in the social world. Indeed, language, or, more appropriately, semiotics (e.g., Saussure, 1969), and power (e.g., Foucault, 1977) are viewed to constitute cultures, societies, knowledge, and their histories as meaningfully organized and as meaningful organizers of everyday practice.

The use of the word *practice* (e.g., Bourdieu, 1990) to describe everyday human activities is a noteworthy related development. Practice offers an alternative to such terms as *behavior, action,* and *performance* commonly used to characterize an individual's activities in the world. Drawing on speech act theory (Austin, 1962), the word *performativity* offers another alternative (e.g., Butler, 1990). The appeal to performativity would appear to be in reaction to the structurally (and utilitarian) focused theoretical employment of *practice* (e.g., de Certeau, 1984) and *performance* (e.g., Goffman, 1959). Performativity focuses anew on the agency of the subject whose enactments of gender, for example, "are constitutive—not merely attributes—of identity" (Kondo, 1997, p. 7).

Distinctions among these words reflect quite differing orientations to the source of activity (e.g., the mind of the individual or the generativity of structural systems) and thereby positions about the intentionality and meaningfulness of activity and the value of these concepts generally. Words like *behavior* and *action* reflect a view of the person as an autonomous psychological agent with a fixed sense of identity. In contrast, *practice, performance,* and *performativity* appeal to engagement with the world through a set of organizing routines that are not properties of a person but matters of engagement. These words forefront identity, not as fixed or singular, but rather as individuals engaging in the world. These words may be said to theorize in practice, not merely refer. Thus, the struggle over what to call people's activities appears to reflect ontological considerations, a move away from humans as things toward a view of them as relational beings.

Constitutive Views and the Field of Communication

As mentioned at the outset, the research on identity reported in this volume was developed within a constitutive view of communication. Within the field of communication, many scholars have worked within what might be called a constitutive perspective (e.g., Cronen, 1995; Gergen, 1991, 1994; Pearce, 1989; Shotter, 1996; Sigman, 1995). Craig (1999) and Deetz (1994) noted the general relevance of such a view for the study of communication, with identity a key concern for both. However, these two articulations of a constitutive view are quite distinct from each other and this is reflected in how identity as an issue is relevant for each.

Craig (1999) argued for the usefulness of a constitutive view in a restricted sense, as a metatheory, namely a theory about theory, that enables a discussion space within which to reconcile contradictions apparent among the multiple phenomena-oriented or problem-focused approaches in the field of communication. His concern with identity, in this context, is the communication field's internal and external image—fragmentation and lack of impact—and the practices that support that image.

Although Deetz (1994) is clearly concerned with the field's image as well, his proposal of a constitutive view offers an explanatory framework for communication, one that expands the communicational focus, explanatory possibility, and practical impact of what he called the informational view, what others have called the transmission model. His proposal for the development of communication explanations of psychological and sociological phenomena by attending to communication, rather than psychological or sociological explanations of communication phenomena, for example, merits broad consideration no matter how one positions oneself. However, his use of the term *constitutive* to characterize both a general perspective and also specific types of communication processes and practices signals a noteworthy difference from the view presented here, a difference that is not merely a matter of potential semantic confusion.

This difference is reflected in how identity as a research problem is approached. For Deetz (1994), identity negotiation identifies a current salient social problematic that results from the inadequacies and erosion of modernism as a source of generalized stability, resulting in a perceived climate of fragmentation within postmodernity (cf. Gergen, 1991). To address this, Deetz (1994) envisioned that: "Communication analysis would emphasize progressive self-differentiation, self-redifferentiation, and identity negotiation as an ongoing process in all interaction. The conception of 'process' subjectivity' invites a responsive self, living the many me's in a dynamic relation with others" (p. 586). The problematic suggests intervention, with the goal of research apparently the dissemination of an already formulated resolution of the problematic.

Suppose instead for a moment that identity is an historically enduring practical problem relevant within all moments of lived experience and that communication might offer explanations why this is so. This is the spirit in which this chapter embraces constitutivity and identity. This presumption is motivated by a read of history and everyday lives that suggests identity's relevance has been at best underappreciated, and quite possibly, at times, if not consistently, suppressed through resolution of the perceived problematic.

This targets interest in identity as an emergent property of communication and approaches identity as relational, a property not of an individual but of interaction itself, very much in the sense of Goffman's (1967) concept of face. A key challenge of this endeavor is the development of ways to describe the emergence and relational nature of identity within communication, not through accounts about communication. The emphasis and approach of this research has distinct parallels with considerations of identity in conversation analysis (e.g., Mandelbaum, 1996), although it is developed within a notably different tradition (e.g., Duncan, Fiske, Denny, Kanki, & Mokros, 1985; McQuown, 1971; Scheff, 1990) and is concerned with a broader set of communication practices.

This view is grounded in the description, analysis, and interpretation of communicative activities or practices as they are instantiated within interactional engagements. The focus is on interaction, not as an event, or an effect parameter as in studies of mutual influence (e.g., Kenny & Malloy, 1988), but as a system. As noted elsewhere, "Conceptualization of interaction in these terms is antithetical to a constitutive perspective. A constitutive perspective rejects the priority of events and objects and instead posits the priority of an interactional system within which events and objects are achievements (of identity), not as stable entities, but as contingent realizations" (Mokros, 1996, p. 6).

IDENTITY MATTERS: A CONSTITUTIVE VIEW

A Working Model of the Constitutive View

A quite simple working model of the constitutive view of communication offers a framework for conceptualizing identity to assist this approach to inquiry. This model identifies three interactive and interacting levels. The relation between levels is assumed constitutive. That is to say, description at each level is contingent on and reproductive of the other two. The model identifies the following levels: discourse, interaction, and reflection.

The level of discourse does not reference worldly communication practices. It is instead the structuring or generative influence of macro systems in the sense of Foucault's discussion of discourse formations (1972) and the disciplining power that these exercise on the expression of everyday communication practices (1977). Interaction is the site of study. What is studied are engagement practices, with one's self, with other(s), or with communication product(s). It is observable interaction, wherein practices intermingle, that provides the focus of microanalytic attention, and wherein realizations of identity are situated for analytic purposes. Reflection refers to meta-practice, engagement with qualities of engagement, which is thus engagement with discourse as well. Reflection is assumed to be observable within interaction through interpretation, as is, of course, also the case for discourse.

The positioning of "reflection" as a level in this model and its choice as a descriptive term merit reconsideration. This is because reflection invites a view of mental activity or mind and thereby a private, individually located experience. This is not to deny the heuristic and practical value of mind in scholarship or everyday practice. However, the intent of this view is to position mind in a distributed sense (cf. Gergen, 1994) as located in and developed through social practices. The terms *meta-practice* or *meta-pragmatic discourse* when conceptualized as the structuring and emergent interface positioned between discourse and interaction offer alternatives. However, that requires a pragmatics of communication developed within a semiotics appropriate to a view of communication as practical activity, something that has as yet not been articulated.

In addition to this working model, several theoretical concepts were also introduced to assist in translating the constitutive view to research practice. One is the distinction between "native" and "privileged" theory as a way to further elaborate discourse-level influences on identity in everyday practice (Mokros, 1993). This distinction assumes discourse as composed of multiple, competing discourses (Bakhtin, 1981), with a discourse of one's self, through time—what might be called an *identity constant*—a discourse within discourse. Native theory references discourses that structure everyday assumptions about the world and how it may be explained, what Geertz (1983) called "common-sense" (see also Scheff, 1997, p. 219ff.). Privileged theories are those developed by experts. To call these *theories* is to suggest that they generatively guide action and perception in everyday practices. Native and privileged theories are assumed to differ in visibility. Privileged theories, in the sense of documented knowledge and procedures for identifying, diagnosing, resolving and otherwise addressing some worldly problem are public and thereby quite visible in comparison to common sense.

Yet, the assumptions and traditions that serve as foundations for privileged theories may, through time, become invisible. The routinization of privileged practice, possible only to the extent that a theory has perceived practical utility, invites engagement elsewhere (cf. habituation). It is at such times likely that practices become separated from their assumptions. Once such separation becomes generalized, byproducts of practice become problems of individual practice. This also suggests privileged theory as inescapably embedded within and appropriated by native theory and shaped as common sense.

Theories of practice and personhood (Mokros et al., 1995) are two additional concepts introduced, and these relate to the distinction between native and privileged theories previously discussed. Practice and personhood represent ways to conceptualize the situated instantiation of practices in interaction. *Practice* refers to a procedural sense of everyday routines employed to accomplish some specific task, as for example providing medical service (professional practice), getting one's point across in conversation (ordinary practice), or just hanging out.

Personhood refers to a practitioner's (in the general sense of someone performing a practice) relational expectations as revealed through the doing of practice. These are products of native and privileged theories that at the level of the individual represent a history of interactional engagements. Of interest for considerations of professional practices is how privileged approaches to practice that aim to shape professional practices through the development of procedural routines (e.g., corporate training, professional development), explicitly or as byproduct, potentially shape an individual's personhood orientation, or confront its resistance. Hochschild's (1983) study of flight attendants and bill collectors offers an important consideration of this issue and its relationship to the idea of a core sense of self.

Theories of personhood and practice are intrinsically related to the more general concept of *situation*. Situation refers to the relationship between specific individuals, the social situation of their engagement, and the conventional or discursive assumptions that appear salient in accounting for the observed order of the interaction and the types of practices performed. It is assumed that individuals bring to interaction expectations of how to proceed, how to approach others, and how they themselves wish to be approached. Framing definitions refer to an individual's definition of the situation, as this is expressed through his or her practices within interaction. Initial turns at talk in conversations are representative of a type of context where framing definitions may be productively examined and compared. This assumes that individuals differ in the framing definitions they bring to any engagement. This then also means that the definition of the situation is continuously relevant and a potential focus for negotiation during the course of interaction. Such negotiations punctuate, in the sense described by Bateson (1996), the natural history of interaction. And these punctuations are then sites for observing reflection in action as well. Thus, situation is viewed as dynamic, in the sense of its moment-to-moment definition, and always implicative of a person's identity viewed thereby as an ongoing positioning of self in relation to other within the social bond. Here, Scheff's

(1990, 1994, 1997; see also Retzinger, 1991) consideration of shame as a barometer of the quality of the social bond proved useful to multiple researchers as it offers not only a way of thinking about reflection but of also observing reflection within the natural history of interaction.

identity Matters Research Data

Each study that served as a basis for subsequent chapters in this book systematically examined some permanent communication record or communication product. These included audio- and videotapes of face-to-face interaction, computer-generated logs of participant activities on Internet sites, and copies (and inscriptions) of communication products publicly available. Each research project contextualized these recordings through participant-observation. Additionally, Chelton (1997), Cockett (2000), Maynard (2001), Mokros (1980), and Thomas (1996) studied settings "familiar" to them based on occupational experience. Coan (Stephenson, 1998), Cockett (2000), Karetnick (2000), Lemesianou (1999), and Rumsey (2001) studied sites they had each participated in over multiple years. Some studies also generated data through auto-ethnography, interviews, focus groups, and document review and most made use of some form of graphic and mathematical modeling (both as modes of mapping and facilitators of pattern recognition).

Studies based on engagements with *communication products* included a single sign, namely the term *Generation X* studied through the analysis of 26,544 titles of articles containing this term, published over a 7-year period (chap. 2); 1,858 unique advertisements appearing over a 1-year period across 116 issues of six Japanese magazines aimed at young adults (chap. 3); and internal and external features of building design across nine public, school, and academic libraries (chap. 4).

Studies of *mediated engagements* were based on computer-generated logs of such engagements and included 492 messages posted by 70 individuals during the first 6 weeks of an online cancer support site (chap. 5); and 1,733 turns of meaningful activity during a "meeting" among 60 participants held one day on a multiuser dungeon (MUD) fantasy site (chap. 6).

Finally, studies based on audio and video recordings of *face-to-face engagements* included 153 librarian encounters and 123 circulation desk encounters with adolescent students that occurred one day over roughly 3 hours in one high school library (chap. 7); a 74-minute intermediate level ballroom dance lesson involving 22 students and 3 instructors (chap. 8); a 25-minute committee meeting including 11 participants and 29 speaking turns (chap. 9); and a selection of brief encounters between salesmen and buyers around one sales desk at a wholesale produce market from among 30 hours of videotaped encounters at this site (chap. 10).

Natural History Method and Interpretive Microanalysis

The data described here were methodically collected with the aim of pursuing some form of microanalysis. This did not, however, involve the application of any coding schemes, purposeful researcher interventions (with recording the notable exception), or any other procedures that would precondition the data. Instead, the collection process selected relevant units of everyday communication (i.e., "entextualized" units of communication or records) and sought, to the extent possible, to preserve the form and meaning these units held in their everyday contexts. Each study involved microanalysis of such units, and many used an interpretive microanalytic approach, developed from three primary influences, those of Bateson, Duncan, and Scheff, as discussed later.

The Natural History of an Interview's (McQuown, 1971) attention to meaningful units of communication, the importance of context, and inquiry based on systematic description involving minimal theory in data collection (Bateson, 1996) is foundational to the development of interpretive microanalysis. Interpretive microanalysis treats natural history as both an approach to research and as a unit of study. In this latter sense, communication events may be thought to have a life that is framed by a moment of birth and some subsequent demise. Conversations and meetings are prototypical examples. It is the natural history then, conceived as a meaningful real-world unit, that identifies the unit examined through microanalytic inquiry. Finally, microanalytic study, as a method, is made sensible through the *"assumption that the microscopic will reflect the macroscopic"* (Bateson, 1996, p. 67).

Duncan focused the natural history approach specifically on the study of interaction, namely the study of its organization or structure through transcription-based analysis of participants' activities. His methodological developments and proposed metatheory (Duncan & Fiske, 1977) for face-to-face interaction represent the most direct influence on the development of interpretive microanalysis and the approach proposed for "identity matters" research generally. He conceived of everyday interaction as a coordination problem, that, in the context of dyads, may be thought of as a question about how two individuals are able to construct a cohesive, organized sense of a common communication space such as a conversation, for example. This represents a structural orientation to interaction, namely a concern with the principles by which coordination is achieved. Duncan viewed interactional coordination as achievable in everyday practices only to the extent that conventions (i.e., a system of rules and procedures that guides interaction), as an organizer of individual choice and agency, are shared or held in common between interactants. His work thereby offers a theory-based methodology that directly engages the micro–macro problem, the relationship between the individual and the social, discussed earlier as an enduring problem of scholarship within the human sciences.

Duncan additionally argued that the coordination problem is important as well for research of individual differences that base inferences about such differences on interaction-based measures of individual activity. He showed empirically how such research is prone to an interpretive error referred to as *pseudounilaterality*, namely the potentially false assumption that measurements of the actions of an individual are interpretable outside the interactional context from which they were obtained (Duncan, Kanki, Mokros, & Fiske, 1984). To the extent that the study of individuals is always interactionally situated, this interpretive error is not merely an issue of method but a foundational misconstruing of what an individual is, and thereby what identity is. Identity is, in other words, not observable as a fixed attribute of a person once one views the person as interactionally situated. Common sense denies "its self" as being but a perspective. This is evident when identity is implicitly approached as a fixed attribute of an autonomous being who resides within a world that reflects things—things that may be understood mechanically and reshaped "techniquely." This assumption neglects to consider interaction as a system (in relation to macro-systems), and thereby the practical and explanatory possibilities of such a view. Again, this is a view that sees identity not as attributes of an individual but as contingent realizations—always—and in all ways based in relational being.

The development of a method appropriate to the exploration of this relationship between the micro and macro is also a focal concern of the third influence on the development of interpretive microanalysis, namely Scheff's (1990) microsociology. Scheff's concept of the social bond as a continuous feature of everyday interaction extends Duncan's appreciation of interaction as a coordination problem. In this regard, he offered a number of generally useful contributions. Part–whole analysis presents an impressive logic of inquiry for addressing the micro–macro problem. Scheff viewed morphological study as the foundational stage in this approach to inquiry with microanalysis the methodological tool. This invites interesting parallels between microanalysis and systematic approaches applied in such fields as archeology, astronomy, biology, geology, geography, and the like. His applications of microsociology and part–whole analysis, in each case I know of, involve the study of natural histories of meaningful units of communication.

His view of the social bond, and approach to studying it, positions solidarity, Durkheim's (1951) theorized generative process to account for the structure of individual activities and societal forms, squarely in the context of everyday interaction. In other words, everyday experience is not merely a matter of coordinated moves, but also coordinated regard for social being, for one's experience of legitimacy in the world. Finally, Scheff's advocacy of contextualized interpretation, through the positing of hypotheticals or counterfactuals in relation to observed interactional features, represents an important and productive extension of the logic of microanalysis as conceptualized by Bateson.

Based in these influences, the application of interpretive microanalysis involves three stages of inquiry: systematic description of a communication record in relation to the phenomenon of interest through the development of multiple transcripts or maps of the phenomenon; systematic analysis of features of these maps, the interactional terrain; and, finally, interpretation through the positing of plausible observable alternatives to observed, contextualized, interactional features revealed through description and analysis.

The first stage aims to preserve the said and done of that which occurred in the record studied, with particular emphasis on the preservation of activities in context in terms of sequencing and co-occurrence of interaction based activities. This is achieved through mapping, namely the application of various transcription techniques, whose aim is to represent the contours and life course of the natural history of the activities captured through some form of permanent recording. This natural history provides a representation of the activities under investigation, attending to context at every mapping stage.

The second stage involves the systematic analysis of these maps with the aim of identifying the organizational properties and principles of the interaction studied and how these relate to the practices of individuals within this interaction. This could, for example, involve posing questions about who speaks to whom and when, and always, conversely, who does not speak when and to whom. In a sense, a set of experiments is conducted—natural experiments in that the control or contrast situations are identified in the data and not imposed through external measures. Mathematical modeling and statistical summaries provide a useful tool for examining organizational properties that are often not easily recoverable through mapping alone.

Finally, the approach involves interpretation wherein alternative possibilities are explored at meaningful junctures within the terrain of the maps. At these points, interpretive and critical questions are raised about the specific shape of the observed landscape, the specific unfolding of the natural history through the researcher's positing of plausible alternatives to what is mapped. The placement of interpretation as a third stage of inquiry is not meant to imply that interpretation is merely a phase of the research. For interpretation, as Geertz (1973) suggested, is quite simply unavoidable (cf. Sacks, 1984). The goal of interpretive microanalysis is to enable reflection, in a somewhat manageable way, on the pronounced ordering and contradictions that common sense imposes. The research act is thereby an important and lasting site for such reflection. Here, achieving recognition that one holds assumptions, and that these assumptions make a difference in seeing is not as easy as it seems, and yet, it is also the only place to start.

The natural history approach, as a methodological tool, renders *a* natural history, not *the* natural history of whatever is being studied. There is nothing natural, as in given, about the natural histories constructed through this line of inquiry. They are meaningful arrangements of distinctions viewed as meaningful, wherein the very idea of meaning should be understood as involving artificial constructions (i.e., interpretations and workings of a semiotic world), as something other than reflections of an observable physical reality (see D'Andrade, 1986)—even as they are claimed to be descriptive accounts of observable traces of human activity.

How Identity Matters

Remarkable across subsequent contributions is the wide-ranging and inescapable presence of representations of identity in the context of communicative engagement with products and others. This implies that identity is continuously relevant in interaction as suggested early on. This is not meant to deny the noteworthy salience of specific moments when identity becomes the explicit focus of engagement between individuals in interaction. Indeed, it is precisely such moments that are analyzed in detail in many of the subsequent chapters. However, the unpredictable occurrence of such moments makes the ongoing relevance of identity for interactants a logical antecedent condition. Rather than focus on any specific example, the following "wanders along the trail" that the subsequent chapters define, with momentary stops at each so as to bring to light what they appear to offer about identity.

At the head of the trail, Lemesianou (chap. 2, this volume) provides a glimpse into the invention of a sign that represents identity, a type of communication product, that in everyday practice functions as an identity marker. Lemesianou specifically exposes to scrutiny a sign that indexes an age cohort, "Generation X," and achieves meaning in contrast to other generation markers such as "Baby Boom Generation," for example. She shows how "Generation X," once invented, gains expanded meaning historically as it is interactionally appropriated within multiple, competing, and often contradictory everyday and privileged systems of meaning or signification. Its symbolic use indexes these appropriations and thereby positions and iconically represents an individual's self in ways that had not previously existed. "Generation X: Generation unimportant or even Generation illiterate if you truly look at the connotations behind our little title" writes one individual, as she experiences her identity positioned within what Lemesianou calls the semiotic landscape(s) where markers of identity feature the terrain.

From here, the trail leads to two further considerations of signs of identity as communication products contained within communication products. First, Maynard (chap. 3) offers a view of Japanese cultural identity within the semiotic landscape of advertising aimed at young adults. This semiotic landscape seeks to influence the consumption of purchasable products it represents by those who engage with an ad. Yet, the landscape presented represents much more than a capitalist product. It includes varied representations of Japanese identity juxtaposed to representations of the occidental or Western world, particularly the United States—its identity as culture and place. The ads are viewed from this perspective as multicultural or global semiotic spaces within which Japanese identity is situated within a globalized marketplace. Maynard invites us to sit for a moment, and examine some ads in specific magazines and appreciate their relevance as meaningful spaces that locate identity. He suggests that these ads not only urge the consumption of goods and services but also images of otherness (representations of the West) and sameness (representations of Japan). This semiotic consumption is inescapably part of engaging with an ad, and offers a taste of self as a cultural positioning through selected flavors of otherness.

Our travels continue to a different kind of semiotic landscape where representations of identity may be examined within communication products. Here, Thomas (chap. 4) leads us on an eyes wide open stroll up to and through a set of libraries. She asks that we not attend to the stored knowledge or expert service available in each but to the features of building design and how these may be read as a landscape of discourses within which identity matters are represented and continuously relevant to our sense of self as we engage these design features. What she reads for us "in design" along the way is the representation of moral value, self-control, and expected being through systems of meaningful identification. It is the entanglement of discursivity, of the present and the past, of the institution and its positioning of the individual, and the myriad contradictions this promotes that Thomas brings into relief. These contradictions, nevertheless, reveal a constant source of influence in relation to the practices of potential users of these libraries. This constant is the expectation of self-discipline and the development of self-focus, not relational being. It is an expectation that orders user practices not just institutionally, but that also institutionalizes disciplinary approaches to the self as a regulated unit of being in the world.

Together, Thomas, Maynard, and Lemesianou open to view the pervasive positioning and pronounced complexity of identity as, and within, communication products. They suggest that we are virtually surrounded, so to speak, by representations of identity that enliven these semiotic land-scapes and that engagement with them arouses the relevance of our sense of identity or "being" within their presence, productively and reproductively.

New terrains of communicative practice and identity representation are opened to view as we encounter two social settings or spaces wherein engagements with others are primary activities through computer media-tion. Although these types of mediated settings present new possibilities of engagement and expression, it appears that how individuals engage each other in these two spaces is much more a timeless quest for the situated meaning of personal being, expressed here in contexts of crisis and play.

Efforts to come to terms with cancer through the assistance of medi-ated others define the activities of individuals in the space Rumsey (chap. 5) brings us to. She shows how these efforts that are motivated by specific needs for information and/or the generalized support of others also implicate and reveal the representation and relevance of identity as social membership. For example, entry into the semiotic landscape of illness situates the individual in membership with similar others. This membership, a sameness of identity defined through shared traumatic experience, is necessary for access to mem-bership within the online cancer support community Rumsey allows us to visit. Yet the statement of one's legitimacy as a member is, for many who par-ticipate within this space, a search for the erasure of the positioned identity ill-ness imposes. Legitimacy and the struggle it presents is inseparable from self-other orientation, the positioning of one's self relationally as this is inevitably, it seems, revealed through the practice of introduction in pursuit of social membership. That is to say, individuals do not merely state informational needs or request specific types of support. On every occasion they also state who they are in relationship to others. They thereby present an expected form of "relational commons" within which what they seek, and offer others is "spa-tial in character." Who they are is only visible through contrast with the rela-tional commons that others project. This is apparent when we speak of an engagement as lacking closeness, or characterize an engagement as if the par-ticipants were in different worlds.

Encountered next is what would seem to be a quite different medi-ated community, an electronic playground of guided fantasy where "a bright green cabbage ponders your existence." Here, Karetnick (chap. 6) shows, quite surprisingly, how the pulls toward and constraints of membership motivate and position the identity of players in this playground. This world "elsewhere," commonly perceived as without constraint and thus "an identi-ty workshop" where the systemic constraints of "RL," namely, "real life," are voidable, is, to the contrary, shown to reproduce the working world. Indeed, play is work within this community playground as questions about one's legitimacy, one's competence, one's aggression, one's deception, one's caring, one's desire, one's employment of possibilities ground identity through membership. What is cared about is relational being, through the public positioning of self, in the foreground and shadows, within a practicing community that attends forcefully to matters of identity as it does elsewhere—"out there"—as Karetnick makes so very apparent.

The possibilities that technology opens for the practicing of membership in newly settled human communities is quite often perceived as signaling a radical transformation. From one perspective, this transformation is a removal of the experiencing self from the world and furthers the experience of alienation in modern societies. From another perspective, the adoption of communication technologies "saturates" the immediacy of the self (Gergen, 1991) with diverse and multiple relational expectations and obligations that have the potential to transform our fixed sense of what identity is. Rumsey and Karetnick offer a different take, one that points to the profound sameness of generalized desire, the desire to be real in relationship to others as revealed through communication practices that inevitably represent and struggle with identity as position and possibility.

The trail at this point leads away from these mediated, virtual communities to ones characterized by face-to-face engagements, where "I" and "you," as instances of identity within the situation speech produces, shift back and forth. These instances or moments of identity, as shifting positions, are embedded within identity frameworks of pronounced constancy. These frameworks systematically structure the practical formulation of identity within interaction, as the forays along the paths of each of the four remaining chapters bring to the realm of the senses.

Chelton (chap. 7) takes us first to yet another library, one located in a high school, where she asks that we attend to the observable encounters between library staff and adolescent students. What we see is unsettling in its settledness but fully expected to the extent we take Foucault seriously. One of the foundational missions of librarianship is assisting people with informational needs. Yet, among the activities observed such acts of assistance account for less than 3 in 100 librarian–student encounters. The majority of the rest involve disciplined and disciplining practices to secure the achievement of order, in handling equipment, through checking out books, and, most notably, in the framing of the adolescent self. Suspicion about adolescent motive, and surveillance of students' activities appear to be the primary (pre-)occupation of librarianship when viewed through the lens that Chelton provides. What is observed is not bad professional practice but the realities that led Foucault (1977) to ask, "Is it surprising that prisons resemble factories, schools, barracks, hospitals, which all resemble prisons?" (p. 228).

At this point, Coan (chap. 8) offers what seems to be a kinder, gentler world as she leads us from this institution-based learning environment to the dance floor whereupon students step, through self-motivation, to practice the disciplining techniques that enable them to "become" dancers and enjoy the gaiety of ballroom dancing. The activities on the floor, we quickly discover, involve more than achieving technical expertise. Students are segregated by gender, they perform an idealized sense of a gender as a dance partner, they are instructed in groups by gender, and they are approached differently, by each other and the instructor by gender. Indeed, the instructor's engagement with them, individually or as a group, is framed throughout by gendered distinctions. Identity is continuously represented through gender by the very conventions of ballroom dance. Identity becomes relevant for all present through gender as a positioning of the self that is evoked through the instructor's efforts to guide and remediate student performance. The relevance of gender at these moments is only observable through the comparison of the instructor's practices over time and across individuals, and is complicated, experientially, by the very gendered discourse or conventions of ballroom dancing. As Coan argues, there are hypothetical alternatives to the instructor's observable practices that would easily avoid the interactional dilemmas that his gender-tailored practices arouse. These alternatives would not disrupt the ideals of the dance as gendered performance. That such alternative practices are not observable says much about how the constancy of personal identity, as an orientation of self in relationship to others, is of relevance for thinking about professional education and practices generally. Instructors do not just instruct—they unavoidably make identity relevant, through their instructional practices and position of authority, in particular ways that relate to their own constancy of being in the world as this is constituted through the dance of communication from birth forward.

The complexities entailed by positions of authority are precisely what Cockett (chap. 9) invites us to observe on our penultimate stop along the identity matters' trail. She takes us into a committee meeting of a group of professionals whose task, in this meeting, is to decide how it is that they are going to go about making some quite specific public policy recommendations. Cockett asks that we attend specifically to the chair of this committee in terms of what she says, when in the course of the meeting she says what she does, and to whom she directs her comments. She also asks that we attend to the complement of what is observable, namely, what the chair does not say, and when and to whom she does not speak. The chair's orientation to her institutionally vested authority, in conjunction with her idealized sense of authority as this relates to an idealized sense of collaborative decision making, presents a dilemma of practical complexity not only for her but the entire committee. This is a dilemma of contradictions that become apparent through the shifting qualities of her interactional practices over time, through the unfolding natural history of the meeting. Cockett illuminates for us the observable tensions between control and collaboration, between autonomy and relatedness exhibited in the exercise of authority in the course of this meeting. She offers us yet another sobering illustration of how identity is an inescapable aspect of instrumental practice, be it providing service, instruction, or heading a committee.

Our final stop, as the path soon leads to a mapping of the spaces we've encountered (i.e., the index), involves a visit to a produce market before dawn during the spring and summer months more than 20 years ago. This is a place I explored for a variety of reasons, including reasons of identity. We specifically visit one large, respected and successful "house" or business within the market and focus attention on how the denizens, the salesmen, workers and buyers who frequent this place view themselves through otherness, in contrast to who they are not. "The house is not a home" we discover while talking to and observing these individuals intently at one social oasis, namely a sales desk. Home, for them, is a place of order, civility, and women and this place is something else. This is a man's place, where swearing constitutes an aspect of membership, where action, in the sense of unpredictability, is ongoing, where lifetime friends meet on a daily basis while most everyone else is asleep, where some "real characters" enliven the everyday for all present. It is a house that women enter, as buyers and not infrequently as visitors unknown to the community. These women are welcomed, although to hear them swear is simply not acceptable. The unfamiliar women are especially welcomed, for everyone knows that such visits mean that "the mouse in the house" will soon produce a good chuckle for all.

Yet, the pace and unpredictability of activities not uncommonly lead to confrontation that at times leads to violence. But this is a very cohesive community and enormous efforts are made to maintain this cohesion even though it may appear otherwise. We watch business as usual, fast and friendly, at the social oasis that is the sales desk. Suddenly tension fills the air as a buyer overhears, by virtue of his presence, details of a petty and oft committed crime perpetrated by a worker just moments ago for the benefit of the head salesman at the desk, a most esteemed member of the community. The buyer realizes the crime affects him financially and accuses those present of a serious offense. Within moments, the offense is recast into a mythic space wherein a nonpresent, situationally innocent scapegoat is offered as a sacrifice that allows the recovery of cohesion and order among the parties present. The identity of the group, and of the individuals present are again fixed. Within minutes, social unraveling is arrested and the harmony and relational caring among individuals is restored through otherness.

Harmony, we come to see, is foundational, along with the craziness that characterizes the house and the identities constituted within it, through quite particular appeals to otherness.

Our brief journey through the spaces and places of identity matters is over. Hopefully, this guided tour provides a glimpse of what a more in depth stop at each space and place might usefully offer and how the research reported there may indeed be said to share in common an approach to identity from a constitutive perspective of communication.

CONCLUSION

Identity represents a profound concern of everyday life. The contributions to this book are products of dissertation research that in each case reconsidered personal interests through the lens of identity. Each approached identity matters through the study of meaningful everyday activities guided by the constitutive view of communication discussed in this chapter. These are the threads that bind this chapter with those that follow. Apparent throughout is a commitment to communication as a mode of explanation and site of exploration. This commitment suspends the common tendency to approach communication through the "dream of communication" (Peters, 1999), of how communication should be. Suspending the restrictions that this dream places on the "identity of communication" brings into view contradiction and irrationality as ordinary features of communication that contribute to our situated and enduring lived experiences—our experiences of identity.

REFERENCES

Austin, J.L. (1962). *How to do things with words*. Cambridge, MA: Harvard University Press.

Bakhtin, M.M. (1981). *The dialogic imagination*. Austin: University of Texas.

Bateson, G. (1996). Communication. In H.B. Mokros (Ed.), *Interaction and identity: Information and behavior* (Vol. 5, pp. 45-70). New Brunswick, NJ: Transaction.

Becker, K. (1932). *The heavenly city of the eighteenth-century philosophers*. New Haven, CT: Yale University Press.

Benedict, R. (1959). *Patterns of culture*. Boston: Houghton Mifflin.

Berger, P.L., & Luckmann, T. (1966). *The social construction of reality: A treatise in the sociology of knowledge*. New York: Doubleday.

Bourdieu, P. (1977). *Outline of a theory of practice*. Cambridge: Cambridge University Press.

Bourdieu, P. (1990). *The logic of practice*. Stanford, CA: Stanford University Press.

Butler, J. (1990). *Gender trouble: Feminism and the subversion of identity*. New York: Routledge.

Carbaugh, D. (1996). *Situating selves: The communication of social identities in American scenes*. Albany: State University of New York Press.

Chelton, M.K. (1997). *Adult–adolescent service encounters: The library context*. Unpublished doctoral dissertation, Rutgers, The State University of New Jersey, New Brunswick.

Cockett, L. (2000). *Self, other and situation in collaborative contexts: A study of personhood in a group decision-making meeting*. Unpublished doctoral dissertation, Rutgers, The State University of New Jersey, New Brunswick.

Craig, R.T. (1999). Communication theory as a field. *Communication Theory, 9*, 119-161.

Cronen, V.E. (1995). Coordinated management of meaning: The consequentiality of communication and the recapturing of experience. In S.J. Sigman (Ed.), *The consequentiality of communication* (pp. 17-66). Hillsdale, NJ: Erlbaum.

D'Andrade, R. (1986). Three scientific world views and the covering law. In D.W. Fiske & R.A. Shweder (Eds.), *Metatheory in social science: Pluralisms and subjectivities* (pp. 19-41). Chicago: University of Chicago Press.

de Certeau, M. (1984). *The practice of everyday life*. Berkeley: University of California Press.

Deetz, S.A. (1994). Future of the discipline: The challenges, the research, and the social contribution. In S.A. Deetz (Ed.), *Communication yearbook 17* (pp. 565-600). Thousand Oaks, CA: Sage.

Duncan, S.D., & Fiske, D.W. (1977). *Face-to-face interaction*. Hillsdale, NJ: Erlbaum.

Duncan, S.D., Fiske, D.W., Denny, R., Kanki, B, & Mokros, H.B. (1985). *Interaction structure and strategy*. Cambridge: Cambridge University Press.

Duncan, S.D., Kanki, B., Mokros, H.B & Fiske, D.W. (1984). Pseudounilaterality, simple-rate variables, and other ills to which interaction research is heir. *Journal of Personality and Social Psychology, 46*, 1335-1348.

Durkheim, E. (1951). *Suicide: A study in sociology*. New York: The Free Press.

Elias, N. (1991). *The society of individuals*. Oxford: Basil Blackwell.

Faubion, J.D. (1995a). Introduction. In J.D. Faubion (Ed.), *Rethinking the subject: An anthology of contemporary European thought* (pp. 1-27). Boulder, CO: Westview.

Faubion, J.D. (Ed.). (1995b). *Rethinking the subject: An anthology of contemporary European thought*. Boulder, CO: Westview.

Foucault, M. (1972). *The archeology of knowledge*. New York: Pantheon.

Foucault, M. (1977). *Discipline and punish: The birth of the prison*. New York: Vintage.

Geertz, C. (1973). *The interpretation of cultures*. New York: Basic Books.

Geertz, C. (1976). "From the native's point of view": On the nature of anthropological understanding. In K.H. Basso & H.A. Selby (Eds.), *Meaning in anthropology* (pp. 221-237). Albuquerque: University of New Mexico Press.

Geertz, C. (1983). *Local knowledge*. New York: Basic Books.

Gergen, K.J. (1991). *The saturated self: Dilemmas of identity in contemporary life*. New York: Basic Books.

Gergen, K.J. (1994).*Realities and relationships: Soundings in social construction*. Cambridge, MA: Harvard University Press.

Giddens, A. (1979). *Central problems in social theory*. Berkeley: University of California Press.

Giddens, A. (1984). *The constitution of society*. Cambridge: Polity Press.

Giddens, A. (1992). *The transformation of intimacy*. Stanford, CA: Stanford University Press.

Goffman, E. (1959). *The presentation of self in everyday life*. New York: Anchor.

Goffman, E. (1967). *Interaction ritual: Essays on face-to-face behavior*. Garden City, NY: Anchor.

Habermas, J. (1987). *The philosophical discourse of modernity*. Cambridge, MA: MIT University Press.

Hecht, M.L. (1993). 2002—A research odyssey: Toward the development of a communication theory of identity. *Communication Monographs, 60*, 76-82.

Hochschild, A.R. (1983). *The managed heart: Commercialization of human feeling*. Berkeley: University of California Press.

Jakobson, R. (1990). *On language*. Cambridge MA: Harvard University Press.

Karetnick, R. (2000). *Identity in cyberspace: An ethnographic and microanalytic study of participation in a virtual community*. Unpublished doctoral dissertation, Rutgers, The State University of New Jersey, New Brunswick.

Kenny, D.A., & Malloy, T.E. (1988). Partner effects in social interaction. *Journal of Nonverbal Behavior, 12*, 34-57.

Kondo, D. (1997). *About face: Performing race in fashion and theater*. New York: Routledge.

Lemesianou, C.A. (1999). *The geographies of discourse and lived experience: A communication approach*. Unpublished doctoral dissertation, Rutgers University, The State University of New Jersey, New Brunswick.

Mandelbaum, J. (1996). Constructing social identity in the workplace: Interaction in bibliographic database searches. In H.B. Mokros (Ed.), *Interaction and identity: Information and behavior* (Vol. 5, pp. 145-169). New Brunswick, NJ: Transaction.

Maynard, M. (2001). *The consumption of otherness and preservation of self: Images of America in Japanese teen magazine advertisements*. Unpublished doctoral dissertation, Rutgers, The State University of New Jersey, New Brunswick.

McQuown, N.E. (Ed.). (1971). *The natural history of an interview* (Microfilm Collection of Manuscripts in Cultural Anthropology). Chicago: Regenstein Library.

Mead, G.H. (1934). *Mind, self and society*. Chicago: University of Chicago Press

Mokros, H.B. (1980). *Microanalysis in context*. Unpublished research proposal, University of Chicago, Chicago.

Mokros, H.B. (1993). The impact of a native theory of information on two privileged accounts of personhood. In J.R. Schement & B. Ruben (Eds.), *Between communication and information: Information and behavior* (Vol. 4, pp. 57-79). New Brunswick, NJ: Transaction.

Mokros, H.B. (1995). Suicide and shame. *American Behavioral Scientist, 38*, 1091-1103.

Mokros, H.B. (Ed.). (1996). *Interaction and identity: Information and behavior* (Vol. 5). New Brunswick, NJ: Transaction.

Mokros, H.B., & Deetz, S. (1996). What counts as real? A constitutive view of communication and the disenfranchised in the context of health. In E.B. Ray (Ed.), *Communication and the disenfranchised: Social health issues and implications* (pp. 29-44). Hillsdale, NJ: Erlbaum.

Mokros, H.B., Mullins, L., & Saracevic, T. (1995). Practice and personhood in professional interaction: Social identities and information needs. *Library and Information Science Research, 17*, 237-258.

Ortner, S.B. (1996). *Making gender: The politics and erotics of culture*. Boston: Beacon.

Pearce, W.B. (1989). *Communication and the human condition*. Carbondale: Southern Illinois University Press.

Peters, J.D. (1999). *Speaking into the air: A history of the idea of communication.* Chicago: University of Chicago Press.

Retzinger, S.M. (1991). *Violent emotions: Shame and rage in marital quarrels.* Newbury Park, CA: Sage.

Ricoeur, P. (1981). The model of the text: Meaningful action considered in text. In J.B. Thompson (Ed.), *Human sciences: Essays on language, action, and interpretation* (pp. 197-221). New York: Cambridge University Press.

Rumsey, E. (2001). *Making sense of health and illness online: A study of patterns of participation and use on one computer-mediated cancer support site.* Unpublished doctoral dissertation, Rutgers, The State University of New Jersey, New Brunswick.

Sacks, H. (1984). Notes on methodology. In J.M. Atkinson & J. Heritage (Eds.), *Structures of social action: Studies in conversation analysis.* Cambridge: Cambridge University Press.

Said, E. (1979). *Orientalism.* New York: Random House.

Sapir, E. (1949). *Selected writings of Edward Sapir in language, culture, and personality.* (D.G. Mandelbaum, Ed.). Berkeley: University of California Press.

Saussure, F. (1969). *Course in general linguistics.* New York: McGraw-Hill.

Scheff, T.J. (1990). *Microsociology: Discourse, emotion and social structure.* Chicago: University of Chicago Press.

Scheff, T.J. (1994). *Bloody revenge: Emotions, nationalism, and war.* Boulder, CO: Westview.

Scheff, T.J. (1997). *Emotions, the social bond, and human reality.* Cambridge: Cambridge University Press.

Shotter, J. (1996). In J. Stewart (Ed.), *Beyond the symbol model: Reflections on the nature of language.* Albany: State University of New York Press.

Sigman, S.J. (Ed.). (1995). *The consequentiality of communication.* Hillsdale, NJ: Erlbaum.

Silverstein, M., & Urban, G. (Eds.). (1996). *Natural history of discourse.* Chicago: University of Chicago Press.

Stephenson, H. (1998). *Guiding becoming: One instructor's approach.* Unpublished doctoral dissertation, Rutgers, The State University of New Jersey, New Brunswick.

Stewart, J. (1996). The symbol model vs. language as constitutive articulate contact. In J. Stewart (Ed.), *Beyond the symbol model: Reflections on the nature of language* (pp. 9-68). Albany: State University of New York Press.

Thomas, N. (1996). *Reading libraries: An interpretive study of discursive practices in library architecture and the interactional construction of personal identity.* Unpublished doctoral dissertation, Rutgers, The State University of New Jersey, New Brunswick.

Vygotsky, L.S. (1978). *Mind in society.* Cambridge, MA: Harvard University Press.

Vygotsky, L.S. (1962). *Thought and language.* Cambridge, MA: MIT Press.

West, C. (1994). *Race matters.* New York: Vintage.

Whorf, B.L. (1956). *Language, thought, and reality: Selected writings of Benjamin Lee Whorf* (J.B. Carroll, Ed.). Cambridge, MA: MIT Press.

Wittgenstein, L. (1958). *Philosophical investigations.* New York: Macmillan.

II

ENGAGEMENTS WITH COMMUNICATION PRODUCTS

2

Sign Matters

The Shift in Semantic Landscapes of the Sign "Generation X" Through Time

Christine A. Lemesianou

A distant mountain range under a broad sky. . . . It "is." Wherein consists the being? When and to whom does it reveal itself? To the traveler who enjoys the landscape, or to the peasant who makes his living in it and from it, or to the metereologist who is preparing a weather report? Who of these apprehends being? All and none.

—Heidegger (1987, p. 34)

Questions of identity continue to frame the cultural, economic, and political scene on both the local and global levels. But, as Heidegger suggested in the opening quote, identity, the question of being, continues to elude us in a definitive sense. For people can variably understand, experience, and evaluate identity depending on the contingencies of the moment and the ways they apprehend the world. On the local level, the ways we conceptualize and talk about the self engender various signs, identity markers that position the self geographically, relationally, aesthetically, morally, and socially. "I am American," "I am the mother of three," "My favorite painter is Picasso," "I oppose the death penalty," "I am a Generation X-er." These are all unavoidable examples of everyday positionings of the self, accompanied by a host of meanings.

On a more global level, identity wars are rampant. Take for instance the introduction of the "euro," the common currency of the European Community (EC), into the economic landscape. Although from a financial perspective the euro may have been successfully integrated into the world of currencies, the identity struggles its actual design incited should not be overlooked. The EC comprises 15 member states, 12 of which have adopted the euro, each with a rich cultural tradition and history. The euro to some extent makes invisible ethnic and national identities, at least on the economic level. The compromise reached for this unifying currency attempts to preserve the best of both worlds. Thus, the eight euro coins of various denominations will have a common European face while on the obverse side each member state will imprint its own motifs. As stated in the EC's Europa literature, "No matter which motif is on the coins they can be used anywhere inside the . . . Member States. For example, a French citizen will be able to buy a hot dog in Berlin using a euro coin carrying the imprint of the King of Spain" (Europa, 2001). Although the common currency may be an indication of the spirit of cooperation amongst these member states, the wish to preserve symbolically within this new community their unique identity and positioning in the pantheon of history is also clearly communicated.

This chapter focuses on just such matters of identity through an examination of the sign "Generation X" from a constitutive perspective of communication. Such a perspective recognizes the power of shared and enduring linguistic practices to create a "commons of participation" in the larger social order and dominant discourses that frame our potential identity claims in interaction (Mokros, 1996). And such a perspective draws on a long tradition of theorizing identity matters through, for example, examinations of linguistic structures and practices that are intricately and intrinsically linked to power and ideology (Bakhtin, 1981; Foucault, 1970, 1972; Jakobson, 1985; Lyotard, 1993; Saussure, 1974; Whorf, 1956). What this study affords is the unique opportunity to trace the path traveled by a linguistic expression that serves as an identity marker, namely Generation X. This sign is traced through its "travels," from its moment of inception and its first 7 years (i.e., 1991-1997), to gain a glimpse of the very processes and struggles of meaning production and reproduction encountered through time.

SEMIOTIC LANDSCAPES

Identity markers that delineate gender, race, or ethnic origin might be just simple "words" but the battles they incite are very real to people. People understand that the recognition and positionedness provided by such categorizations that "objectify" can have serious repercussions in the everyday through widely held stereotypic expectations and routinized, relational practices associated with these markers. Consider, for example, the following statement by a Generation X-er (excerpt from C. K., September 6, 1996):

> I am the first person in my family to graduate from college. I have a degree in English and a certificate to teach high school in the state of Georgia. I am also a member of Generation X: Generation unimportant or even Generation illiterate if you truly look at the connotations behind our little title.

C. K. was a participant on an Internet site developed explicitly for Generation X-ers in 1996. The site was titled "Politics and the X Generation" (Politics and the X Generation, 1996). C.K.'s reflections on the sign Generation X, as an identity marker that creates a less than desirable position in the social and political landscape, clearly resonates with the primary focus of this chapter—sign matters. As Goffman (1963) suggested, certain identity markers can stigmatize and reduce a person from "a whole and usual person to a tainted, discounted one" (p. 3). Generation X constitutes a "tribal" stigma, a generational stigma that differentiates by age, one that is difficult to hide and thus subjects its carriers to the "plight of the discredited" (pp. 4-5).

These concerns are very relevant to a constitutive perspective that recognizes the power of enduring semiotic practices to frame the "real." Mokros (1996) proposed that communication should be viewed as the opening up of a space, "as a site within which experience achieves a sense of coherence, structure and meaning" (p. 4). That is, in communicative moments reality, identity, and a sense of place come to be realized not as predetermined and static but as emergent and fluid realizations. The theoretical framework that follows examines the constitutive power of signs to objectify and reference the "real" and the "placeness" such semiotic practices claim and occupy within social life generally.

Signs, Diffusion, and Travel

The social constructionism movement placed communication as central to meaning-making processes in everyday interactions and language as key to constituting humans' relations to their social and ideological surroundings (Berger & Luckmann, 1966; Harre, 1986; Shotter, 1989). The symbolic nature of language that allows for abstraction from the immediacy of experience also creates ideal systems of categorization and structures of knowledge that are perpetuated and lead to truth claims and native theories that go largely unexamined (Bourdieu, 1977; Foucault, 1972; Geertz, 1983; Lyotard, 1993). From a constitutive perspective, language is not a mere explanatory tool that is employed to reference an existing reality (Mokros & Deetz, 1996). As Heidegger (1987) warned, such an understanding reduces language to "an indispensable but masterless means of communication that may be used as one pleases, as indifferent as a means of public transport, as a street car which everyone rides in" (p. 51). Rather, language shapes the very ways we construct our reality and creates for us structural positions that help us locate the self in relation to others, issues, and the social context. We are thus, relational selves functioning in what Taylor (1989) called "webs of interlocution" (p. 27).

Peirce's (1991) work in semiotics begins this travail into the power of language through the philosophical investigations of signs and their constitution as meaningful markers of identity. He defined a sign as "something which stands to somebody for something in some respect or capacity" (p. 141) and identified three "types" of signs—icons, indexes, and symbols. These three types differ in the extent of arbitrariness defined in the relationship of the sign to that for which it stands. Thus, icons represent physically, indexes point to or locate, and symbols conventionally mean that to which they refer. Icons, a hallmark of art, are rare in language, with indexes a small but important set, and symbols constituting the vast majority of signs.

Furthermore, Peirce proposed semiosis as an ongoing process of production and reproduction, structuration and destructuration, an infinitely divisible time and space continuum whereby signs come to be dialogically transformed through Firstness (e.g., position), Secondness (e.g., velocity), and Thirdness (e.g., acceleration). In his articulation of Thirdness, Peirce (1931-1935) recognized the embeddedness of linguistic systems within larger systems of signification and influence and rejected the idea that language is a homogeneous and self-contained system that functions independent of its surroundings or users. Signs thus exist in environments of conditionals. Analytically, this underscores the need to situate signs in time and space, to appreciate that signs have a natural history, in order to adequately account for the function and meaning of any given (cf. Jakobson, 1990; Scheff, 1996, 1997).

Peirce's account of the dialogical, diachronic articulation of signs introduced a sense of dynamism into the conceptualization of language that may be examined through an analysis of the processes of diffusion and travel of signs over time. The sign "Generation X" represents an innovation, introduced into our vocabularies in 1991 with the publication of Coupland's (1991) book *Generation X: Tales for an Accelerated Culture*. The diffusion process of any innovation involves the spontaneous or planned, centralized or decentralized spreading of a new idea through certain communication channels over a period of time. This diffusion impacts the existing social system and may produce numerous anticipated or unanticipated, desirable, or undesirable effects according to Rogers (1983, 1995). The basic elements of his model of diffusion involve an innovation, communication channels, time, and a social system. These elements correspond in this chapter to the diffusion of the sign "Generation X" in different databases between 1991 and 1997 and the potential consequences of this discourse on the perceived members of this generation as well as other social spectators.

The diffusion and accumulation of a sign comes to constitute a body of knowledge, what Foucault (1972) theorized as a "technology of domination," that results in forms of discipline and constraints on the identity claims and social positionings of those it represents. The diffusion process involves both local and global travel. In the contemporary scene, a scene characterized by globalizing tendencies, economic and political upheavals, media conglomerates and the abundance of high technology, it is not just the individual that finds herself dislocated, displaced, appropriated, and reconstructed. Signs are subjected to these same forces. Signs can no longer, if they ever could, be contained within the realm of inception: They travel. Thus, to understand the natural history of a sign one has to follow its traveling path, a path that Deleuze and Guattari (1987) suggested is not predetermined and linear, but rather rhizomatic, a complex web of heterogeneous connections branching out in unpredictable "lines of flight." In this traveling activity the meaning of signs such as "Generation X" have the potential of being appropriated, drastically transformed, and even co-opted (Kaplan, 1996).

These diffusion and travel processes provide a framework for the analysis of how signs come to materialize semantic landscapes. Although this sign emerged in the title of a fictional work, it quickly made inroads into multiple media realms, including initially popular outlets, such as newspapers, magazines, and television shows and subsequently in academic journals with research reports, appropriating this sign as an index of a generational cohort. This attention and continual engagement with the sign's semiosis rendered further legitimacy to the realness of the semiotic landscapes into which it entered, engaging with and offering an age cohort a previously absent marker of cohort identity, albeit a marker that suggests a lack of definition in contrast, for example, to the "baby boom" generation. This contrasts notably with the "baby boom" cohort marker with its clarity of reference as a historically situated demographic and notably felicitous associations. And whereas "boomer" appropriated a variety of psychosocial descriptors associated with those it identified, its clear indexicality of an historical phenomenon tempers, in a sense, the shadow of subsequently appropriated psychosocial associations to this generational index, and those it marks, when in use. Such is not the case with Generation X. Here, there is no clear sense of indexicality to historical events but rather a sense of unclear fit historically. And, as the quote from C. K. presented earlier suggests, the psychosocial descriptors linked to Generation X in the everyday are not a great source of pride for its members.

The Currency of Signs

Through the operation of discursive formations and "bipower," life, for Foucault (1980), eventually encounters the workings of capital, manifested in two processes. The first is an anatomo-politics of the body that disciplines and normalizes everyday life. The second is a bio-politics of population that utilizes administrative mechanisms to regulate and provide justification for techniques of discipline. In contrast to Foucault's concern with the utility and accumulation of bodies in the service of capital and profit that sustain a capitalist mode of production, the focus of the communication exploration and explanation within this chapter is on the utility of signs and their accumulation into a semantic landscape, a terrain of "common sense." As Mokros (1996) suggested:

> The relative value of any token of information (including the concept of information as a token) is thereby seen to not be a function of the economy, parsimony, and objectivity in its ability to represent external reality for "knowing" individuals. Instead its value derives from its preferential use, its currency in discourse. This then implies that information tokens are politically and ideologically laden and dependent, discursive realizations within the constitutive moments of communicative action. (pp. 3-4)

Lash and Urry (1994) also gestured toward an economy of signs that they saw primarily directed by information and communication structures, network flows and the accumulations of organized expressive symbols. This economy of signs only appears to be locally based. Drawing from the work of Appadurai (Lash & Urry, 1994), who identified five dimensions of flows—ethnoscapes, finanscapes, technoscapes, mediascapes, and ideoscapes—Lash and Urry argued that mediascapes that enable the flow and dissemination of cultural images and signs predominate. Thus, the power of mediational industries to thrust a particular sign into circulation and to promote its travel in local and global realms may be a strong factor in constructing a unifying and unidimensional semantic landscape for Generation X. And in turn, the power of Generation X-ers to redirect the sign's semiosis into more positive directions, reflected in the dimension of ideoscapes, the realm of common sense, is largely diminished. -

How are we then to understand the currency of the sign "Generation X?" Coupland (1991) drew strict boundaries for Generation X membership and defined it as the group born between 1961 and 1971. Coupland's invention of the sign "Generation X" was inspired by Fussell's (1983) sociological treatment of U.S. social class structure wherein he identified as "X" those groups who reject a highly competitive, modern mode of existence. Coupland co-opted this conceptualization in his fictional treatment of "Generation X," with an intent to reference the qualities of people, not generational positioning per se. He expressed this explicitly in a *Details* (Coupland, 1995) magazine article writing there that "marketers and journalists never understood that X is a term that defines not a chronological age but a way of looking at the world" (p. 72). Subsequent considerations of Generation X have nevertheless shown great interest in anchoring the sign "accurately" within the flow of history. Thus, one observes a concern with precise historical frames as for example the shift in the birth year that delineates Generation X membership from baby boomers from 1963, 1964, 1965, and even 1972 (see Bennett, Craig, & Rademacher, 1997). Reportedly then, estimated numbers for Generation X range from 46 million to 79.4 million depending on chronological markers of inclusion and exclusion.

The chronological delineation for this generation is only one element that produces uncertainty. Unlike previous generations, such as the baby boomers, Generation X is an amorphous and highly diverse mass, difficult to easily characterize and lacking in consumer and politically oriented predictability. For example, research indicates that Generation X-ers defy expectations of political involvement, partisanship, and consistency in decision making (Bennett & Rademacher, 1997; Dennis & Owen, 1997; Miller, 1991; Owen, 1997; Rice & Hamilton, 1996; Spiker & McKinney, 1999). Such findings suggest an ambivalence toward the existing political system, a characterization apparent in the words of one female Generation X-er shortly before the 1996 presidential elections: "I have a lot of conservative views; I have a lot of liberal views. If people would recognize that we're all like that, I'd have a lot more faith in our political system" (Leland & McCormick, 1996, p. 33). Thus, the currency of the sign in popular discourse may be in part driven by its ability to capture a blurring of traditionally distinct ideological positions among this huge segment of the population.

AN APPROACH TO THE ANALYSIS OF SEMIOTIC
LANDSCAPES: THE CASE OF "GENERATION X"

Naturalistic Inquiry

Any living system, whether the human body, a family, a city, or a sign can be said to have a "natural history," a natural unfolding (Bateson, 1996). Natural, in these terms, should not be understood as normative or socially sanctioned but rather as naturally occurring, that is to say uninterrupted by research requirements or preframed by theoretical demands (Blumer, 1969; Lincoln & Guba, 1985; Schutz, 1976). An inquiry of this sort begins with the most concrete of data and develops within these data more abstract and theoretical considerations. Naturalistic inquiry calls for systematic attention to the detail and the minuteness with which the empirical world presents itself and advocates representation of this detail and minuteness as an effort to capture the "morphology" of the phenomenon being considered (Scheff, 1996, 1997).

Databases Examined

Consistent with the premises of naturalistic inquiry, the data discussed in this chapter were gathered in an unobtrusive manner that preserves the ongoing traveling path of the sign "Generation X" and its interactions with other systems of signification. Five databases that are available through Dialog (an online compilation of databases that represent diverse professional communities and readerships) were selected and examined. These databases are as follow:

1. Newspapers in all regions of the United States (70 databases available including such publications as the *Washington Post, Los Angeles Times,* and *Newsday*).
2. Foreign newspapers (8 databases available including such publications as *The Times* from the United Kingdom and the *Toronto Star* from Canada).
3. Journals and magazines (18 databases available including such publications as the *Harvard Business Review* and *Consumer Reports*).
4. Major newswire services (16 databases available including such services as Reuters and AP News).
5. The Social Science Index (44 databases available including Art Abstracts, Social SciSearch, and ERIC).

Distribution of "Generation X" Titles Across Databases From 1991 to 1997

All databases were searched from 1991 to 1997 for articles whose titles made reference to the identity marker "Generation X." Titles were chosen as they provide a relatively accessible, manageable, and uniform unit of analysis across databases and time. As shown in Table 2.1, these searches yielded 2,853 articles containing the sign Generation X in the title across databases and years. The U.S. newspaper database accounted for 36% of these articles, with the Social Science Index containing the second highest frequency (28%) across all five databases.[1] Articles containing the sign Generation X although low in number the first 2 years, increase dramatically in frequency thereafter with 1994 the peak year for such articles within the 7 years examined. Given the sign's extensive diffusion into collective consciousness, the total number of articles contained in these databases is in some sense surprisingly small. The merits of such a conclusion are an empirical matter that would require comparative study of other comparable signs.

This discussion now considers the complete titles of articles including Generation X. This provides a way of mapping the semantic contexts "encountered" by the sign "Generation X" as it traveled through time.

TABLE 2.1
Frequency of Article Titles Containing "Generation X" for Selected Databases from 1991 to 1997

Database	Year							Total
	1991	1992	1993	1994	1995	1996	1997	
U.S. newspapers	13	9	128	381	189	181	125	1,026
Foreign newspapers	6	21	66	142	62	48	25	370
Newswire services	3	0	8	37	28	47	26	149
Journals and magazines	4	8	63	104	133	113	96	521
Social sciences	11	21	97	177	178	147	156	787
Total	37	59	362	841	590	536	428	2,853

[1]The titles of articles were not explicitly examined for redundancy. Because each database represents the work of different professionals and addresses varied readerships, the extent to which one can find redundancy in articles is not a concern. Rather, what is of interest is the natural path of the sign's travel, consistencies in the manner in which information professionals engaged with the sign "Generation X" and the overall availability of the sign for public consumption.

Mapping the Travels of "Generation X" Through Time

The full titles of articles containing "Generation X" offer a unit of analysis for mapping the semantic contexts within which the sign appeared through time. This mapping involved the application of semantic network analysis. Semantic network analysis examines clusters of words in a given unit (in this case a particular title) as a measure of the relationship between words and higher order concepts (Rice & Richards, 1985). Of particular concern here is the identification of the types and range of concepts in which "Generation X" was situated and if and how this situatedness or positioning shifted over time. Specifically, this line of analysis identified those words that occurred with "Generation X" in the titles and how these words may relate or cluster into semantic units. What such analysis also makes apparent are the types of words that do not appear in these titles, words that hypothetically might have been part of the semantic landscape frequented by "Generation X."

One cautionary remark merits consideration regarding mapping procedures. They are laden with political decision making and implications (Deleuze & Guattari, 1987; King, 1996). As Wood and Fels (1992) pointed out "There is nothing natural about a map. It is a cultural artifact, an accumulation of choices made among many choices every one of which reveals a value: not the world, but a slice of a piece of the world; not nature but a slant on it; not innocent, but loaded with intentions and purposes" (p. 108). This is certainly relevant to the current examination given that certain decisions were made regarding the unit of analysis, the bracketing of a time frame for the examination, and the method of analysis. The seven structural mappings of titles developed through semantic network analysis from 1991 to 1997 that organize the following discussion are thus not meant to imply a definitive representation of the totality of the discourse surrounding Generation X. Rather, they highlight certain aspects of the territory.

THE SEMANTIC LANDSCAPE OF "GENERATION X" OVER TIME

Given the theoretical and methodological considerations just cited, the chapter now explicitly considers the analysis of "Generation X" in the titles of articles drawn from multiple databases between the years 1991 and 1997. Specifically, the analysis identified regularities in semantic spaces surrounding the sign "Generation X" reported here according to the clustering and ordering within clusters of the most closely associated terms appearing in these titles (see Lemesianou, 1999, for a fuller explication of these analyses).

Maps of the Semantic Travels of "Generation X" by Year

Semantic Contexts for 1991. Coupland's fictional treatment, *Generation X: Tales for an Accelerated Culture*, appeared in 1991. As noted in Table 2.1, 37 titles contained "Generation X" that year (with none the previous year). Table 2.2 presents the results of the semantic network analysis for these 37 titles and offers a glimpse at the semantic associations noted for "Generation X" this initial year of its appearance.

Table 2.2 shows that the most frequent terms in titles for 1991 represent words from the extended title of Coupland's book. What's notable is the low frequency of the remaining terms found in these titles. However, of interest are the clusters of additional words, the first referencing age and links to the baby boom generation and the second referencing a consumer orientation.

This analysis suggests a number of things. First, the diffusion of "Generation X" through additional mass media, including newspapers, magazines, and scientific journals, was most closely associated with Coupland's book, presumably through book reviews and interviews of the author. The emergence of two additional clusters marks, however, the decoupling of the sign from its literary source. This may be said to represent a divisional terminology that moves to develop Generation X in terms of age-cohort discriminations as evidenced in the second cluster and toward consumptive practices in the third. This divisional terminology does not only function on the level of abstract discourse but rather is translated into very concrete, economically related terminology of target market, and links to one of Coupland's chapters in the fictional book titled "I Am Not A Target Market." Thus, the terms in general are strongly associated with Coupland's book and terminology. This pattern of semantic associations will be seen to shift drastically through time.

TABLE 2.2
Semantic Contexts of "Generation X" in 1991

Cluster 1	Cluster 2	Cluster 3
Accelerated		
Tales		
Culture		
Boomers		
	Age	
	Adolescence	
	Angst	
		Target
		Market
		Yuppie
		Excess

Semantic Contexts for 1992. A shift in semantic associations or contexts is already apparent in the next year examined as shown in Table 2.3, which reports data for 1992 with 59 titles containing "Generation X" appearing that year in the databases examined. Again, three dominant clusters are revealed with the most prominent, again, as in 1991, linked to Coupland's book. However, the other two travel in new directions with the second cluster including such terms as *primary, market,* and *aging* and the third cluster including terms like *trends* and *style, inspired* and *fashion.* These clusters of terms signal an initial rupture of the relationship between "Generation X" and its literary source. The sign had begun to enter into new constitutive relationships.

Although the second cluster links to Coupland's book through his name, the remaining terms accentuate a move also seen in 1991 toward delineation among generational cohorts. Within 1992, this delineation is not related to cohort characteristics but rather to the formation of a primary target market. Generation X as a target market is especially supported by the third cluster, which gestures toward consumerism through fashion, style, and trends. Of interest is how this moves away from a central thesis of Coupland's book, that sees Generation X-ers as people who retreat from the center and are resistant to being treated as a target market. Thus, the spotlight that Coupland's fictional heroes worked hard to evade by leading inconspicuous lives on the periphery is denied in public discourse through the primacy and significance Generation X-ers are given as a distinct group.

TABLE 2.3
Semantic Contexts of "Generation X" in 1992

Cluster 1	Cluster 2	Cluster 3
Boomers		
Accelerated		
Tales		
Culture		
	Primary	
	Market	
	Aging	
	Post	
	Baby	
	Coupland	
		Style
		Trends
		Fashion
		Inspired

Semantic Contexts for 1993. This rupture from the fictional becomes far more pronounced in the following year, 1993, a year in which titles containing "Generation X" increased sixfold over the prior year. Table 2.4 presents the results of semantic analysis for the 362 titles from that year.

Most striking in these data was the absence of any clear reference to Coupland's book. Whereas "Generation X" was closely associated with its literary origins in the previous two years, by 1993 the three most dominant clusters make no reference to this realm of inception. By 1993, the sign "Generation X" had assumed in a sense an autonomous "realness." The three clusters observed in 1993 titles signal an adversarial, contradictory relationship with each other. The dominant cluster includes such terms as *boomers, crude, portrait,* and *stereotype.* There is thus recognition that this divisional label that sets apart Generation X-ers from their older counterparts, baby boomers, is an oversimplification of the diversity that could characterize any one generation. In contrast to this, the second cluster re-inscribes Generation X-ers as a distinct group of consumers with such terms as *advertising* and *marketing, group* and *market.* The third cluster consisting of *targets, freeze,* and *frame* furthers the contrast to the first cluster, as it indicates that although there is a recognition of the crudeness involved in trying to capture a whole generation, attempts to freeze frame the moment and take advantage of perceived similarities, desires, fears, and so on are not abandoned. These contradictions may be indicative of negative reactions toward this sign or attempts by Generation X-ers to subvert its potential power.

TABLE 2.4
Semantic Contexts of "Generation X" in 1993

Cluster 1	Cluster 2	Cluster 3
Young		
Baby		
Boomers		
Crude		
Portrait		
Stereotype		
	Advertising	
	Marketing	
	Group	
	Market	
		Magazine
		Targets
		Freeze
		Frame

Semantic Contexts for 1994. In the next year, "Generation X" continued to move away from its literary source and travel into new semantic spaces. The year 1994 saw more than a doubling of articles compared to 1993 with nearly a 33-fold increase when compared with the first year assessed, 1991. As noted earlier (see Table 2.1), 1994 represents the peak year for "Generation X" articles over the course of the 7 years examined. The 3 years after 1994 show a decline in articles each year. Nevertheless, the frequency of articles in these years remains higher than any observed during the first 3 years studied. Analysis of the 841 titles in 1994 identified two dominant clusters, as shown in Table 2.5. The first cluster includes a mixture of terms—*baby, boomers, reality, bites, magazine,* and *marketing*—that suggest a tightening of the consumer association. The second and third clusters introduce a whole new realm of semantic associations not previously represented and include *health, social, security,* and *work.*

The travel of the sign into new semantic spaces may be related to the general public and political discourse surrounding the congressional elections in 1994. As in 1993, an inherent contradiction in the regularities of articulation concerning Generation X is apparent. On one hand, the reaffirmation of Generation X as consumers becomes apparent in links to Ben Stiller's movie *Reality Bites,* a movie supposedly directly targeting Generation X-ers while giving voice to their perceived realities, lives, fears, and potentialities. On the other hand, there is a broadening of the terrain entered as the terms seem to suggest Generation X-ers as a potentially growing group of political and workforce participants, concerned citizens who critically examine issues of social security and health care.

TABLE 2.5
Semantic Contexts of "Generation X" in 1994

Cluster 1	Cluster 2	Cluster 3
Young		
Baby		
Boomers		
Reality		
Bites		
Magazine		
Marketing		
	Health	
	Ads	
	Social	
	Security	
	Age	
		Old
		Work

Although the link of "Generation X" to Coupland's book seems to have gone underground, it remains evident. A major buzzword associated with Generation X in Coupland's (1991) novel was that of "McJob," defined by the author as "a low-pay, low-prestige, low-dignity, low-benefit, no-future job in the service sector" (p. 5). Generation X-ers had by now been characterized as overeducated and underemployed, a generation that had grown increasingly resentful of the promise of the American dream that never materialized. Thus, oftentimes, Generation X-ers were portrayed as whiners and slackers.

Semantic Contexts for 1995. This more serious treatment of Generation X continued to make itself apparent in the following year—1995. Nevertheless, the contradictory associations of Generation X-ers to consumerism as opposed to social and political participation remained. They manifest themselves in the context of referencing new consumer markets. Table 2.6 displays this in the semantic clusters derived from the 599 titles appearing that year. The most prominent cluster consisted of such terms as *targets, baby, boomers, marketing, job, market,* and *future.* These associations merge the distinction between Generation X-ers as marketing targets and citizens with employment concerns while reaffirming the generational division from their older counterparts, *baby boomers.* The second cluster consisted of the terms *Internet* and *software* and thereby introduced a new association to technologies and, in particular, the explosion of attention to the World Wide Web at roughly this time. As these new communication technologies made significant inroads into everyday modes of relating, both in the workplace and socially, more

TABLE 2.6
Semantic Contexts of "Generation X" in 1995

Cluster 1	Cluster 2	Cluster 3
Targets		
Baby		
Boomers		
Marketing		
Job		
Market		
Future		
	Internet	
	Software	
		Entrepreneurs
		Workers
		Security
		Post
		Boom

attention was devoted to understanding those segments of the population that embraced these new technological means of communication. This included consideration of what triggers interest in, and what needs were being fulfilled through such mediated engagements. Thus, a whole new industry, that of communication technologies, had turned its attention to Generation X. The final cluster included such terms as *entrepreneurs, workers,* and *security* indicating that Generation X-ers may have been perceived as pursuing alternative routes to employment.

So far, the assessment of the semantic travels of "Generation X" has established associations with three key themes. The first referenced the fictional story by Coupland and was prominent only in the first 2 years, from 1991 to 1992. A second theme of target market emerged in 1991 that initially remained closely aligned with the fictional treatment of Generation X and functioned as a negation in terms of identity formation. This theme subsequently became an affirmation of identity formation, assumed naturalness, and was affirmed in connections to the fashion, advertising, marketing, entertainment, and communications industries. A third prominent theme implicated Generation X as a significant group of citizens and workers, with less explicit connections to the realm of politics.

Semantic Contexts for 1996.   The relative disattending to the realm of politics through 1995 was counteracted in the year 1996, the year of the presidential elections in the United States. During this year, the travel of "Generation X" involves multiple associations to the semantic realm of politics and political participation. Table 2.7 presents semantic clusters for the 536 titles appearing in 1996.

The first cluster includes the terms *baby* and *boomers* and suggests a clear and definitive generational division between Generation X and baby boomers. This division stands alone as a significant part of the discourse surrounding Generation X for the first time in 1996. The second cluster references a new context of associations for the sign "Generation X" with such terms as *political, target, consumers, television, liberals,* and *strategy,* blending the realms of politics and business, the roles of people as citizens and as consumers. Managed, as consumers, by the business industry and strategically manipulated, as citizens, by politicians, Generation X-ers were characterized as being at the mercy of the powers that be. The final cluster includes such terms as *sidelines, coverage, anonymous, election,* and *jobs.* These associations take the connection to politics one step further and indicate again a contradiction of a different type. Are Generation X-ers now characterized as participants or mere observers in the political process? The term *sidelines* was a strong determinant of the discourse surrounding "Soccer

TABLE 2.7
Semantic Contexts of "Generation X" in 1996

Cluster 1	Cluster 2	Cluster 3
Boomers		
	Political	
	Target	
	Consumers	
	Television	
	Liberals	
	Strategy	
		Coverage
		Sidelines
		Election
		Anonymous
		Jobs
		Employees

Moms" in 1994, yet another group perceived to exercise political clout (Lemesianou, 1997). Yet, as the term suggests, the role of spectator does not afford much legitimacy or power to those it represents. Furthermore, are we to infer that Generation X-ers were characterized as occupying the spotlight in the upcoming elections or were they simply an anonymous group with no voice? Were they being catered to or ignored?

Semantic Contexts for 1997. Regardless of the contradictions indicated in the new semantic associations in 1996 relating to the political territory, this potentially newfound significance of Generation X-ers as political creatures did not last long. With the elections taking place in October 1996, the travel path of the sign in 1997 is particularly marked by the absence of any explicit references to politics. Table 2.8 displays the networks of terms for 428 titles appearing in the databases for that year.

The first 1997 cluster included the terms *market, culture,* and *financial;* the second, such terms as *entrepreneurs, funding, management, work, advertising, marketing,* and *women;* and the third, terms such as *plan, college, social,* and *slackers.* These clusters continue themes already observed in earlier years. The exploration of Generation X-ers as students or employees or entrepreneurs as well as their perceived impact on the culture had already appeared in the semantic travels of previous years that juxtaposed consumer and citizen roles.

TABLE 2.8
Semantic Contexts of "Generation X" in 1997

Cluster 1	Cluster 2	Cluster 3
Members		
Culture		
Market		
Financial		
	Entrepreneurs	
	Funding	
	Management	
	Work	
	Advertising	
	Marketing	
	Women	
		Social
		Slackers
		Plan
		College

Unique in 1997, the final year examined, was an emergent characterization of Generation X-ers as social slackers, a characterization that had existed in the broader discourse surrounding Generation X since the initial introduction of the sign "Generation X." It is a characterization that emerged from Coupland's fictional stories of characters in his book and one that had circulated extensively by word of mouth. It is not important that the frequent references to Generation X-ers as social slackers may be ones of affirmation or negation. Even in negation there is the recognition that a particular frame exists, as readily available to the public and requiring intervention. Thus, even attempts to sanitize and reconstruct the image of Generation X-ers, by redirecting the sign's path and infusing its semantic landscape with positive meanings, need to contend with the "context of availabilities" and in some sense re-inscribe the negative, the problematic, the orthodoxy.

A Summary of the Semantic Travels of "Generation X" Across Years

To summarize, the analyses just presented describe a pattern of shifting semantic spaces within which "Generation X" was situated over time, from 1991 to 1997. Although these semantic spaces preserved certain semantic associations, the shifts were notable, and indicative of an ongoing indexical relationship to Coupland's fictional realm that initially manifest itself explicitly in corresponding and complementary terms in 1991 and 1992, but that by 1993 had become invisible and antagonistic. Thus, by 1993, the sign "Generation X" assumed a certain degree of "realness" that rendered references to its fictional inception irrelevant. The antagonism to the fictional realm of inception was particularly evident in references to Generation X as a target market for advertisers generally, producers of popular culture and the fashion and technologies sectors in particular. This emphasis completely subverted Coupland's (1991) presentation of Generation X-ers as intentionally striving to abstain from a consumerist mode of existence: "We live small lives on the periphery; we are marginalized and there's a great deal in which we choose not to participate. We wanted silence and we have that silence now. . . . [N]ow that we live in the desert, things are much, much better" (p. 11).

This antagonism was furthered in the contradictions that kept emerging regarding characterizations of Generation X-ers and their consumer, professional, and political status signaling the contested manner in which semiotic spaces are produced. These contradictions, however, although reasserting the multiplicity of meanings, also reified through time what is taken for granted regarding this generation. The regularities observed in the traveling path of the sign into new territories suggest how semantic spaces are co-opted in an organized manner and come to constitute a discursive formation (Foucault, 1972). Such discursive formations are not isolated but rather in constant interaction with the larger public realm. Their ongoing reproduction and reconstitution is responsive to cultural, economic, and political transformations.

SIGN MATTERS AND SIGNS MATTER

The process of constitution and reconstitution of the semantic landscape as a path traveled by "Generation X" has been mapped in a sense through the rendering of a natural history of the sign. The prevalence of Thirdness as conceptualized by Peirce, namely the contingency of a sign's travel path on some conditional, provides the mechanism through which the sign's semiosis is motivated. The embeddedness of the sign within shifting relationships into larger realms of discourse, such as politics and culture, indicate the complexity of semiosis. A number of conditionals emerge from this examination, such as the advertising, marketing, entertainment, and new technologies industries, indicating that there is a struggle to appropriate and redefine this semantic landscape and the "currency" of the identity marker. The natural history of "Generation X," as a sign, was impacted by multiple systems of signification guided by their own histories and economies, driven primarily by concerns of power and capital. That is politicians, marketers, media professionals, and social scientists, all have a vested interest in segmenting the society, albeit for different purposes.

The power of these contenders in defining the semantic landscape of Generation X becomes particularly revelatory if one considers that the author, Coupland, declared the death of this generation in 1995 in an article in *Details* magazine. In this article he wrote "And now I'm here to say that X is over. I'd like to declare a moratorium on all the noise, because the notion that there now exists a different generation X, Y, K, whatever—is no longer debatable" (p. 72). No one was listening by then! For Coupland, this may be viewed as a strategic move, since his declarations came just in time for announcing a new catchphrase and book "Microserfs," a label that never achieved the recognition of "Generation X" and has not incited any pronounced struggles. Engagements with the semiosis of "Generation X" continue today. One might argue that the Pepsi slogan introduced in January 1997 "Generation Next" may have had more of a chilling effect on the sign's currency in public discourse than the declarations of its author. Coupland's inability to reclaim the sign and dissolve its potency makes a strong statement about the matter of signs.

Many have theorized the current epoch as a highly technocratic era that propels the individual into an isolated state of being (e.g., Bellah, Madsen, Sullivan, Swindler, & Tipton, 1985; Riesman, 1973; Sennett, 1992). It is this condition that shifts attention from modes of production and active participation to modes of consumption and spectatorship. Faced with an overabundance of constructions, the self turns inward, where the inner self now becomes the new frontier to explore and rewrite, resulting in what Lasch (1979) referred to as a "narcissistic preoccupation of the self," Simmel (1971) the "tragedy of culture," and Marcuse (1964) as "repressive desublimation." Thus, struggles that used to be incited over the accumulation of and access to products of labor, are replaced by struggles over the accumulation of and access to symbolic forms. As Goffman (1963) suggested, the perceived control over the production and dissemination of information concerning self-identity is fundamental. He wrote that stigmatized identity markers result in disempowerment given that "personal identity can and does play a structured, routine, standardized role in social organization" (p. 57). And, in part, this is a struggle for members of Generation X and how they contend with the stigmatized associations of the sign.

If signs matter, one might then ask: "What can members of this perceived generational cohort do to rehabilitate or transform the semantic landscape their generalized identity marker frequents?" "What control do Generation X-ers have over media conglomerates and how much voice are they afforded?" Given the dynamic nature of semiosis, I argue that the power of Generation X-ers to redefine the identity marker is limited to the personal level. Consistent with Lash and Urry's argument, I suggest that local communication practices and struggles that fail to tap into the more global mediated flows can result in incremental, personal empowerment but do not have significant impact on the natural history of the sign (Lemesianou, 1999). Rather, organized activism on a more global level is necessary in order to seriously challenge the bounds of the sign and the dominant discourse surrounding Generation X. For Generation X-ers, identity matters will continue to persist. For the sign's matter as a web of complex associations creates the conditions for how it matters in lived experience. Although those who are indexed by the sign may feel validated in everyday contexts, in their roles as hard-working professionals, savvy consumers, and informed voters, they nonetheless will continue to contend with the devaluation and disconfirmation of self that result from the semantic spaces "Generation X" visited in its travels.

REFERENCES

Bakhtin, M.M. (1981). Discourse in the novel. In M. Holquist (Ed.), *The dialogic imagination: Four essays* (pp. 259-422). Austin: University of Texas Press.

Bateson, G. (1996). Communication. In H.B. Mokros (Ed.), *Interaction and identity: Information and behavior* (Vol. 5, pp. 45-70). New Brunswick, NJ: Transaction.

Bellah, R.N., Madsen, R., Sullivan, W.M., Swindler, A., & Tipton, S.M. (1985). *Habits of the heart: Individualism and commitment in American life.* New York: Harper & Row.

Bennett, S.E., Craig, S.C., & Rademacher, E.W. (1997). Generations and change: Some initial characteristics. In S.C. Craig & S.E. Bennett (Eds.), *After the boom: The politics of Generation X* (pp. 1-20). New York: Rowman & Littlefield.

Bennett, S.E., & Rademacher, E.W. (1997). The "age of indifference" revisited: Patterns of political interest, media exposure, and knowledge among Generation X. In S.C. Craig & S.E. Bennett (Eds.), *After the boom: The politics of Generation X* (pp. 21-42). New York: Rowman & Littlefield.

Berger, P.L., & Luckmann, T. (1966). *The social construction of reality: A treatise in the sociology of knowledge.* New York: Doubleday.

Blumer, H. (1969). *Symbolic interactionism: Perspective and method.* Englewood Cliffs, NJ: Prentice-Hall.

Bourdieu, P. (1977). *Outline of a theory of practice.* Cambridge, MA: Cambridge University Press.

Coupland, D. (1991). *Generation X: Tales for an accelerated culture.* New York: St. Martin's Press.

Coupland, D. (1995, June). Generation X'd. *Details, 14,* 72.

Deleuze, G., & Guattari, F. (1987). *A thousand plateaus.* Minneapolis: University of Minnesota Press.

Dennis, J., & Owen, D. (1997). The partisanship puzzle: Identification and attitudes of Generation X. In S.C. Craig & S.E. Bennett (Eds.), *After the boom: The politics of Generation X* (pp. 43-62). New York: Rowman & Littlefield.

Europa. (2001). [On line]. Available: http://europa.eu.int/euro/html.

Foucault, M. (1970). *The order of things: An archaeology of the human sciences*. New York: Random House.

Foucault, M. (1972). *The archaeology of knowledge and the discourse of language* (A. M. Sheridan Smith, Trans.). New York: Pantheon.

Foucault, M. (1980). Questions on geography. In C. Gordon (Ed.), *Power/knowledge: Selected interviews and other writings 1972-1977* (pp. 63-77). New York: Pantheon.

Fussell, P. (1983). *Class: A guide through the American status system*. New York: Ballantine.

Geertz, C. (1983). *Local knowledge: Further essays in interpretive anthropology*. New York: Basic Books.

Goffman, E. (1963). *Stigma: Notes on the management of spoiled identity*. New York: Simon & Schuster.

Harre, R. (1986). An outline of the social constructionist viewpoint. In R. Harre (Ed.), *The social construction of emotions* (pp. 2-14). New York: Basil Blackwell.

Heidegger, M. (1987). *An introduction to metaphysics* (R. Manheim, Trans.). New Haven, CT: Yale University Press.

Jakobson, R. (1985). Language and culture. In S. Rudy (Ed.), *Roman Jakobson: Selected writings* (pp. 101-112). Paris: Mouton.

Jakobson, R. (1990). *On language* (L. R. Waugh & M. Monville-Burston, Eds.), Cambridge, MA: Harvard University Press.

Kaplan, C. (1996). *Questions of travel: Postmodern discourses of displacement*. London: Duke University Press.

King, G. (1996). *Mapping reality: An exploration of cultural cartographies*. New York: St. Martin's Press.

Lasch, C. (1979). *The culture of narcissism*. New York: Norton.

Lash, S., & Urry, J. (1994). *Economies of signs and space*. Thousand Oaks, CA: Sage.

Leland, J., & McCormick, J. (1996). The children of gridlock. *Newsweek, 1*, 33.

Lemesianou, C.A. (1997). *What's in a buzzword? The rise and fall of the "Soccer Mom" in the 1996 presidential election media coverage*. Unpublished manuscript, Rutgers, The State University of New Jersey, New Brunswick.

Lemesianou, C.A. (1999). *The geographies of discourse and lived experience: A communication approach*. Unpublished doctoral dissertation, Rutgers University, The State University of New Jersey, New Brunswick.

Lincoln, Y.S., & Guba, E.G. (1985). *Naturalistic inquiry*. Beverly Hills, CA: Sage.

Lyotard, J.F. (1993). *The postmodern condition: A report on knowledge* (G. Bennington & B. Massumi, Trans.). Minneapolis: University of Minnesota Press.

Marcuse, H. (1964). *One-dimensional man*. Boston: Beacon Press.

Miller, W.E. (1991). Party identification, realignment, and party voting: Back to the basics. *American Political Science Review, 85*, 557-568.

Mokros, H.B. (1996). From information and behavior to interaction and identity. In H.B. Mokros (Ed.), *Interaction and identity: Information and behavior* (Vol. 5, pp. 1-22). New Brunswick, NJ: Transaction.

Mokros, H.B., & Deetz, S.A. (1996). What counts as real? A constitutive view of communication and the disenfranchised in the context of health. In E.B. Ray (Ed.), *Communication and the disenfranchised: Social health issues and implications* (pp. 29-44). Hillsdale, NJ: Erlbaum.

Owen, D. (1997). Mixed signals: Generation X's attitudes toward the political system. In S.C. Craig & S.E. Bennett (Eds.), *After the boom: The politics of Generation X* (pp. 85-106). New York: Rowman & Littlefield.

Peirce, C.S. (1931-1935). *Collected papers of Charles Sanders Peirce* (Vol. 1-6; C. Hartshorne & P. Weiss, Eds.). Cambridge, MA: Harvard University Press.

Peirce, C.S. (1991). *Peirce on signs* (J. Hoopes, Ed.). Chapel Hill: The University of North Carolina Press.

Politics and the X Generation. (1996). [On line]. Available: http://www.xgeneration.org/index.html.

Rice, R.E., & Richards, W., Jr. (1985). An overview of network analysis methods. In B. Dervin & M.J. Voigt (Eds.), *Progress in communication sciences* (Vol. 6, pp. 105-165). Norwood, NJ: Ablex.

Rice, T.W., & Hamilton, T.A. (1996). Partisanship over time: A comparison of United States panel data. *Political Research Quarterly, 49,* 191-202.

Riesman, D. (1973). *The lonely crowd: A study of the changing American character.* New Haven, CT: Yale University Press.

Rogers, E.M. (1983). *Diffusion of innovations* (3rd ed.). New York: The Free Press.

Rogers, E.M. (1995). *Diffusion of innovations* (4th ed.). New York: The Free Press.

Saussure, F. (1974). *Course in general linguistics.* London: Fontana.

Scheff, T.J. (1996). Part/whole analysis: Stages of inquiry. In H.B. Mokros (Ed.), *Interaction and identity: Information and behavior* (Vol. 5, pp. 25-44). New Brunswick, NJ: Transaction.

Scheff, T.J. (1997). *Emotions, the social bond, and human reality: Part/whole analysis.* New York: Cambridge University Press.

Schutz, A. (1976). *The phenomenology of the social world* (G. Walsh & F. Lehnert, Trans.). London: Heinemann.

Sennett, R. (1992). *The fall of public man.* New York: Norton.

Shotter, J. (1989). Social accountability and the social construction of "You." In J. Shotter & K.J. Gergen (Eds.), *Texts of identity* (pp. 133-151). Newbury Park, CA: Sage.

Simmel, G. (1971). *On individuality and social forms* (D.L. Levine, Ed.). Chicago: The University of Chicago Press.

Spiker, J.A., & McKinney, M.S. (1999). Measuring political malaise in the 1996 presidential election. In L.L. Kaid & D.G. Bystrom (Eds.), *The electronic election perspectives in the 1996 campaign communication* (pp. 319-334). Mahwah, NJ: Erlbaum.

Taylor, C. (1989). *Sources of the self: The making of modern identity.* Cambridge, MA: Harvard University Press.

Whorf, B.L. (1956). *Language, thought, and reality.* Cambridge, MA: MIT Press.

Wood, D., & Fels, J. (1992). *The power of maps.* New York: Guilford.

3

Culture Matters

Cultural Multiplicity and Local Identity in Japanese Advertising

Michael Maynard

Culture matters addresses the question of how a local culture preserves its identity in the face of cultural multiplicity. The question is important because it deals with issues of homogenization of culture, the prospect of a one-world culture, and the supposed loss of national and cultural identity. Through technological, commercial, and cultural "synchronization" (Hamelink, 1983), the impetus for which comes from the West especially the United States, the rest of the world is supposedly becoming increasingly Americanized (e.g., Barber, 1995; Ritzer, 1998).

Advertising and Globalization

Specifically, these types of culture matters are examined in the context of Japanese advertising. Advertising certainly represents one example or site where a multiplicity of signs, symbols, and icons taken from various cultures, and then mixed and matched to suit the needs of advertisers is apparent. But do the advertisements then precipitate a *cultural* globalization? Some would claim that individual societies are losing their local cultural identities as a result of a heightened globalization process through which media convergence and the marketing imperative are making everyone on the planet part of the same consumerist culture. The problem with this claim lies in the specifics. Aside from the McDonalds, Disneyworlds, and Pizza Huts that have cropped up with increasing frequency in non-Western cultures (Ferguson, 1992), where is the evidence that the world is becoming one world culture? Where does one look for empirical support? Anecdotal information and hearsay do not make a very compelling case either for or against the notion that, beyond our control, the world has become one big village.

Even more problematic is the question of identity. Are people around the world incrementally becoming the same because a worldwide consumer culture is eroding their native cultures? The rise of ethnic identification movements and religious fundamentalism offers sobering evidence of resistance to forces of globalization (e.g., Friedman, 1994; Giddens, 2000).

To make sense of the big issues of cultural globalization and identity, we need to examine specific sites where these abstractions become reality. The rationale for this study, therefore, is that any theoretical claim about globalization must be based on cultural artifacts that promote senses of identity. Evidence of cultural globalization may then be researched, for example, in the iconic representations found in the print advertisements of a non-Western nation. The specific question addressed in this chapter is "How common (and in what form) are non-Japanese iconic representations in advertisements targeted to Japanese teenagers?" This leads to a second question, "How is Japanese self (local identity) preserved in advertisements that incorporate otherness, and are targeted to its own youth culture (global space)?" It is assumed, of course, that in the analysis of identity in the Japanese case that non-Japanese representations will be predominantly, if not exclusively, Western—particularly American.

Advertising as Discursive Multicultural Spaces

These questions are grounded in the assumption that advertising texts represent discursive spaces that display a variety of cultural values and beliefs, not merely product pitches. To address these questions, this chapter reports efforts to deconstruct these discursive spaces to show how they may be regarded as contested territories of cultural identity. The aim is to identify the types and frequency of icons of Western culture, predominantly American culture, placed in one Japanese advertising outlet, namely, magazines targeted to Japanese teenagers. It is assumed that advertisements in magazines aimed at Japanese teenagers will be especially rich in representations of American culture, although the rightness of this assumption is not specifically considered here.

Advertising self-consciously projects images of culture's ideal Self. Yet, advertising also complicates this by incorporating idealized images of Otherness within its product pitches. Assuming Harris' (1998) logic, that peers have more effect on childhood personality development than parents, and that what the young person experiences outside the home in the company of peers is what matters most, mediated peer images such as appear in magazine advertisements would seem to play a significant part in the development of a person's self-image.

The study conceptualizes the advertisement as a multicultural space. This is because advertising is the modernist vanguard to consumer culture, a culture of consumption that traverses the globe. The very existence of an advertisement as we know it represents a global culture. Placed within a magazine, a medium for mass communication—yet targeted to a specific demographic group—the advertisement is part of a global network of consumerist communications. Advertisements are embedded within a standardized consumerist culture, which can be found anywhere in the world where civilizations are sufficiently developed to support mass media communications. Magazines, after all, are largely financed by the sale of advertisements. Advertisements represent multicultural space insofar as they, by definition, embody a global lifeworld. Within this already multicultural space, then, how does a local culture preserve its unique identity? This study examines just how the Japanese anchor their self-identity within the multicultural spaces of advertising.

Why Japan?

Japan's long history of active Western cultural importation and occasional direct intervention, makes it a prime candidate for an investigation of Western cultural influence. In addition to being described as insular and different, Japanese culture has also been described as quintessentially postmodern in that the Japanese freely appropriate styles, trends, icons, systems, philosophies, and so forth from other cultures (Barthes, 1982). Ivy (1993) noted that many (intellectuals) speak of Japan as thoroughly postmodern in its cultural forms. The de-centering, fragmented, pastiche aspects of Japan's postmodern condition as applied to its mass media production offer fertile ground for study (Ben-Ari, Moeran, & Valentine, 1990; Horne, 1996).

CONSIDERATIONS OF CULTURAL MATTERS:
A COMMUNICATION FRAMEWORK

Culture is expressed, in part, through a body of texts, signs, icons, and symbols that conveys its values. The expression of culture here includes the specialized and professional discourses of the arts, and the commodified output of the culture industries (e.g., the advertising agencies). Communication, in this context, refers to the ways in which these texts, signs, icons, and symbols are moved through time and space and the processes whereby they are constituted.

In conducting this descriptively anchored, interpretive study of the discursive practices extant in the Japanese advertising text, I draw from textual analysis. The task is approached from what Mokros (1996) called a constitutive theory of communication, with clear antecedents and links to a social constructionist perspective (Berger & Luckmann, 1966). A constitutive approach to communication recognizes that the significance of communication resides in human interaction and sees the communicative event as the site of both meaning and identity. The interpretation of print advertising appearing in Japanese youth magazines starts from the premise that advertising is not merely a physical product or an informative or persuasive sales pitch, but is a socially and culturally constituted semiotic sphere. Within this sphere, semantic, social, and cultural values are embedded, reproduced, and negotiated. Identity, as well, is negotiated both "within text" and "without text" within this semiotic sphere. "Without text" refers to the interplay between the ad and its audience. To understand the advertising text communicationally, one must realize that the "within-text" site reflects, overtly and covertly, the cultural lifeworld of both the source and the recipient. Seen as such, the advertising text exists as a constitutive process of cultural communication between the Self (Japanese) and the (Western) Other, "within text," not only with its audience.

The communicational approach applied in this study follows ontological assumptions of the Japanese (as well as all peoples) as relational beings (e.g., Deetz, 1994; Mokros, 1995, 1996; Mokros & Deetz, 1996; Mumby, 1997). Applying Carey's (1975, p. 10) social constructionist claim, that "communication is a symbolic process whereby reality is produced, maintained, repaired and transformed" to the advertising text, I take the position that the icon-selection act, when creating an advertisement, although prompted by the logic of the marketing imperative, is, after all, a communicatively derived social construction. The words, icons, and claims constitutive of the total communication artifact (the ad) do not simply represent a reality "out there." Rather, advertising reflects what Schudson (1984) called a fictive *capitalist realism* whereby the actors, the action, the plot are not real, but hyper-real, in what Schudson described as their constructed glorification of the pleasures and freedoms of consumer choice.

The theoretical perspective taken in this research follows the logic of the distinction between information and communication (Deetz, 1994; Mokros, 1996). It conceptualizes advertisement not merely strategically—as a tool or process of message exchange—but as constitutive, as a (within-text) site "within which experience achieves a sense of coherence, structure and meaning" (Mokros, 1996, p. 4).

Given that advertisements strive to identify with their target audience, a process of self-identification is at work when readers consume advertising. The next section addresses theoretical perspectives on the Self that guided the development of this research (Maynard, 2001).

Identities: Mediated, Imagined, and Culturally Negotiated

Obviously the within-text identities are mediated and imagined. Even the without-text "consuming" identity the magazine reader is expected to relate to, is a "constructed" identity. Instructive for the understanding of these multiple mediated and imagined images of self is the postmodern discourse that views identity as contingent (White, 1992) and as discursively and interactively constituted (e.g., Gergen, 1991). Derrida's (1976) deconstruction of self, Foucault's (1972, 1978) death of the author, and Baudrillard's (1981, 1988) concept of the individual as merely a point in a vast network of images, to cite some of the major French postmodern writers, all suggest an erosion of subjectivity, agency—or the contestation of "I" (Taylor, 1989, 1991). The erosion of subjectivity and annihilation of autonomous identity offer useful heuristics in researching how the Japanese ideal type, the within-text youth persona, is constructed and negotiated with the American ideal type, the within-text persona of the Other, within the space of the advertisement. These identities are not fixed, but are contested and negotiated through a linguistic and visual grammar. Applying Gergen's (1996) conceptualization of the "relational sublime," thus placing into prominence the significance of "relatedness" to the postmodern advertising text of ads directed to Japanese teenagers, affords a rich field of analysis where the focus of study is on how identities are formed through relatedness. Gergen (1996) emphasized the centrality of "relatedness" to meaning and culture, stating "the capacity to give life to words, and thus to transform culture, is usefully traced not to internal resources but to relatedness" (p. 138).

Particularly significant to my research project is the concept of intertextuality, where different "imagined" and constructed cultural identities are represented. As suggested in the postmodernist literature, Japanese advertising freely incorporates images (identities) of the Other, and intertextualizes them through cultural appropriation. My concern is with studying which cultural signs of the (mediated) Other are selected, and how they are linguistically and visually represented in the Japanese advertising text.

AN APPROACH TO THE EXPLORATION OF CULTURAL MATTERS IN ADVERTISING

Assuming then that advertising is imbued with identity, and that globalization remains a murky concept unless grounded in empirical data, the approach follows a logic of classification which calibrates how and to what extent the West, as the Other, is presented in advertising directed at Japanese teenagers. Specifically, in this chapter I show how an analysis of iconic representations offers a view of the intertextuality of the advertising, thus capturing the relational qualities between represented Self and Other. This involves examining what kind of, and to what extent, Western icons interpenetrate the space of the advertisement. Here, I limit consideration to icons of place. Icons of place are coded according to temporality, as either referencing contemporary or nostalgic places, and according to source, as either Japanese or Western, that is, Self or Other.

In this way, I consider Japanese advertising in magazines aimed at teens to assess how Otherness, Western icons, are integrated into the ads. This includes differentiating ads according to types, and also involves conceptualizing ads as semantic spaces with predictable features.

The Case of Japanese Advertising

Magazines, according to Dentsu (1994), are a $14 billion industry in Japan. With the exception of comic magazines, lifestyle is the largest selling category of magazines in Japan (Rosenberger, 1992). The youth-oriented market, driven by fashion and trendy lifestyle targeting young men and women separately, tends to feature four-color glossy monthlies, bimonthlies and weeklies. The colorful style and design of Japan's popular youth-oriented magazines are calculated to attract attention on the display rack, Japan's primary distribution channel for such magazines. Many pages, including special inserts, feature multiple products and prices giving sections of the magazine the look of a quality catalogue.

Narrowly targeted magazines in Japan such as the six whose ads are considered in this chapter are popular and widely read (Johansson, 1994). Moreover, in comparison to broadcast media, loyalty is print's strongest selling point. Quoting Robert Brennan, president of Starcom Media Services, a unit of Leo Burnett, Bounds (1999) said, "With a magazine, you seek it out, and it talks to you about very specific things in your life. This choice by consumers, to spend uninterrupted, focused time with magazines, is the most powerful thing the industry has going for it" (p. B3). Given the high literacy rate in Japan, these conclusions no doubt apply also to Japanese teens and young adults. These conclusions also support the point made earlier that magazines, as a highly segmented form of advertising, encourage "interaction" between content and reader.

The six magazines whose ads were studied are representative of today's Japanese youth market. They include *Fineboys, Hot Dog Press*, and *Popeye*, for young men; and *PeeWee, Seventeen*, and *Puchi Seven*, for young women. *Fineboys* and *PeeWee* are monthlies, and *Hot Dog Press, Popeye, Seventeen*, and *Puchi Seven* are semi-monthlies. Analyses reported subsequently are based on all 116 issues of these magazines published between July 1996 and July 1997, including 58 issues directed at young men and 58 at young women. Gender differences, however, are not considered in this chapter.

In reviewing the titles of these magazines one is already led to appreciate the prominence of Western penetration. The titles appear as seen here, in English, and are themselves part of a linguistic trend in Japan for naming new things in English (Burton, 1983; O'Barr, 1994). Titles such as *Hot Dog Press* and *Popeye*, two of the young men's magazines selected for this study, are indicative of how American cultural tokens (hot dog, as American food; Popeye, as American cartoon character) are appropriated into the Japanese media stream. Even *Puchi Seven* (*puchi* is the Japanese rendition for the French word *petite*) is a Westernized title.

The six magazines examined are general interest (as opposed to comic or sexually oriented) teen/young adult magazines that provide lifestyle information relevant to adolescents. The publishers of *Seventeen*, for example, report that the magazine is for high school girls, and that it addresses "problems and interests of girls at the turning point of their life" (Dentsu, 1994, p. 307). According to *Zasshi Shinbun Sookatarogu* (1993), the combined total circulation of the six magazines is about 2.8 million. All are available in convenience stores (24-hour outlets such as Family Mart and Seven-Eleven), train station kiosks, and other easily accessible locations that Japanese teenagers are likely to frequent.

The Coding of Icons of Place

All nonredundant ads were examined within the issues of these six magazines. Icons of place were coded according to one of six types of settings and included four identifiable real-world settings defined according to culture and time. (Icons of the West were, in fact, overwhelmingly of America and I use this term subsequently to avoid confusing "the West," with the American West.) Culture was coded as either Japanese or American and time was either contemporary or nostalgic/romantic. According to these two dimensions, identifiable real-world settings included Japanese contemporary, Japanese nostalgic/romantic, American contemporary, and American nostalgic/romantic. The two remaining coding categories included unidentifiable real-world settings and settings that had no resemblance to real-world environments, referred to as Limbo settings. Each is explained briefly here.

Japanese Nostalgic/Romantic Settings. Icons of a nostalgic or romantic Japan capture historical or imagined scenes of traditional Japanese culture, a culture that is separated out from Western culture. Thus, a *torii* (gate to a shrine), a *tatami*-matted room, rice paper sliding doors, a person performing the tea ceremony, a noodle shop or sumo wrestling arena, and other such scenes were coded as nostalgic/romantic Japanese settings. Also coded as instances of such settings were ads that referenced geographic (and architectural) icons associated with a traditional/romantic sense of Japan, as, for example, a small oval shaped illustration of Mt. Fuji situated within the contact information at the bottom of an ad for *sake*.

Japanese Contemporary Settings. Icons that represent present-day Japanese settings included such familiar places as the Tokyo Tower, *Shinjuku* Train Station, or the *Ginza*. The Bullet Train was also coded as a Japanese contemporary setting. Less well-known settings such as street corners, apartments, retail stores, or office environments were coded in this category if it was clear that these were contemporary Japanese settings.

American Nostalgic/Romantic Settings. Icons rendered as either photographs or illustrations of historical scenes of America, such as the pilgrims, frontier settlements, New York City in the 1920s, and so forth were coded as examples of an American nostalgic/romantic setting. This category of settings also included romanticized representations of American geographic landmarks such as Mount Rushmore, Monument Valley, the Grand Canyon, or Arizona's highways. The concept of "place" in these settings includes mythical places, the past, and nostalgic recreations—as was also the case with comparable Japanese settings. Scenes and artifacts that were obviously indicative of America's past were coded in this category. Here, 1950s vintage artifacts such as soda fountains, hoop skirts, drag racing cars, and old Coca-Cola serving trays were common examples. A small illustration of an Edwin's jean patch depicting the American West was also coded in this category (Edwin is a Japanese company that markets primarily in Japan, with an invented English name).

American Contemporary Settings. Photographs and representations of the West and America today fall under this category. They included such portrayals as the Golden Gate Bridge, Times Square, Chicago's State Street, or contemporary suburban strip malls.

Unidentifiable Real-World Settings. Some advertisements appealed to a sense of place—an exterior location, or an interior setting—without clarity as to where this place was culturally situated. These are referred to as culturally unidentifiable settings. Typically, such ads presented an out-of-focus or blurred background photograph showing greenery or an urban street that revealed no features by which to determine a sense of place or a sense of time.

Limbo Settings. Many ads contained no sense of real-world place or time. Often, the background was the set in which the product or the model was photographed. These types of ads are referred to as settings in limbo.

REPRESENTATIONS OF CULTURAL SETTINGS IN JAPANESE ADVERTISEMENTS

Table 3.1 presents the classification of 1,858 nonredundant advertisements contained in the magazines according to three general types of settings defined by the classification system just introduced. These were limbo settings, identifiable real-world settings, and unidentifiable real-world settings. The majority of ads ($N = 1,167$), 63% of the sample, included only a limbo setting, with no hint of any real-world sense of place. Identifiable real-world settings were present in 512 (28%) of the advertisements with the remaining 179 ads (9%) presenting real-world but unidentifiable settings. Thus, the background presented to Japanese teens is, most commonly "limbo," a nowhere place, neither in Japan nor a foreign country—indeed a place not of the world as we tend to imagine it.

TABLE 3.1
Background Settings of 1,858 Japanese Ads

Limbo settings	1,167	(63%)
Identifiable settings	512	(28%)
Unidentifiable settings	179	(9%)
Total	1,858	(100%)

Among those 512 ads where a Japanese or American place could be identified, 326 (64%) explicitly depicted a Japanese setting. American settings accounted for the remaining 186 (36%) ads with identifiable settings and represented roughly 10% of all ads examined.

Table 3.2 cross-classifies these 512 ads containing culturally explicit settings as backgrounds by the time frame reflected in these settings, as either contemporary or romantic/nostalgic. Contemporary ads were more common (66%) than nostalgic ads (34%). However, the data in Table 3.2 clearly suggest an association between cultural setting and time frame. This was born out by a chi-square test of these data that showed significant association ($\chi2 = 72.7$, $df = 1$, $p < .001$), with Japanese settings more likely characterized by a contemporary time-frame and American settings more likely in the nostalgic time-frame.

To summarize what has so far been reported, most of the products in the 1,858 advertisements studied were set in a nowhere space, a neutral, limbo environment devoid of explicit cultural place markings. Those containing explicit place settings were nearly twice as likely (1.75 to 1) to depict a Japanese rather than an American context. These ads containing explicit place settings were also nearly twice as likely (1.91 to 1) to be situated in contemporary rather than nostalgic contexts. Although one would expect that Japanese contexts would be more commonly portrayed than American contexts in these ads, the ratio of Japanese to American contexts is smaller than one might expect. It is certainly noteworthy that 1 in 10 of the number of ads examined had an American setting as a background and that these accounted for more than a third of those ads containing a culturally identifiable background. Additionally, ads with American contexts as background stand out from their Japanese counterparts as they are significantly more often set in nostalgic settings and significantly less often in contemporary settings. It would seem that contemporary or (post)modern time would have greater appeal to teenagers than tradition or nostalgia and that advertisers would capitalize on this. That something much more complex is represented is clear as contemporary times

TABLE 3.2

**Identifiable Background Settings for 512 Japanese Ads
Cross-Classified by Culture (Japan or America) and Time
(Contemporary or Nostalgic)**

	Japan	America	Total
Contemporary	258 (79%)	78 (42%)	336 (66%)
Nostalgic	68 (21%)	108 (58%)	176 (34%)
Total	326 (100%)	186 (100%)	512 (100%)

are associated with Japan and nostalgic times with America, within a broader context of nowhere, a world of limbo. Something more would seem to be going on here than just marketing newness to teenagers who are assumed to have a taste for the contemporary, the modern.

The ads invite the young Japanese reader to identify not merely with matter-of-fact, current icons of another culture, but particularly with idealized nostalgic icons of that culture. Although these are advertiser choices, the patterns observed have interesting relevance for how identity is constructed. While scenes of American culture constitute a prominent part of the visual imagery targeted to Japanese youth, Japanese culture nevertheless sustains its identity. That is, the iconic representations of America are highly selected views of the Other, as filtered through the cultural lens of Japanese ad-makers.

The analysis to this point says little directly to the question posed at the outset, namely, how a local culture (Japan) preserves its identity within a context of cultural multiplicity. To address this question directly the next section offers a fine-grained analysis of two specific ads, both depicting nostalgic American settings. This analysis, at first glimpse, suggests how profoundly culturally contested these advertising spaces are. Indeed, when the language represented in the ads is considered, all of the ads contain an English presence in some form (i.e., Web sites) and most contain English words elsewhere within the ads (see Maynard, 2001). However, a closer look begins to reveal how apparent cultural tensions, and impositions of Otherness, are managed so as to preserve a very firm sense of Japanese identity.

DOMESTICATING AMERICAN NOSTALGIA

Two ads for Japanese domestic products help to show how Japanese identity persists even when iconic (and linguistic) representations of the West (i.e., scenes of America, and English text) are prominently displayed. The first, Nissan's Datsun automobile ad, exemplifies iconicity of place (or so it seems). The second, Honda's City Scrambler (Benly CL50) motorcycle ad provides an example of how Japanese ad makers harness nostalgic iconicity of Otherness (American identity itself set in limbo) in the creation of a retro image for a vintage Japanese product.

Nissan and the American West

The first ad considered (Fig. 3.1) markets a Nissan automobile, a Datsun, with both visual and textual images of the nostalgic American West prominent. This ad appeared seven times (four times in *Hot Dog Press*, twice in

FIG. 3.1.
Reprinted by permission of Nissan Jidoosha Kabushikigaisha.

Fineboys, and once in *Popeye)* between July 1996 and June 1997. This is but one of many automobile ads contained in these magazines, with 86 Nissan automobile advertisements alone in the three male teen magazines that carried this specific ad. Within these three male teen magazines, Nissan automobile ads accounted for about 8.3% of the 1,035 ads contained in these magazines. The ad aims to introduce a new model in the Datsun automobile line: a 4 x 4 pick-up.

The layout of the ad is divided into two parts. The upper half presents a photograph of a scene from the American West, which was coded as nostalgic. The lower half is a "beauty shot" of the pick-up, along with copy, signage, and small print. Superimposed over the photograph of the American West are three textual configurations.

Starting on the left, in the upper corner, are the manufacturer's logo (NISSAN) and above it, in an even larger font, the byline, in English, "Life Together." Below the Nissan logo is the philosophical phrase, written in Japanese, "Human tenderness to the car." Skipping down, one reads, also in Japanese, part of Nissan's corporate public service message, "Controlled speed, good driving," and "Wear your seat belt."

On the right-hand side of the top half of the ad, running vertically down the page in traditional Japanese writing style is the headline, which literally translates "Call it (me) Hot Dat!" The largest text in this upper photograph, and in fact, the largest text in the entire ad (all caps and at about 72-size font) is in English, and reads: HOT DAT. Thus, HOT DAT is represented here in both Japanese, in its *most traditional syllabary* (see Maynard, 2001), and English. The content text HOT DAT is clearly contemporary although represented in both traditional and contemporary icons. These words, HOT and DAT, are stacked and placed in the center of the photograph. A bolt of lightning is shooting through the "O" in the word "HOT." Immediately below this prominent display are the words "On Route 66," a reference to the fabled American road from Chicago to Los Angeles that captured the American imagination prior to the interstate highway system.

The ad's primary text is positioned between the bottom edge of the photograph and the contour of the truck in the lower half of the page. The lines are not arranged in the traditional horizontal alignment, but are placed somewhat diagonally. The copy is in Japanese. This is how it translates into English:

Sub-Headline:
Like the expression of this guy [vehicle], discover your HOT self.

Copy:
Route 66, the legendary highway that crosses the American continent, 2,500 miles from Chicago to Los Angeles. Once to the west, and to the west, the people heading to the new world rushed through with big dreams and hopes in their heart. The new pick-up truck that makes you experience the strong and powerful spirit etched on the highway is this guy [vehicle]. More than anything else, the fearless and firm attitude [of the vehicle] is great. The vehicle runs even tougher than before, and that is great. It is almost as if the entire body is filled with "adventure mind" [adventurous spirit]. The name is HOT DAT. Those who sustain never-cooling passion, we wish for you to drive this masterfully.

Although no person is visible in the advertisement, the copy explicitly refers to the new Datsun as *koitsu*, a "guy," a person, assumedly of course, a Japanese person. Both in the sub-headline and the copy, the vehicle is treated as a rough-and-tumble masculine male. Thus, metaphorically, the ad situates the prototypical male Japanese self in the "legendary" environment of the Other, where, in this case the Other represents a kind of untamed, rugged, yet spiritual, adventurer. In doing so, the copy reifies the positive associative values of "dreams" and "hopes," what the American travelers were assumedly imbued with as they headed west along the open road.

The copy, in fact, repeats the call to "go west" as if to suggest, on a higher level of abstraction, that the ad is imploring the Japanese readers to go to America. This call to action is made positive by describing such a choice (as well as the vehicle) as "fearless" and "firm." These representations are also made explicit in the sub-headline, which literally invites the reader to "discover your hot self." The subtext for "hot" is a passionate, never-ending quest for adventure. The word "hot" (in red), prominently displayed in the photograph, refers both to the "tougher" truck and the adventurous self and figuratively places the Japanese Datsun driver in the space of the Other (i.e., the American West).

The iconicity of place, in terms of Otherness includes the broad geographic region known as the American West. The sweeping landscape provides a seemingly limitless backdrop to the explicit iconicity of place, namely, "On Route 66," as indicated in the headline. Confirming this, a road sign reading "Route 66" is clearly visible in the photograph. The exact location along Route 66 where the photograph was taken is unclear although the arid landscape with sagebrush and the open road heading toward the distant mountains on the horizon suggests the Rocky Mountains. The train in the photo conveys a sense of the vastness, and, along with the road, the only signs of human existence within a great openness.

What is important is not the exact location, but what transports the reader to this spirited place. What transports the reader to this imagined Other place is both Route 66 and the new Datsun pick-up. Route 66 is then double valenced in that it embodies the legendary and historically factual 2,500-mile thread connecting Chicago to Los Angeles, and second it embodies the nostalgic and appealing symbolic thread connecting a passion for adventure to the new Datsun pick-up. The character of both the Datsun and its hoped-for owner, presumably a young Japanese male, is described as "hot" in the sense of having a never-ending passion. Both the vehicle and its intended owner are also filled with "adventure-mind," a Japanese linguistic invention (written in *katakana*) that means "a frame of mind willing and open to adventure."

This photograph occupies nearly half of the advertisement's space. Because it is uppermost, and in color, it strongly attracts attention, and seems to do so in a constant back and forth with the truck, presented in a limbo, nowhere scene in the bottom half of the ad. Significantly, more than half of the photograph is taken up with the sky. Back-lit as if the sun is setting in the west, the pale blue sky, warm clouds and yellowish sunlight offer a picture of America that the Japanese seem to like to imagine: wide open spaces and long horizon lines—an image quite distinct from the Japanese experience.

The lower half of the ad, a white space in limbo, features a "beauty shot" of the truck, the copy, and the large display signage: "New Datsun Pick Up [is born]." Given the ad's premise, that the vehicle personifies the positive traits of young Japanese males who have a passion for adventure, and that, figuratively the pick-up is a young Japanese male, Japan and America would seem to be distanced by the visual separation of a bordered photograph versus free-flowing white space.

But, in fact, the identity of Japan is superimposed over the iconicity of America (the Other) throughout. First "HOT," though an English word, is interpreted as identifying the fiery spirit both of the vehicle and the reader. Second, "DAT" is a Japanese identity marker, the first part of the name for the Japanese-made truck. Third, the ad overtly invites us to read "HOT DAT" as the embodiment of a sort of spirit combining Japanese person and auto. In addition to "HOT DAT," in large letters occupying the center of the photograph, the vertically arranged Japanese script headline, guides us in the identification process, "Call it [me] Hot Dat." The semantic space opened by the possibility of reading the line as meaning "me," the truck as an anthropomorphic representation of a (Japanese) person, invites the Japanese consumer to imagine his or her experience as plausibly placed in America, somewhere out West, at some indeterminate spot along Route 66.

The image of Route 66, as a pathway through adventurous spaces, wide open and inviting, is emblematic of how Japan, through its ad makers, domesticates images of Otherness. Cultural icons from the United States, such as Route 66, are chosen for their positive value in imaginatively creating a world in which the Japanese can enjoy and, in a real sense, incorporate the Other.

Honda's Engagement with Norman Rockwell's America

The second ad examined, as shown in Fig. 3.2, uses nostalgic place in a quite different way. Here the depiction of nostalgic Americana is not anchored in a tangible place such as Route 66, but instead is evoked through the illustrative period style of Norman Rockwell. This is a one-page

FIG. 3.2.
Reprinted by permission of Honda Giken Koogyoo Kabushikigaisha.

ad for Honda's motorcycle, the City Scrambler, that appeared in three issues of *Hot Dog Press*. (Honda motorcycles and automobiles represent 4.7% of the ads in the young men's magazine sample.)

Visually, this advertisement presents a limbo environment, shaded a pale yellow. In the top left corner is the manufacturer logo and byline. It reads in English "Come ride with us. HONDA." Honda is all caps and relative to the rest of the byline, is in an enlarged font. Immediately below, in large red Japanese characters and script are two headlines stacked on top of each other. They read (translated into English):

Ride it quickly.
Ride the City Scrambler.

Immediately below, in smaller, black type is the body copy which translates as:

Freedom, light, smart, smile, friendship, toughness, refinement, functional beauty, flexible.
And so on, the new Benly CL50 is filled with a variety of charm (attraction).
The fashionable and enjoyable City Scrambler, you can be with it anywhere, anytime.
Our imagination and cruising radius expand greatly.
On a clear fine day, if you happen to want to scramble, let's take off (to a destination).
If you have a City Scrambler, you can move easily and quickly.

Immediately below this text is an image of the bike, with another smaller image below that. The people in the advertisement replicate the sort of line-art drawings of people in U.S. popular paintings, posters, calendars and advertisements during the 1950s (the halcyon days of Route 66). The ad incorporates Norman Rockwell-like illustrations, of, assumedly, Americans. In the smaller illustration at the bottom of the ad, a father dressed in a suit, complete with a newspaper under one arm, with a raincoat draped over the other and an umbrella in hand, eyes the motorcycle from one side. From the other side, three young children (two boys and a girl) similarly focus on the bike in an admiring manner.

Most prominent of the Norman Rockwell-like icons, however, is the nappy young man in the main visual. Attired in a preppy blazer and dress slacks, and carrying a tripod, strap bag, field notebook, and small canvas frame, this icon of a clean-cut young American male in the 1950s is presented bending stiffly toward the motorcycle, poised as he prepares to take its picture with his camera. He and the motorcycle are facing each other, both on the same plane, both in profile. His overly determined, and unnaturally mannered posture creates the impression that the young man is "investigating" (face-to-face, almost as if about to mount or be mounted) the City Scrambler. Bending precisely from the waist, with one arm held stiffly behind his back, he strikes the pose of someone who is, within a sense, quotation marks, in "studied observation." The small instant camera, held in one hand, appears to be aimed at a point somewhere behind the motorcycle. This off-hand way of taking a photograph—with one hand—alerts us to the possibility that something is amiss.

In fact, he is in no position to take a photograph of the City Scrambler. Close inspection of the proximal relationship between this young man and Honda's motorcycle suggests that the two do not actually fit together—or belong on the same plane. Put differently, the Japanese motorcycle and the nostalgic icon of this American appear simply to be thrown together to create a sense of symmetry. Yet to look even closer suggests that the direction the camera is pointed, the object most probably appearing in its lens is the City Scrambler's model name: Benly CL50. It should be pointed out that "City Scrambler" is rendered in *katakana*, the Japanese script designated for foreign words. The *katakana* phonetic spelling and pronunciation for City Scrambler is "*shitii sukuranburaa*." Yet, the model name, "BENLY" is presented in English script, with BENLY presenting a presumed English word.

No doubt the advertisers purposefully created this one name that looks as if it were English, but most likely derives from Japanese vocabulary. The word "*benri*" in Japanese means "convenient." The reason the motorcycle is named "Benly" as opposed to "Benri," is a common example of the appeal that product names in English have for the Japanese (Haarman, 1984; Loveday, 1986). English product names carry an aura of modernity, whereas traditional Japanese names, and words turned into product names, such as "benri," carry overtones of what is non-modern (see, e.g., Quackenbush, 1974). This represents an interesting contrast to the preference for American nostalgic, and Japanese contemporary icons of place within the ads studied.

This advertisement suggests a Japanese preference for iconicity of the Other, both in terms of person and text, in creating an appeal to Japanese teenagers. The Norman Rockwell-like figures are merely props, icons of nostalgic Americana, which, presumably, add a distinctive look to Honda's City Scrambler campaign. The switching of the Japanese transliterated letters "r - i" to that of the English "l - y" to form the neologism, "Benly," shows how Japanese "symbolic analysts" (Reich, 1992) domesticate the Other, and turn it to their own use.

The question of why these Norman Rockwell-like representations might have been chosen for this product, is possibly answered through a closer look at the motorcycle. Its design suggests a classic model. The Benly CL50, even its numeric suffix, reminiscent of the Oldsmobile 88, or the Rocket 90, and so forth, appears almost as a vintage reproduction. Because the product, itself, conveys nostalgia, the Japanese ad makers most likely decided upon a nostalgic "look" to the ad. This is where the notion of cultural multiplicity comes into play. The advertisers, through common sense as cultural agents or through strategic choice based on what is known to appeal to the Japanese, determined that a representation of nostalgic

Americana (and not nostalgic Japan) would serve the purpose of creating a favorable aura for the Japanese vintage reproduction motorcycle.

CONCLUSIONS

Despite the cultural multiplicity evident in the icons of Otherness in the ads generally (of which the two discussed are but prototypical examples), Japan, as the local culture, appears firmly in control of the process in the context of the ads studied. That is, in the response to the question of global cultural homogenization raised at the beginning of this chapter, the evidence in this study suggests that Japanese local identity is well intact.

At first glance the appearance of Route 66 in the Nissan ad, and the Norman Rockwell-like figures in the Honda ad, might be read as an indication of how overrun Japanese advertising is with American cultural icons, and that Japan is experiencing an American-led cultural incursion. Closer examination, however, reveals that these icons of other cultures, though present, play a rather minor role in the broader "textual landscape" extant in Japanese advertising.

Moreover, when iconicity of Western place is employed in the image-making, it is done so within the cultural framework of the host culture. Analyses of these ads suggests that the incorporated iconicity of Western culture in advertising as a Japanese move, is calculated. It would appear to serve the purposes of how Japan prefers to view the world and how Japan prefers to incorporate a nostalgic world. Accordingly, any thought that Japan is on the receiving end of an unwanted cultural homogenization misses the point. A more nuanced reading of the appearance of cultural icons of the West in Japanese advertising strongly suggests that it is done because that is how the Japanese want to imagine the world outside of Japan.

In short, Japan appears to be in control of how it identifies with the West, through nostalgia and linguistic inventions that smack of modernity. Icons representing the West are part of the mosaic of cultural multiplicity pervasive in a globalized world. At least in the case of Japan, identity of self would appear to be firmly intact, and firmly in control.

The advertising spaces examined in this study are sites of communication where cultural iconicity is readily mixed and matched. In this mediated space, Japanese culture (represented by products) and American culture (providing the contextual space) are contested. Yet, ultimately Japanese cultural identity overrides and domesticates the West. This message is constitutively integrated and negotiated within text. Although the product and the place are not inherently related, the creative juxtaposition of these elements creates "relatedness" and leads to the construction of such reality.

Recall that in the case of the Nissan ad, the product is identified through the (constructed) relatedness between the pick-up truck and the nostalgic Route 66. In the case of the Honda ad, as well, the product's identity is negotiated through the (constructed) relatedness between the motorcycle and the nostalgic Norman Rockwell-like world of a 1950s America.

At the same time, given that the youth magazines encourage interaction between content and reader, it is reasonable to posit that a Japanese identity is negotiated without-text as well. That is, Japanese youth are encouraged to identify with a self that is steeped in relatedness with the West, but only to the extent that the Japanese self domesticates it. In this way, multiple and complex images of Self and Other—an intimacy of local culture and global influence—produce a mediated reality of the Japanese self that is repeatedly produced, maintained, and endlessly transformed—while remaining thoroughly Japanese.

REFERENCES

Baudrillard, J. (1981). *Simulations*. New York: Semiotext(e).

Baudrillard, J. (1988). *Selected writings*. Cambridge: Polity Press.

Barber, B.R. (1995). *Jihad vs. McWorld: How globalism and tribalism are reshaping the world*. New York: Random House.

Barthes, R. (1982). *Empire of signs* (R. Howard, Trans). London: Jonathan Cape.

Ben-Ari, E., Moeran, B., & Valentine, J. (Eds.). (1990). *Unwrapping Japan: Society and culture in anthropological perspective*. Manchester: Manchester University Press.

Berger, P.I., & Luckmann, T. (1966). *The social construction of reality: A treatise in the sociology of knowledge*. Garden City, NY: Doubleday.

Bounds, W. (1999, April 12). Magazines seek to demonstrate efficacy of ads. *The Wall Street Journal*, pp. B1, B4.

Burton, J. (1983, February 7). Buy any other name? Not in Japanese. *Advertising Age*, p. 42.

Carey, J.W. (1975). A cultural approach to communications. *Journal of Communication, 2*, 1-22.

Deetz, S. (1994). Future of the discipline: The challenges, the research, and the social contribution. *Communication Yearbook, 17*, 565-600.

Dentsu. (1994). *Dentsu Japan Marketing/Advertising* Yearbook. Tokyo: Author.

Derrida, J. (1976). *Of grammatology*. Baltimore, MD: Johns Hopkins University Press.

Ferguson, M. (1992). The mythology about globalization. *European Journal of Communication, 7*, 69-93.

Foucault, M. (1972). *The archaeology of knowledge and the discourse on language* (A.M.S. Smith, Trans.). New York: Pantheon.

Foucault, M. (1978). *The history of sexuality: Vol. 1. An introduction* (R. Hurley, Trans.). New York: Vintage.

Friedman, J. (1994). *Cultural identity and global process*. London: Sage.

Gergen, K.J. (1991). *The saturated self: Dilemmas of identity in contemporary life*. New York: Basic Books.

Gergen, K.J. (1996). Technology and the self: From the essential to the sublime. In D. Grodin & T.R. Lindlof (Eds.), *Constructing the self in a mediated world* (pp. 127-140). Thousand Oaks, CA: Sage.

Giddens, A. (2000). *Runaway world: How globalization is reshaping our lives.* New York: Routledge.

Haarman, H. (1984). The role of ethnocultural stereotypes and foreign languages in Japanese commercials. *International Journal of Sociology of Language, 58,* 107-121.

Hamelink, C.J. (1983). *Cultural autonomy in global communications: Planning national information policy.* New York: Longman.

Harris, J.R. (1998). *The nurture assumption.* New York: The Free Press.

Horne, J. (1996). "Sakka" in Japan. *Media, Culture and Society, 18,* 527-547.

Ivy, M. (1993). Formations of mass culture. In A. Gordon (Ed.), *Postwar Japan as history* (pp. 239-258). Berkeley: University of California Press.

Johansson, J.K. (1994). The sense of "nonsense": Japanese TV advertising. *Journal of Advertising, 23,* 17-26.

Loveday, L. (1986). *Explorations in Japanese socio-linguistics.* Amsterdam: John Benjamins.

Maynard, M. (2001). *The consumption of otherness and preservation of self: Images of the West in Japanese teen magazine advertisements.* Unpublished doctoral dissertation, Rutgers, The State University of New Jersey, New Brunswick.

Mokros, H.B. (1995). Suicide and shame. *American Behavioral Scientist, 38,* 1091-1103.

Mokros, H.B. (1996). From information and behavior to interaction and identity. In H.B. Mokros (Ed.), *Interaction and identity: Information and behavior* (Vol. 5, pp. 1-22). New Brunswick, NJ: Transaction.

Mokros, H.B., & Deetz, S. (1996). What counts as real? In E.B. Ray (Ed.), *Communication and disenfranchisement: Social health issues and implications* (pp. 29-44). HIllsdale, NJ: Erlbaum.

Mumby, D. (1997). Modernism, postmodernism and communication studies: A rereading of an ongoing debate. *Communication Theory, 7,* 1-28.

O'Barr, W. (1994). *Culture and the ad: Exploring otherness in the world of advertising.* San Francisco: Westview Press.

Quackenbush, E. (1974). How Japanese borrow English words. *Linguistics, 131,* 59-75.

Reich, R. B. (1992). *The work of nations.* New York: Vintage Books.

Ritzer, G. (1998). The McDonaldization thesis: Is expansion inevitable? *International Sociology, 13,* 291-308.

Rosenberger, N. (1992). Images of the West: Home style in Japanese magazines. In J.J. Tobin (Ed.), *Remade in Japan* (pp. 106-125). New Haven, CT: Yale University Press.

Schudson, M. (1984). *Advertising, the uneasy persuasion: Its dubious impact on American society.* New York: Basic Books.

Taylor, C. (1989). *Sources of the self: The making of modern identity.* Cambridge, MA: Harvard University Press.

Taylor, C. (1991). The dialogic self. In D.R. Hiley, J.F. Bohman, & R. Shusterman (Eds.), *The interpretative turn: Philosophy, science, culture* (pp. 304-314). Ithaca, NY: Cornell University Press.

White, H.C. (1992). *Identity and control: A structural theory of social action.* Princeton, NJ: Princeton University Press.

Zasshi Shimbun Sookatarogu. (1993). Tokyo: Media Research Center, Inc.

Design Matters
Projections of Identity in Library Environments

Nancy P. Thomas

This chapter examines design matters in the context of academic and public libraries. Design matters refers to how the design features of a building, its architecture, and both fixed and temporary adornments relate to and implicate considerations of identity. This suggests that libraries, and buildings in general, are not merely physical entities with functional purposes but are also sources of meaning. That is to say, people construct meaningful "images" for libraries just as they do for churches, hospitals, fast-food chains, and shopping malls. For example, Gutman (1969) noted that symbolic meanings are inevitably a part of the environmental experience of all buildings and "have an important influence on people's perceptions, attitudes and behavior" (Becker, 1977, p. 10).

In a very real sense, a library's building constitutes its public "face," and as some researchers have suggested, there may be elements present in the environmental aspects of libraries with which both positive and negative responses may be associated. For his part, Becker (1977) asserted that designing buildings "without attempting to understand the kinds of symbols that elicit desired reactions, rather than negative ones, and the range of people for whom these symbols are meaningful is to ignore a fundamental component of people's evaluations of buildings" (p. 10). Of course, individual users may respond in different ways to the same architectural forms and design features. For some, monumental buildings may "resonate," embodying, for example, connections with the past, community values, or personal aspirations. For others, these same edifices may seem overwhelming and alienating, and for still others, as gratuitous and wasteful.

The relationship between library architecture and library use has been of professional interest to the library community for a long time. A testimonial to this interest is the annual issue devoted to library architecture and design in *American Libraries*, a major publication of the American Library Association. However, scholarly interest in this issue, within library and information science research, has been more restrained. Those who have approached this topic have made apparent the relevance of scholarly investigation and theorizing. For example, Davidson and Budd (1991) argued that monumental structures and archival functions, together constitute a pervasive stereotype of the library that represent a "major barrier" between an "institution and its potential audience" (p. 146). In a similar vein, Miller (1978) suggested that physical location, "building design and landscaping" have the power to "influence the user in either a positive or negative way in his/her approach to the institution" (p. 20). "Once inside," Miller continued, "the user may encounter any number of physical features which "encourage or discourage information seeking" (p. 20).

Empirical investigations of such implied social and communicative functions of architecture and the meanings that commercial and service environments hold for people have been reported in the literature on library facilities (Crumpacker, 1994; Sever, 1987; Wagner, 1992), and organizations (Steele, 1986; Upah & Fulton, 1985). The orientation of this line of research is consistent with long-standing, multidisciplinary efforts to examine the behavioral, cultural, and symbolic aspects of the built environment. Especially notable have been contributions in the fields of architecture (Eco, 1980; Gowans, 1992; Gutman, 1969; Jencks, 1980, 1984, 1985; Raskin, 1974; Ruesch & Kees, 1970), psychology (Bolan, 1980), environmental psychology (Altman, 1975; Duncan, 1985; Rapoport, 1976, 1977, 1982; Wener, 1985), social psychology (Hall, 1966; Zeisel, 1975), object relations theory (Csikszentmihalyi & Rochberg-Halton, 1981; Norman, 1988), and semiotics (Wagner, 1991, 1992). Concern for users' everyday experiences of buildings, as pioneered in the work of Jacobs (1961), along with "postmodernist" considerations of the expressive qualities of architecture and the social and relational aspects of buildings, have stimulated both academic (e.g., Gergen, 1991, 1995; Russell & Gaubatz, 1995) and more popular writings (e.g., Martin, 1994; Muschamp, 1994).

Scholarly considerations both within and outside of the library context suggest a variety of questions. How can we account for this range of meaning, these disparate reactions in the ways people sense places? More specifically, what physical elements contribute to the creation of a library's image? What symbolic meanings may library buildings, ornaments, and arrangements have for their users? What might be the outcomes for users as a result of environmental engagement? In short, what tales do libraries tell about themselves and about their potential users? These are the questions that guided the larger study (Thomas, 1996) from which this chapter is developed. My assumption is that architectural and environmental elements of a library contain or implicate, to some extent, that library's mission, its values, and its expectations of its users and their activities and that these implications may be recovered through a careful "reading" of these design elements.

To say that a library may be read suggests that architecture, and design features more generally, may be regarded as texts. Additionally, three premises linked to this assumption are central in my own approach to such a reading. First, interactions between people and between people and institutions arise in social situations within which environmental clues are used in making sense of their experience. Second, as social constructs, libraries have embedded within them social, political, and cultural values. And, third, within social situations the personal identities of participants are at stake.

Within this framework, I approached the reading of a library as initially involving interpretation based on descriptive investigation of how architectural and design features may be said to contain situation-defining practices. I assumed such practices to be embedded within these features, and that they project a sense of institutional identity or public face of a specific site along with expectations of, and attitudes toward its users. Thereafter, critical interpretation served to gauge how a user's experience of these practices might be internalized as confirming or disconfirming of self and implicate future patterns of use. My aim through such interpretive reading is meant to offer practical guidance in design and planning. In other words, the exploration and interpretation of situation-defining practices within architectural features may provide a way to enhance the sensitivity of library environments for users (Gutman, 1969; Wagner, 1992) by offering plausible user-centered criteria for the evaluation of library facilities (Doll, 1992; Goldstein, 1964).

A CONSTITUTIVE THEORY OF COMMUNICATION

The interpretive reading approach to design matters in library environments is theoretically grounded in a constitutive view or theory of communication (e.g., Deetz, 1994; Mokros, 1996; Mokros & Deetz, 1996), which seeks to offer communication explanations through communication explorations of central phenomena and problems of everyday being. A constitutive view regards communication as a central process through which psychological and social realities (e.g., systems of knowledge, personal identities) are constructed. Such a view of communication differs significantly from the informational or "conduit" model as, for example, articulated by Shannon and Weaver (1949). The conduit model considers communication instrumentally, as a "tool" used by people in making connections with one another, and sees language as essentially representational, reflecting and reflective of a concrete reality that exists "out there" (Mokros & Deetz, 1996). Within this understanding, the primary focus is on the information "transferred" rather than in meaning and its construction. In contrast, a constitutive view focuses primarily on meanings, which inhere not in "messages" as products of individual cognitive activity but as constructions arising in, and through, communicative engagement with social others (e.g., Watzlawick, Beavin, & Jackson, 1967). Additionally, language in use is regarded as neither neutral nor exclusively representational but value-laden and semiotically charged even though such "valuing" proceeds out of awareness and is seldom explored.

Applying a constitutive approach to the exploration of library architecture and design features suggests that traditional institutional concerns with storage and programming consider additionally the character of the interactions that take place between users and systems on a daily basis, particularly the byproducts, as types of outcomes, of such interaction. This concern is wholly consistent with the paradigm shift in library and information science research toward user considerations as, for example, developed by Dervin and Nilan (1986), Kuhlthau (1993), and Belkin (1980). What distinguishes the focus of the efforts described in this chapter from these lines of research is its explicit concern with questions of identity, the identity a library projects of itself, of the culture within which it is situated—both locally and more generally—and of the "generalized user," the self that engages and interacts with and within it. The consideration of identity at these levels seeks to explicate how features of library environments may come to interact with real users. Through such interactions, users experience both reproductive and challenging projections of identity, projections that confirm or disconfirm aspects of their legitimacy. It is in this sense that one can talk about the byproducts, generally, of encounters with design as matters of identity—considerations that have been largely ignored within literatures that consider, and limit, assessments of facilities in terms of productive, functional use.

Orientation to the Constitutive View

My orientation within the constitutive view is influenced by a number of traditions, particularly the social constructionist (e.g., Berger & Luckmann, 1966), postmodernist (e.g., Foucault, 1972), and symbolic interactionist (e.g., Blumer, 1969; Mead, 1934) movements in social science and social theory. Social constructionists, for example, hold that all knowledge is subjectively known and recoverable in everyday experience through language. Acknowledging the phenomenological emphasis on the primacy of communication in the construction of reality, social constructionist theory construes meaning as essentially social, based not in individual perceptions of experience but arising in social interaction over time. A social constructionist approach also provides useful insights into the development of personal identity. From this perspective, images of self are interactively constructed, first in response to attitudes of one's significant others' expressions of confirmation or disconfirmation, and later in response to encounters with norms and codes in one's social world. Environmental interaction may be appreciated within this perspective as constitutive of social institutions as well as the individuals who engage with them.

Foucault. My appreciation for the textuality of human experience is inspired by postmodernist thought. The writings of Foucault (e.g., 1972), with his attention to the power that discursive formations wield over everyday lived experience, are particularly noteworthy and influential within this tradition. Foucault (1972) developed the term *discursive formation* to capture the routinized or rule-governed, historically and societally bound links between knowledge systems and everyday practices. Discursive "practices" are interpreted broadly to include not only "written and spoken discourse," but also nonverbal gestures including architecture, the use or appropriation of spaces, "institutional practices, and social relations" (Foss & Gill, 1987, p. 387). The logic of discursive formations defines appropriate objects of discourse, acceptable vocabularies, styles of presentation, and the conditions and circumstances under which discursive practices may proceed. Discursive formations establish relations, specify and order practices, establish standards, and create roles of privilege for certain kinds of social agents. In these ways, the instantiation of discursive formations, such as medical knowledge or social systems of etiquette, establish what counts as knowledge or truth at a given place and time. A discursive formation empowers agency through social conventions or norms as implemented in discursive practices yet may not be overtly manifest in the articulated rules of institutions, societies, or cultures.

Foucault's (1972, 1980) theory permits the analysis of experienced reality as it is formed discursively in societal or institutional practices and the consideration of assumptions and ideological values embedded therein but frequently lost in the "taken-for-grantedness" of daily life. Indeed, Best and Kellner (1991) asserted that an essential goal in analyzing discursive formations is to encourage the "proliferation of differences," to recover "autonomous discourses, knowledges, and voices suppressed through total-izing narratives," and to explore "the operation of power and domination working behind neutral or beneficent facades" (p. 57). Foucault's theory encourages a broadened sense of textuality and invites consideration of the complex and competing systems of environmental features found in libraries "discursively." His theory offers an analytic frame for the exploration of everyday experience through the rules and roles librarians and users employ, these regarded as extensions of the system of norms and values characteris-tic of a discursive formation.

Social Interactionists. Foucault's (1972) interest in social roles is, however, essentially limited to those who represent the institution or system and are therefore considered "rhetors" within the discourse. The symbolic interactionist tradition offers a way to address this limitation. For example, the work of Shibutani (1987) suggests some ways in which aspects of the built environment repeat and reify conventional roles for both users and librarians. His emphasis on the importance of identity and control in social settings has applications in the present instance in that libraries, as institu-tions, usually operate according to well-established conventions. In fact, conventions that define roles for librarians and for users are so pervasive that they have become widely acknowledged stereotypes. Echoing the social constructionist paradigm proposed by Berger and Luckmann (1966), Shibutani argued that culture itself emerges in communication in terms of norms of behavior. Social control is exerted every time an individual attempts to live up to group expectations in the form of norms. Although the internalization of culture represented by adherence to group norms enhances group activity and interaction, it also excludes those who are not privy to the same assumptions and lack a priori knowledge of their roles, or awareness of norms of acceptable behavior within a given situation. Because social coordination depends on the degree to which participants in the interaction fulfill the roles that are expected of them, and because in differ-ent cultures roles are learned differently, intercultural misunderstandings frequently occur.

The conceptualization of the unforeseen "byproducts" of users' interactions with the environment and their importance for the construction of the self is also informed by the work of Erving Goffman (1959, 1973), who views the institution's presentation of itself as representing its "defini-tion of the situation." This "definition" instantiates an institution's claims and promises. In engaging library facilities, it can be argued that users seek clues for framing the situation in which they find themselves, not only in terms of where to go and how to do something, but also in terms of how to act and how they may be judged. Thus, an experience of library architec-ture, here broadly defined to include all physical aspects of library facilities, is not simply a "backdrop" that engages or fails to engage a user aestheti-cally. Rather, it constitutes part of a "semiotically loaded" communicative moment, wherein users experience themselves and come to understand themselves in interaction with a "generalized other" (Mead, 1934), an extended context (Scheff, 1990) of embedded institutional and societal, that is to say discursive, values.

Finally, the work of Scheff (e.g., 1990) has proved especially relevant for my considerations of design matters. According to Scheff, individuals orient themselves to social settings in ways that reflect a relationally based, personal sense of social responsibilities and the value of connectedness with others. It is within and through social interaction that individuals strive for and achieve a sense of connectedness or "bond" with others. The specific qualities of the bond may be characterized as optimally differentiated, with relatedness based on the acknowledged autonomy and legitimacy of self and other. Conversely, the qualities of the bond may implicate the isolation of the self from the other or the loss of self through enmeshment with the other. It is then in and through the qualities of the social bond, the qualities of relational connection that indi-viduals develop and experience a "self," a sense of who one "is." All interaction-al moments present for individuals the potential to experience a sense of belonging or not, a sense of confirmation or disconfirmation, of affiliation or alienation, of being valued or de-valued. And individuals orient themselves within interactional contexts in ways that reflect a history of such experiences, albeit all individuals are motivated, according to Scheff, to achieve secure social bonds. Thus, individuals differ in the qualities of bonds they seek, and differ in how experiences of confirmation or disconfirmation, for example, matter for the experience of one's self. Thus, whereas Foucault encourages consideration of the value-laden invisible systems that shape everyday practices, experiences, and identities, Scheff encourages an appreciation of the impact that everyday interactions have upon the emotionally and relationally experienced qualities of self. Scheff's approach offers then a way to theorize experience-near identity issues that arise from an individual's interaction with library architecture and design.

These theoretical developments provide a foundation for a constitu-tive approach to communication-based explanations of design matters in the library contexts discussed next.

STEPS TOWARD A "READING OF DESIGN MATTERS" IN LIBRARIES

The interpretive "reading" approach applied to the study of library design matters represents a type of phenomenological investigation. Precedents for applying a phenomenological approach to investigations of environmental experiences in every day settings (Gerson & Gerson, 1976) and the acknowledgment of multiple, interpretive, realities come from research in environmental psychology (Gerson & Gerson, 1976; Tuan, 1976) and geography (Relph, 1984).

An Interpretive Reading Approach

My orientation to the development of an interpretive reading approach was guided by the first three steps of Scheff's (1990, 1996) proposed four-step approach to inquiry. This approach, which incorporates both morphological and analytic perspectives, suggests that research in real-world settings should begin with the preliminary exploration of a single case, followed by a microscopic exploration of several "specimen" cases, involving description and interpretation. A third step calls for the generation of a "micro–macro theory," grounded in the "description and interpretation" developed in the two prior stages, in order to place a specific specimen in the "largest parts of the system" (p. 39), guided here by the theoretical frameworks and insights just discussed. The fourth step Scheff proposed involves quantitative testing of the "abstract theory" (p. 39) developed in this third stage. Although quantitative analysis may certainly be applied to an analysis of design features within and across sites, a formal quantitative test of the theoretical argument would seem to be at odds with the interpretive reading approach advocated here.

The link between description and interpretation within the context of the earlier stages of this model involves the application of "abduction," the "extremely rapid internal dialogue between observation and imagination" (Scheff, 1990, p. 142). This process takes advantage of what people do on an everyday basis in making sense of experience. This may be thought of as a "juggling" of theory and data (Scheff, 1996, p. 39) through a consideration of "counterfactuals." Influenced by the pioneering microanalytic work of Pittenger, Hockett, and Danehy (1960) and extended by Mokros, Mullins, and Saracevic (1995), this approach involves the proposal of plausible alternatives, counterfactuals or hypotheticals, to what was observed and descriptively inscribed. This then broadens morphological description so as to consider, at any given point, what was observed in a context of what might have been observed. As such, it invites the kinds of reflexivity in thinking reflective of phenomenological considerations of possible alternatives at any point of engagement with phenomena and is consistent with the postmodernist recognition of multiple interpretations of what is observed.

Library Sites Studied and Modes of Observation

Within this approach, observations were undertaken at nine separate sites in three different types of settings: school, academic, and public libraries. Specifically, observational sites included four school libraries (a primary school, a kindergarten through eighth-grade school, a middle school, and a high school), three academic libraries (the undergraduate library serving a women's college, and two specialized research libraries, one devoted to art and art history and the other to science), and two public libraries (one located in an urban area and one in a suburban area). The choice of these libraries did not involve any effort to capture a representative sample of libraries. Instead, I sought to develop detailed descriptions of specific environments created to serve a variety of potential library users. In addition, when viewed together, the sites indexed a sort of "developmental progression" of library experience, stretching from early childhood to maturity, available within a single geographic region.

Observations at each site initially involved viewing the exterior of the building or room, and then entering the facility, following a path a user might take when encountering the site for the first time, paying attention to the sequence of experiences as well as the overall context available to library visitors. Although observations in the school libraries required only one visit, the size and complexities of the other sites necessitated several observational sessions. In all, 31 visits were made across sites. The data generated through this process included scratch notes created "in the field," audiotaped interview data, and publicly available documents. An extensive photographic record was created for each study site to capture the library in context and record my encounter with the site externally and internally. After each observation session, detailed fieldnotes were created from scratch notes and "head" notes with the photographic record and collected documents coordinated to these fieldnotes. Interview data were subsequently incorporated within the fieldnotes. These data created a text open to analysis and interpretation.

AN INTERPRETIVE READING OF LIBRARY DESIGN MATTERS

The interpretive reading of library design matters summarized here was guided by the theoretical and methodological considerations previously discussed. The account of this interpretive reading will first summarize design feature dimensions identified through observation. These design feature dimensions coalesced as "domains" of design practice within which library architects, planners, and staff designers made specific choices as to the physical appearance, the organization and articulation of space, the furniture and decorative appointments, and the signs at each site. Thus, this approach recognizes as design features not only the fixed and permanent architectural environmental forms that provide structures and frames for library activities but also the permanent and ephemeral furnishings and objects that are assumed to condition or contextualize the user's experience of libraries in terms of use, aesthetics, and relational regard. The discussion then considers how knowledge, norms, roles, and rules, that is, expressions of control reflective of the operation of discursive formations in everyday life, are coordinated to or settled within these design domains and the dimensions they frame. The discussion of design domains and dimensions and expressions of control embedded within them does not consider specific library sites. Instead, what is reported may be thought of as a framework for attending to design matters more generally.

This initial discussion is followed by a consideration of each library site visited. My aim in this discussion is to offer an account of the uniqueness of each site, to suggest how each site may be said to have meaning, and to consider trends, themes, and narratives across libraries as an aspect of professional discourse. Essentially, I argue that an interpretive reading within these sites should seek to recover from aspects of the physical context that surrounds and structures the provision of library services and a library user's activities those general features (or domains) that have a communicative function as well as the themes exhibited in the range of specific choices or dimensions within each domain. Of specific interest is how "relational projections" are recoverable within these themes. That is to say, the interest here is not motivated by a desire to represent the essence or defining image of each library as something apart from its potential users. Rather it is to consider how the structures of power and control, created discursively, are represented in the physical context as a form of communicative action. I then suggest how the users' senses of their own identities might be implicated given the expectations for library use articulated in aspects of the library settings created for them. Of specific interest in this reading are the "relational projections" (i.e., clues to how one may be regarded and may regard oneself in the setting, and thereby one's relationship to the institution). This concerns how these libraries, through their design features, orient themselves to users of these libraries, and in a sense prescribe what is possible and permissible, in terms of user activity, within them. Of concern as well is whether and to what extent it is possible to locate or recover across themes the sense of a primary or dominant narrative. The search here for themes and narrative structure thus transcends local choices among design features and instances of control to identify instead how design matters implicate ideological orientations, manifestations of discursive formations in Foucault's sense, for users as to their being within the larger social world. In short, in interactions with library settings the selves of users are inevitably positioned in relation to environmental expectations—a positioning that has consequences for their senses of who they are, can be, and should be in that space, and by extension, in the world.

Design Features as Expressions of Discursive Control

The reading of design features and expressions of control within the nine libraries studied included consideration of both the physical features of each building along with the ways that the administrators (e.g., library staff generally) of these facilities made use of them and thereby further contributed to the building's design structure. Of particular interest in this regard are indications that professionals made choices among design alternatives to alter, shape, or "decorate" their spaces and how these choices were linked to expressions of control.

Domains of Design Practice. Review of the descriptive data suggested four discursive design domains within which architects, designers, and library staff made selections from among design alternatives to achieve or create the specific look and character of each facility. The domains identified were architecture, environment, artifacts, and texts. How choices were made across these reflects in a sense an ongoing history of design decisions. Dimensions within each discursive domain were expressed as design choices. Thus, within the architectural domain dimensions in terms of symbolism, monumentality, architectural kinship with other buildings, accessibility, and interior structure found expression in choices of architectural style, size, scale, and elevation; siting (site and setting); number, types, and character of entrances, exits, and approaches; and, fixed elements of interior spatial design.

Practices within the environmental domain included choices in interior space allocation; the style, character, and disposition of furniture, fixtures, furnishings, and related appointments (e.g., carpeting, drapes); and the presence, location, and types of security equipment observable. Together, these functioned discursively to create the physical experience of the library for library users; establish patterns of interaction and activity; mark as privileged, library staff, certain types of users, certain types of services, and certain types of activities; and to provide for institutional control over library materials and library users. These environmental mechanisms in turn potentially conditioned users' experiences of the library as humane or mechanistic, or as sociopetal or sociofugal, and potentially constituted library visitors as competent or incompetent, advantaged or disadvantaged in their ability to use the facility.

Dimensions or practices of the artifactual domain involved choices as to display of fine and graphic art, antiques, objects of popular culture (e.g., memorabilia, toys) and plaques of commemoration and recognition. Included in addition to choices of genre or character of artifacts on display were choices as to the positioning of such displays. There is a good deal of research literature across a variety of disciplines that discusses the meaning of things and their function in establishing authority (Goodsell, 1977); indexing efficiency, friendliness, warmth, or hostility (Bolan, 1980; Goodsell, 1977) and social and communicational possibilities (Ornstein, 1989, 1992); and reflecting community solidarity (Wagner, 1992), group membership, social values, and cultural norms (Rapoport, 1977, 1982; Zeisel, 1975). Major work on the character of cherished items and the meanings which they have for people has been studied extensively by Csikszentmihalyi and Rochberg-Halton (1981). At the libraries I studied, the presence, arrangement, and manner of presentation of artifacts, displayed items such as fine and commercial arts, objects, and plants functioned discursively to establish a sense of an institution's venerability, legitimacy, or permanence, to express aesthetic values or estimates of what is considered beautiful or art, to express social values, social context and social class, and to express community connectedness.

Finally, dimensions or practices within the textual domain consisted of choices in the character, tone, and deployment of signs (used for informational, directional, locational, or instructional purposes); instructional materials available as handouts, flyers, pamphlets, and brochures; library maps or diagrams; and posted policies and prohibitions. These texts contributed to the discourse at study sites as expressions of institutional authority (in the enumeration of prohibitions, rules, and policies); expressions of professional expertise (in offering specific services and in explanations and definitions of codes); expressions of institutional agency (in messages that indexed supported activities); expressions of validation (in terms of inclusion, accommodation, and way-finding assistance); and expressions of affirmation, welcome, and relational regard (by virtue of their form, tone, and the formal–informal; personal–impersonal; equal–unequal; respectful–disrespectful nature of the relationship between staff and users).

Embedded Control in Domains of Design. It is my argument that the dimensions within architectural, environmental, artifactual, and textual domains represent choices among many possible alternatives, and that those within a given setting not only create a sense of an institution's presence as "place," but also incorporate orientations to, or expressions of control. Such expressions introduce systems of meaning from the larger social world that speak to how roles, rules, norms, and knowledge—the stuff of discursive formations (Foucault, 1972)—operate within designed spaces. These expressions speak to privileged social values, participatory permissibilities, social order, and the ideals of the "generalized user."

Consider, for instance, how design practices across the four domains identified specify the roles that administrators and other staff members assume in a given setting. Where design decisions allocate space to the director of the library that is larger and/or less exposed to public access or view than desks in public areas occupied by library clerks, hierarchical or status roles are invoked. Choices in furniture, artwork, and signage make additionally apparent that the position of director is not merely a matter of institutional function but incorporate as well markers of privileged social status.

This sensitivity to functional (e.g., administrator, patron) and ritual (e.g., status, gender) roles in design choices and practices most certainly suggests the operation of a system of rules that links a grammar of social relationships to design decisions related to issues such as occupancy and activity. These types of decisions further implicate the operation of both institutional and societal norms and differential investments of power. Through this sort of interpretive reading, one comes to see how design practices accommodate themselves to considerations of roles, rules, and norms in the ways design domains are uniquely constructed, and to appreciate how these accommodations implicate a system of knowledge.

The qualities of this system of knowledge, with its related roles, rules, and norms, constitute what Foucault referred to as a discursive formation, which exercises control over and organizes the activities of designers and decision makers, and, through their practices, implicates the activities of the library's staff and visitors. Design decisions are thus matters of discursive practice—practice that positions library users and library staff within the framework of values created through, and expressed in, discursive formations.

DESIGN, MEANING, AND SELF

Although Foucault helped to illuminate the larger social world within which discursive practices place individuals, Goffman's (1967) considerations of deference and demeanor and Scheff's (1990) theory of the social bond, offer frameworks for interpreting the experiencing of design choices. In Goffman's view, deference and demeanor structure individual experience in interaction and define the social status of interactants as well as the situation within which the interaction proceeds. Characterizing Goffman's view, Scheff (1990) wrote "[interactants] are excruciatingly sensitive to the exact amount of *deference* they receive, that is, to gestures of respect and disrespect" (p. 28). Acts of self-reflection or self-monitoring in response to the possibilities for action in a setting are part of each interactive, situation-defining moment, and it is in this sense that personal identity, which in part involves an estimate of one's relation to what Scheff called the social bond, can be interpreted as having been constructed.

Because libraries create structures of use that enable and constrain user activity, they may also be said to project an expected or "generalized" user of the space. Embedded within design domains and dimensional choices, this expectation can be considered as the library's representation of what it expects users to be and to do that engages users, and it is within moments of engagement that library visitors experience the tension between this representation and their own inner experiences of self. As these moments are also experiences of judgment or valuing, of pride and shame as Scheff (1990) explained, they have nontrivial consequences for the selves of library visitors. Thus, design features may be theorized to offer confirmation and legitimation of the self as well as disconfirmation and challenges to one's legitimacy. Moreover, where confirmational or disconfirmational experiences echo or reproduce systems of advantage or disadvantage that are part of the larger social realm within which everyday life, including experiences of libraries, are embedded, they can be considered experiences of this larger social order and those discourses that frame social experience more generally. Seen in this way, design domains and dimensions can be construed as presentation rituals indexical of institutional "attitudes of relatedness, power, and membership" (Mokros et al., 1995, p. 248), that are not only available to library users but are, for everyone, an inevitable part of everyday engagements with institutional environments. Within this line of argument, design clearly matters.

Design Matters: Cross-Context Comparisons

The dimensions of architectural, environmental, artifactual, and textual design domains together created a form and physical aspect for the library, a structure for its activities as well as its resources, a social and cultural context for library use, and informational and relational texts. Together these also contributed to the library's "line," it's projection of its identity as an institution, its culture and social values, and its expectations of use in terms of a "generalized" user.

In engaging with the library environments, one first encounters their exterior presentations, then experiences the library as a place, environmentally; finally encountering objects and reading the texts available as the individual circumstances or information needs necessitate. Together, these encounters create the institutional context, through which one may experience the library in its projection of itself, its projection of culture and social values, and finally its projection of its expected client, the "generalized " user.

These projections are revealed through interpretive readings that take into account a library's integration or distance from its neighbors and community, its monumentalism or minimalism as a physical presence, and the conditions it creates environmentally, artifactually, and textually that may be experienced by library users as experiences of intimidation or invitation, aestheticism or functionalism, hardness or softness. A comparison across libraries may bring these projections more clearly into view. This kind of analysis is useful because it provides a way to move beyond considerations of the visual and perceptual to embrace: "the meaning which people place on environments, the meanings they read from environments, and what is very likely the undifferentiated character of meaning and knowing in the everyday life of most people" (Moore, 1979, p. 41).

Design Matters at Three Academic Libraries

The three academic libraries included in the study were part of a library system within a major research university. Two of these libraries primarily served graduate students in science and art. The third provided library services primarily to undergraduates enrolled in a liberal arts college. The fact that the three shared a number of architectural similarities should not be surprising. They were all designed by the same architectural firm over a 30-year period. However, projections at the three libraries in terms of institutional identity, of social and cultural values, and the ideal or generalized user showed a number of interesting differences.

Identity Projections in Academic Libraries. The College, Art, and Science libraries were notable in their deliberate appropriation of stylistic details that linked them architecturally to other buildings in their academic communities. Although built well before the emergence of a formal postmodern style in architecture, the College and Science library buildings foreshadowed postmodernism in their inclusion of classical elements and local themes in their exterior design.

The identity projected in design domain decisions at the college library, foregrounded the relationship to the college community, an institutional valuing of art and the arts, and a commitment to the attainment of women's education goals. Gestures to the community were reflected in the use of exterior brick, pierced brick screening, and the suggestion of stone "columns" as part of the library's façade. These choices represented a conscious effort to incorporate structural elements and architectural details manifest in other campus buildings, while the overall design and manner of siting were deliberately chosen so that the library would complement rather than obscure a nearby campus landmark. The placement of the library's name label at street level rather than above the door functioned to humanize the building's proportions and reduce institutional pretentiousness.

Design choices that served to set the library apart, if not from its neighbors then perhaps from the world of everyday experience, were seen in the library's elevated entry and the use of a bridge to connect the steps from the sidewalk to the entry doors. Then too, architectural monumentalism was suggested in the two-story ceiling height of reading, reference, and periodicals areas; the use of elevated areas or "mezzanines"; and the open stair at the rear of the library that provided a multistory view of the adjacent ravine.

A concern for the aesthetic experience of library users was acknowledged not only in the art objects and paintings that were available in almost every area of the library, but in the more mundane choices related to user comfort: use of wood trim, upholstered furniture arranged to support social grouping, incandescent as well as florescent lighting, carpeted areas, and green plants. Then too, the placement of study carrels to ensure users' visual access to the landscape surrounding the library indexed a sort of transcendental quality as an expression of the library's identity.

Environmental references to the college's traditional interest in women's issues, women's empowerment and a reverence for the college's past were implicit in: the sign that carried the library's "name," displays of student memorabilia and photographs, the library's collection of antiques, and plaques and memorials to alumnae. Posted acknowledgments of alumnae gifts also made claims about the library's projection of itself.

Although the art library shared with the college and science libraries themes of affiliation in design decisions expressive of an institutional identity, the scale and elevation of the building created for it a very different "line" or presence. For example, the library's cathedral-like elements— the height of its raised entry, its dome-like cupola, and the shape, scale, and glazing detail of its windows—gave expression to its own importance as well as expressing a veneration for art scholarship. Internally, architectural monumentality was reflected in the use of an atrium design and in a monumental stair, which rose to a mezzanine above the main level. The "rotunda" effect was magnified at night when spotlights mounted above the mezzanine illuminated the interior of the cupola. On the other hand, sensitivity to the university community was evident in the postmodern design of the art library and its reproduction of the structural themes observed in nearby historic buildings, as well as in light fixtures and landscaping. Connections to this community could also be seen reflected in the system of sidewalks that linked the library with neighboring buildings. The primacy of the library's relationship with the art history department was underscored in its physical attachment to the building that housed the department; in the double door design of the library's main entrance to allow access directly from the department; and the handouts and flyers that informed users about art-related events and programs.

Interestingly, the art library shared with the science library a sort of environmental rationalism, indexed in the minimalism of interior architectural appointments and design details. As was observed at the science library, a lack of decorative artifacts, displayed objects, memorials, plaques or name-plates added to the overall impersonality of the setting, while the mechanistic, and inorganic quality of the structural materials and appointments, seemed to express a value of efficiency over creature comforts. This environmental formality and spareness seemed especially "hard" (Sommer, 1974) when compared with the attention to the aesthetic and comfort needs of users implicated in design decisions at the college library.

At the art library, an emphasis on efficiency was also apparent in the use of a single "desk" for the management of library services, and the prominence of electronic equipment. Moreover, the neutrality, restraint, and refinement of the decor, and the static nature of the interior arrangement created an institutional anonymity, predictability, and order, which appeared to reflect an essentially intellectual and scholarly approach to art rather than the expressive ebullience and passion of artistic creativity. Surprisingly, few examples of art were part of the furnishings in the public areas of the art library. Observable framed art and prints had architectural themes, one of which appeared to be the architect's rendering of the library building itself. Together, these features functioned discursively to suggest an institutional regard for architecture as art in general and the beauty of the library building in particular. The sparseness of these furnishings also reflected a minimalism consistent with the tenets of modern architecture and with some tenets of upper class aestheticism.

Projections of identity at the science library indexed the immutability of science and rationalism and solidarity with the medical college and science departments, while the recognition of individual academic achievement and an emphasis on information and discovery seemed to be repeatedly expressed in design domain choices. The design choice of modern or international architectural style and its form and composition expressed the library's affiliation with the other "modern" brick and poured concrete buildings with which it shared a campus. Linkages to the community were also implicated in the network of sidewalks that connected the library with nearby buildings, and in the decision to create two entrances, so that the library "faced" buildings that housed the library's two primary constituencies.

By the same token, a monumental presence was achieved through the solidity of the science library's exterior form and the massiveness and verticality of the two-story colonnades that created galleries on two sides of the building. Indeed, the massive quality of the overall design of the library, and the use of brick piers that recalled classical themes, suggested both the preeminence of science and the veneration for scientific knowledge.

Themes of access, efficiency, and functionality abounded at the science library, with a general sense that this library represented access to up-to-date, necessary information. This orientation was underscored by the emphasis on technology and electronic access, not only in the prominent display of recently published science journals, but also in the prominent location of electronic equipment including computer terminals. A sense of order at the science library was realized in the careful labeling of all areas, bookstacks, doors, and equipment; in instructional signs; and in guides that articulated library policies. Finally, an emphasis and acknowledgment of the individual nature of scholarship seemed implicit in the arrangement of study spaces and the placement of service sites that maximize independent use of the facility, the library equipment, and the materials.

The relationship of this institution to the university was apparent in the recognition of individuals in displays, a memorial plaque, and in the maintenance of services for specified user groups. For example, a showcase of documents, photographs, and books had been placed in the lobby to celebrate the anniversary of the discovery of a "wonder drug" and the winning of the Nobel Prize by members of the university's scientific community. This event, which clearly continued to reflect credit on the university, was also construed as the instantiation of the library's expression of community affiliation. The emphasis on individual recognition and academic achievement implied in this display, however, seemed qualitatively different from the focus on group membership, the student experience, and the collective memory of the "daily round" of student life so evident in the choice of contemporary and historical objects displayed in the college library's lobby showcases.

Although there were indications that at some previous time there had been attention paid to the creation of a coherent decor in public areas at the science library, changes over time had substantially reduced the integrity of the design and consistency in style and color scheme. These conditions, the absence of art objects in public areas, together with a general minimalist approach to decoration and ornamentation throughout as design features was noteworthy within the science library, suggesting that aesthetic experience was not valued as a part of the knowledge in this setting. A striking example of the difference in the aesthetic experience of place for uses existed at the college and science libraries in terms of the "decor" of the rooms set aside for student use. At the college library, the main floor reading room featured an oil painting on the wall, a model of the library building, and a display of sculpture. In addition, the room contained a number of large, well-tended plants. Similar attention had been given to the decoration of the "quiet study" room located above the library's lobby, where framed prints adorned the walls and an adjacent area held an archival display of antiques. In contrast, a similar study room located on the main floor at the science library offered two "no smoking" signs and a small bulletin board that was empty of notices. A similar disparity in expressions of amenity was noted in the display of art in the main staircases of these libraries. At the college library, the stairway was a venue for the college's permanent collection of art; its counterpart at the science library held posters warning of the possibility of theft of personal belongings, and admonitions against smoking on the premises.

Projections of Culture, Aesthetics and Social Values in Academic Libraries. That knowledge at the college library was seen to encompass artistic expression as well as intellectual concerns was evident in the large area devoted to the preservation of music resources, and the emphasis on art at the facility in terms of the library's permanent collections, its art gallery displays, and its displays of student art projects. Projections of cultural identity at the art library were expressed in similar ways, although not to the same degree. Indeed, the building itself seemed the instantiation of the library's projection of cultural and aesthetic values. At the science library, on the other hand, the absence of attention to fine or decorative or graphic arts, as well as its utilitarian approach to aesthetic considerations seemed an expression of the valuing of the cognitive and scientific over other ways of knowing.

The expression of social values at the college, art, and science libraries seemed to reflect decidedly different orientations, at least when one considers the environmental support for relational and social activities at these institutions. The contents of display cases in the lobby areas of the college and science libraries are also suggestive of differing social realities. Whereas the college library maintained a number of spaces for social interaction, group tasks, and group study, such spaces were not supported to the same extent at either the science or the art libraries. The public areas of the art library provided only study desks and chairs, and its "interwoven" interior structure and atrium design made private conversations of any kind problematic. At the science library, the only casual furniture was in rooms reserved for quiet study activity. These design choices underscore the valuing of individual study and knowledge creation.

At the science library, objects displayed in the lobby cases evinced a focus on science and a valuing of individual achievement. The "objective" quality of the display was underscored by the choice of artifacts as well: texts, Xerox copies of documents, and photographs. At the college library, the exhibited artifacts were a celebration, not of individual achievement, but of the student experience, so that the focus on group membership and group (women's) academic success and social experience, and the personal items that were used to reflect these experiences (e.g., gym clothes, scrapbooks, personal mementos, photographs of campus life) projected a decidedly different set of social values.

Projections of the Generalized User in Academic Library Settings. In the academic libraries in the study, projections of the ideal or expected user were expressed in design decisions that provided support for certain kinds of users, certain kinds of use and activities, certain kinds of behaviors and behavior levels, certain interests, and certain traditions. At the college library, clues to the user constructed in this setting potentially lay in design choices in displayed artifacts, environmental amenities, and concerns for user safety on campus. For example, the predominance of artifacts and plaques that appeared to reflect the valuing of relationships evinced a gendered quality that was also underscored by the number and prominence of contemplative objects.

An upper class aesthetic in the preponderance of abstract as opposed to representational art forms at the academic libraries also suggested a student or faculty user, typically and traditionally a member of this college community. By the same token, in spite of the ramps to front and rear entrances, there appeared to be a presumption of a youthful, on-campus student user, in the maintenance of mezzanines in the library that did not permit wheel chair access, and the failure to provide parking immediately adjacent to the library's entrance. On the other hand, the provision of permanent "maps" of the library at strategic points in the building argues for an expectation that those who were not necessarily familiar with the library would be among the library's visitors. The variety of choices, in terms of the view, the character and conditions of library use, the types of workspaces, types of furniture, and types of rooms available to library users, seemed to anticipate the individuality and individual preferences of the user population, while the deployment of interactive equipment, the number of bulletin boards to which users could attach messages as well as read them, and the suggestion box, appeared to invite their intellectual participation

At the art library, norms for behavior differed depending on the status of the user. For example, the deployment of reserved, elaborate, and personalizable study carrels anticipated a privileged class of users who would spend substantial amounts of time in the library pursuing independent study activities. This privileged status translated into the measure of environmental control users could exert in this setting, namely, in their ability to personalize the carrels reserved to them, and to maintain a level of privacy in what was otherwise a public space.

At the same time, the nature and disposition of unreserved space indicated an expectation, on the library's part, that the norm for behavior expected of non-art and/or undergraduate students would include solitary study and brief visits. The essentially "unpublic" nature of the art library, that made possible the awarding of "insider" status to a comparatively few students, seemed to be reflected in the very few directional signs, in the modest security gates, and the absence of push bars for entering and exiting library visitors. In addition, the specialized vocabulary (e.g., "elephant folios"), special kinds of shelving (e.g., rollered edges), and special policies (e.g., noncirculation of materials; reserved carrels) not observed at other libraries in the university's system marked this setting, and its users, as unique.

The emphasis on scholarly activity at the art library was recoverable in practices that treated fixed arrangements of study tables, exclusivity in use of single carrels, and privileging of research activity as situated norms. For these reasons, it appeared that knowledge at the art library instantiated a worldview that acknowledged the value of serious scholarship conducted as an essentially individual activity. The lack of casual or sociopetally arranged furniture further suggested that social interaction was not environmentally supported or an expected behavior of library users.

Although the generalized user projected in design decisions at the science library shared with the art library a focus on the solitary, task-oriented, student user, evidence of privilege or insider status was not part of the science library's support for its clientele. The adjacency of a large parking lot, the prolific articulation of library loan policies, library rules, library hours, and the prominent and elaborate library diagrams on each level of the facility, together suggested users from across the university rather than a cohort group of local "resident" users or a cadre of insiders, as was the case at the college and art libraries. This related to the prominence of warnings about theft of personal property and routine backpack searches. Representations of human progress, order, control, and reason contained in the library's public presentation through design were juxtaposed with security practices that expressed expectations of irrationality, disorder, and irresponsibility. In this way, the anomalies of contemporary campus life were reflected in seemingly contradictory practices at the science library.

In the main, the informational and instructional nature of the handouts that the science library provided showed that its policymakers expected student users who sought access to information in online as well as print formats. In addition, an active role for users at the science library seemed implicit in the opportunities for interaction with library systems, with individual library staff members, and with the process of library acquisitions and service delivery evident at this site. Of all the libraries visited, the reference counter at the science library, which was desk height and which provided chairs for both users and librarians, seemed the most conducive to participatory engagement. Users also had choices in terms of seating alternatives that allowed some measure of control over the conditions of use, although the arrangement of tables and the relegation of informally grouped, casual furniture to an area designated for quiet study limited substantially the environmental opportunities for collaborative study or social interaction among library users. Overall, the essentially independent nature of user activity that seemed to receive primary support at the science library was seen in the proliferation of individual carrels and in the generally sociofugal nature of the arrangement of library furniture. In fact, the picnic tables and benches located near the entrance, which provided environmental amenities for users on the one hand, also seemed to suggest that social activities would be best (and most appropriately) undertaken outside the building.

Design Matters at Two Public Libraries

Public libraries are usually thought to share a general approach to service and outreach across contexts. As information agencies with a limited and known clientele, they tend to tailor their activities to the exigencies of the local community of constituents. The two libraries I visited in the study served the needs of adjacent communities; one urban and one suburban. Although located in the same geographical region, their primary constituencies were substantially different. The urban library had been built just after the turn of the 20th century with funding provided in part by the Carnegie Foundation. The suburban library had been built in the mid-1960s. Architectural dissimilarities, immediately and strikingly apparent, were also reflected in differences in their identity projections, and their projections of the generalized user, even though the cultural and social values they projected were remarkably similar.

Projections of Identity at Public Libraries. In overall size, the urban library was relatively "modest" in comparison with urban library buildings in many major metropolitan areas. However, its appropriation of academic architectural forms and classical themes, and its elevation, created a sense of monumentality that clearly distinguished it from its neighbors. The siting of the library, on a spacious, landscaped, and park-like lot and set back some distance from the street, also set the facility apart and suggested

for the library a certain remoteness from the community as well as a uniqueness of status. Although a recent postmodern addition seemed to index the
growth of the library's collection over time, there was little in the physical
aspect of the original library building to indicate that time had passed or
that the demographics of the community had changed since the library was
built in 1904. The urban library's design practices foregrounded themes of
tradition and preservation that seemed to suggest a dominant "high-culture"
narrative. This was apparent in both external and internal design features,
through its temple-like architectural style and formal arrangement, its array
of photographs and maps, its posted rules, memorial markers, and cherished and secured collections.

Inside the urban library, the effect of monumentality was achieved
through the creation of a rotunda-like vaulted ceiling in the lobby, which,
with its walnut paneling, leaded glass, arches, Roman columns, pilasters,
and escutcheons, added a quality of "grandness" and a degree of elegance
which was, albeit, somewhat diminished by the modern, fluorescent light
fixtures that were suspended from the ceiling. Taken together, these architectural strategies transformed both the library building, and by extension
the "library," into a public "sublimity."

The importance of tradition as a standard of value at the urban
library was the dominant theme in the projection of library identity. Thus,
an apparent veneration of traditional forms of knowledge implicit in the
library's temple architecture was reinforced in the array of artifacts, texts,
and behavioral norms represented design decisions at this site. Indeed, the
decision to put the reference department of the library in the new wing of
the library argues for the importance of information services to the library's
sense of itself.

That the history of the community and the development of the city
over time contributed to the library's projection of itself was reinforced environmentally in the library's proximity and affiliation to a landmark building,
its historical markers and plaques, its displays of historical maps and photographs, and in the careful preservation and presentation of historical items
and artifacts. By the same token, allusions to the library's past and traditions
were implicit in the reverential replication of architectural themes in stylistic
elements of the library's recent addition, in the careful preservation of interi-
or design details, and in the amount of space and the care and attention
devoted to the presentation the library's treasured items (its extensive doll
collection, an antique doll house, portraits, wall decorations, and plaques).

In contrast, the suburban library's architectural style and structural
elements reflected those of its neighbors in a municipal complex that
included the municipal building, the senior center, and the public safety
court building. In its proportion, siting, and landscaping, if not in its archi-

tectural style, the library also reflected housing and siting patterns of the garden apartments that surrounded this municipal "campus." This similarity, and the fact that it shared its site with other community agencies, suggested for the library a degree of affiliation with both the community and the other service agencies.

Unlike the urban library, where many references to community reflected historical associations, community relationships at the suburban library, reflected in artifacts, plaques, displayed items and informational literature and brochures, had a contemporary focus. Indeed at this library, even tradition seemed predicated on community terms, marked in memorial plaques that honored both library staff and community leaders. In this way, expressions of venerability were embedded in expressions of affiliation with the community.

Knowledge valued at the suburban library foregrounded effectiveness and efficiency as theories of professional practice. A valuing of efficiency in terms of service delivery were recoverable in the proliferation of service counters, while professional competence and expertise found expression in the prominent display of awards and plaques. In addition, the orderliness in the arrangement of departments and materials and the support for efficient use of the facility was underscored by the proliferation of shelf labels to mark library materials, the posting of diagrams of the facility, large and colorful signs, and uncarpeted "paths" to outline and link areas of the facility.

The essential rationality of institutional knowledge revealed in the library's public presentation was also reflected in the minimalism of its modern architectural style, as well as in the sign on the library's facade which graphically constituted the library (symbolized as a book) user as a thinker (symbolized by a brain). Although there was evidence of the foregrounding of electronic equipment and access to information in the proliferation of OPACs and copiers and the posting of notices which indicated their location throughout the facility, knowledge at the suburban library also included attention to aesthetics, as evidenced in the deployment of plants in all areas of the library, the use of decorative objects and graphics, and the color coordination of library appointments.

If the imposing architecture and interior monumentalism of the urban library projected an archival identity, the tone reflected in design choices at the suburban library was decidedly commercial. Marketing strategies such as the deployment of books for "impulse" check out at the circulation desk, celebrity posters urging people to "READ," plastic shopping baskets, "best sellers" lists, and fabric tapes to channel people into line at a "multi-windowed" circulation desk contributed to this image. The merchandising of stamps, disks, community publications, fax services, and Xerox copies, and the rental of videotape and current "best sellers" evidenced commercial themes observable in other library practices as well. Finally, because rooms were set aside for quiet "study," conversational tones were appropriate for other areas of the library, and this too added to the commercial quality of the library's physical presentation. An important part of knowledge at the suburban library was a service orientation for families, which made materials and spaces for young adults and children an important part of the framework of its environmental presentation.

Projections of Social and Cultural Values at Public Libraries. The predominance of the Western literary tradition in literature and popular culture, largely unenriched by symbols representing other national or ethnic traditions and other gestures of community inclusivity, was notable at the public libraries. Cultural and social values were apparent in the predominance of contemplative artifacts and the creation of spaces that supported restrained, task-oriented activity. Where they were observed, "action" objects were usually limited to utilitarian and task-related items rather than those that might suggest or support recreational, cooperative, social, or creative activities. Evidence of social and gender stereotyping was recoverable in posters, calendars, and other artifacts where males outnumbered females, Anglo-Americans outnumbered minority Americans, and males were generally portrayed in active, often professional activities or settings while females were generally seen as more passive, and portrayed in nurturing roles. Where they were observed, acknowledgement of non-Western cultures in artifacts was most frequently found in relatively ephemeral rather than permanent form (e.g., in paper graphics and posters).

Across libraries, classic markers of the "Puritan-Pioneer" (Sillars, 1991, p. 138) or of middle-class values promoting specific views of success were reflected in the range, nature, and rules of activities offered, and norms of acceptable user conduct. In the main, these libraries defined success as the achievement of individual goals related to reading, the acquisition of academic knowledge, winning, and celebrity. Expressions of social valuing in art and artifacts reflected: individual achievement; economic development; efficiency, order, and social stability; a nostalgic view of childhood; traditional family patterns and roles; as well as social and racial stereotypes. At the urban library, for example, the value of hard work, individual achievement, and faith in the importance of education were presented in the context of two role models: portraits of Abraham Lincoln and Andrew Carnegie.

Social stability and traditional social patterns were also expressed in art and artifact at both public and suburban study sites. However, the most compelling examples were observed at the urban library, where themes of social stability and human progress were expressed in sets of photographs celebrating community growth, industrial development, and urban renewal.

These photographs presented a community of White citizens, engaged in activities that portrayed women as exclusively involved in domestic, nurturing roles (preparing food, caring for children), or as the instantiation of community morality (nuns). Males were, in contrast, shown engaged in professional, creative, and highly energized types of activities (carving wood, making music, building buildings, clowning). In many respects, these same gendered ways of knowing were replicated in library posters and artifacts. Any reference to the multiethnic composition of the contemporary community was entirely missing in this prominent and permanent tribute to progress and development. However, the contemporary community achieved a sort of recognition through library posters, information in brochures and posted notices, and through a displayed collection of international dolls.

The view of childhood in the discourse of the urban library was reflected in a photographic display in the library's reference room. Photographs of a street carnival showed children being greeted by clowns and people in animal costumes were representative of a presentation of childhood as a happy and secure time. This was evident as well in a decorative wall sculpture, in the arrangement of dolls in the dollhouse, and the like. The "reality" of childhood was apparent in the organization of collections and services according to a three-tier developmental model: child, young adult, and adult. The place of children and youth was recoverable as well in policies that excluded unescorted children from some areas and maintained others for their exclusive use. In contrast, the suburban library themes valued intergenerational relationships and family life as expressed in banners, brochures, posted activities, and interactional spaces and furniture.

Library posters represented compelling expressions of social valuing. Although the use of entertainers, musicians and sports celebrities in posters tended to suggest that libraries were attuned to popular culture and contemporary in their outlook, each poster also constituted a powerful statement of cultural and social values and assumptions. These were embedded in the posters chosen, through the person displayed, in the books subjects were shown holding, and the occupations they represented. Examined closely, these posters in many ways perpetuate gender and ethnic stereotypes and support a view of an "entertainment" society where reading supports acting, performing, and playing—other forms of entertainment.

Projections of a Generalized User in Public Libraries. As just explained, projections of an ideal or generalized other were interpreted as being embedded within or expressed in design decisions that ordered the environment to support certain kinds of library activities, certain behaviors and levels of behaviors, and certain kinds of users. It was noted that the projected identity as expressed at the urban library, emphasized its historical traditions and cultural aspects; whereas in the suburban library's presentation, solidarity with the community, commitment to family services, and expressions of professional efficiency and expertise were foregrounded. These differences indexed differences in the projected or generalized user as well.

In both libraries, individual achievement, task orientation, and traditional social patterns found reinforcement in environmental and artifactual design choices. Within this climate, the possibilities of professional-user interaction are shaped (and modeled) by the configuration of service counters into a dispensing of things needed rather than a participatory or mutual problem-solving orientation to service. Designated spaces did support group activity but were only available through scheduling, thus not a spontaneous option. The proliferation of interactive, task-oriented equipment, and the absence of other kinds of interactive objects, suggested the existence of a library norm that limited users to various types of controlled engagements with others and library materials in determined rather than emergent or creative ways. Design decisions that enacted order and process, as in directing users to enter and exit at particular locations, wait for services in designated places, and restrict activity to stipulated times and places, condition the surrender of self through practices of consent that support systemic choices of how to be in the social in the world.

The urban library orientation to users projected a sense of relational separateness, reinforced in its protectively displayed artifacts and collections, and its explicit behavioral norms. An orientation to, and concern for individual achievement seemed evident in the many references to individuals and their contributions to the community, to the library, and to its history. By the same token, expected activities and activity levels were suggested in the generally sociofugal nature and arrangement of furniture as well as in the layout and organization of space. The value placed on appropriate library deportment, as outlined in the posted list of rules, reinforced through contemplative objects, and modeled by the quiescent state of the displayed dolls, suggested the ideal of a quiet, serious, responsible, and passive library user. The lack of space for social interaction and lack of comfortable furniture reinforced this view of the user as well. The library's attitude toward deportment was mirrored in the cultural uniformity of artifacts that projected a White, middle-class, and adult norm. By the same token, these artifacts and texts implicated failure, ignorance, irrationality, irresponsibility, poverty, waste, and self-indulgence as potential (likely) consequences of not engaging the library in this ideal way.

No doubt, users for whom the architectural symbols and artifacts manifest in the physical presentation of the library have meaning find a measure of reassurance, and personal validation, not only in the survival of a landmark building that confirms their historical past, but in its apparent commitment to the preservation and extension of traditional cultural traditions and the social values embedded in them. Likewise, those who can identify with the community members depicted in photographs and artifacts in the library, find in these allusions confirmation for their presence in this setting. However, these constitutive experiences fail to appreciate how much more is being accomplished when practices that are in a sense exclusive and exclusionary are manifest in this way.

In contrast, the suburban library seemed to invite the user into more active levels of intellectual and task-related engagement. The lightweight, casual furniture provided in the children's area encouraged autonomy and creativity through the ability to adapt the environment to suit multiple potential purposes. Nevertheless, a "commercial" model of service delivery was embedded in the design decisions. Environmental and artifactual design domains foregrounded a view of information as a commodity that suggests an ideal of the user as a passive consumer of information. The contrasting arrangement of the young adult section, with its static arrangement of study carrels and tables in contrast to that of the children's section, suggests the embrace of information as a commodity in a rational, controlled manner as a developmental progression.

CONCLUSION

I have applied an interpretive reading approach to explore issues of control, and the ways in which these are enacted through design. This involved a read of four discursive domains: architecture, environment, artifacts, and texts at selected libraries. The aim of this read was to show how design practices embed values of social meanings and desired order that library users continuously confront in their use of these facilities. I sought to show through individual description followed by comparison the differences between libraries in "self-regard," projection of cultural and social values, and projection of an idealized or generalized user identity. How design matters for user identity is a nontrivial concern, theoretically and empirically, that deserves recognition by those who design buildings, contribute to their currency of design, and generally hope to empower rather than reproduce people through the use of libraries is but one example.

Recognizing practices that might be read as disconfirmational or exclusionary by some library users is a first step in re-creating in libraries expressions of positive regard and respect for all individuals who may engage with them. Considered as "confirming" were architectural, environmental, artifactual, and textual practices that expressed welcome and reflected institutional consideration for diversity in users' cultural, activity, comfort, and empowerment needs.

Discursive practices were considered potentially disconfirming when their use potentially: reduced environmental competence and feelings of comfort and confidence through expressions and practices of environmental control; imposed a single standard of behavior on all users; perpetuated asymmetrical relationships between staff and users; depersonalized interactions; and expressed distrust and/or disrespect or, by omissions of cultural references that rendered potential user groups invisible in that setting.

To view the creation of confirmational settings for users as a dimension of library practice calls on library professionals to develop an environmental sensitivity to deference and demeanor issues, to the expression of institutional goals, and to the instantiation of social stereotyping and ethnic and cultural exclusivity that reflect and reify inequities existing "in the larger society" (Latrobe & Laughlin, 1992, p. 155). Especially significant to this line of reasoning is the realization that although the experiences that generate positive and negative images of self are social constructions, they are experienced as "real" and are thus "real in their consequences" (Thomas, 1966, p. xl). This reality organizes the experience of users in such a way that the valuing or devaluing of self that occurs in one setting may be carried into other encounters in different settings, and makes revaluing in other settings more difficult (Coontz, 1992).

Because it allows for a consideration of the interactional outcomes of the user's experience, the employment of an interpretive, interactionist framework may provide a theoretical grounding for the evaluation of library facilities, while the architectural, environmental, artifactual, and textual domains and dimensions identified may suggest a structure for evaluation criteria that addresses the complexities of all kinds of contemporary service institutions, and most especially, libraries.

REFERENCES

Altman, I. (1975). *Environment and social behavior: Privacy, personal space, territory, and crowding*. Monterey, CA: Brooks/Cole.

Becker, F.D. (1977). *Housing messages*. Stroudsberg, PA: Dowden, Hutchinson & Ross.

Belkin, N. (1980). Anomalous states of knowledge as a basis for information retrieval. *Canadian Journal of Information Science, 5*, 133-143.

Berger, P.L., & Luckmann, T. (1966). *The social construction of reality: A treatise in the sociology of knowledge*. New York: Doubleday.

Best, S., & Kellner, D. (1991). *Postmodern theory: Critical interrogations*. New York: Guilford.

Blumer, H. (1969). *Symbolic interactionism: Perspective and method.* Englewood Cliffs, NJ: Prentice-Hall.

Bolan, R.S. (1980). The practitioner as theorist: The phenomenology of the professional episode. *American Planning Association Journal, 46,* 261-274.

Coontz, S. (1992). *The way we never were: American families and the nostalgia trip.* New York: HarperCollins.

Crumpacker, S. S. (1994). The school library as place. *Wilson Library Bulletin, 69,* 23-25.

Csikszentmihalyi, M., & Rochberg-Halton, E. (1981). *The meaning of things: Domestic symbols and the self.* New York: Cambridge University Press.

Davidson, D., & Budd, R. (1991). Libraries: Relics or precursors? In R. Budd & B.D. Ruben (Eds.), *Beyond media* (pp. 138-159). New Brunswick, NJ: Transaction.

Deetz, S.A. (1994). Future of the discipline: The challenges, the research, and the social contribution. In S.A. Deetz (Ed.), *Communication yearbook 17* (pp. 565-600). Thousand Oaks, CA: Sage.

Dervin, B., & Nilan, M. (1986). Information needs and uses. *Annual Review of Information Science and Technology, ARIST, 21,* 3-33.

Doll, C.A. (1992). School library media centers: The human environment. *School Library Media Quarterly, 20,* 225-228.

Duncan, J.S. (1985). The house as symbol of social structure: Notes on the language of objects among collectivist groups. In I. Altman & C.M. Werner (Eds.), *Home environments* (Vol. 8, pp. 133-151). New York: Plenum Press.

Eco, U. (1980). Function and sign: The semiotics of architecture. In G. Broadbent, R. Bunt, & C. Jencks (Eds.), *Signs, symbols, and architecture* (pp. 11-69). New York: Wiley.

Foss, S. K., & Gill, A. (1987). Michel Foucault's theory of rhetoric as epistemic. *Western Journal of Speech Communication, 51,* 384-401.

Foucault, M. (1972). *The archaeology of knowledge and the discourse on language.* New York: Pantheon.

Foucault, M. (1980). *Power/knowledge: Selected interviews and other writings, 1972-1977* (C. Gordon, Ed.). New York: Pantheon.

Gergen, K.J. (1991). *The saturated self: Dilemmas of identity in contemporary life.* New York: Basic Books.

Gergen, K.J. (1995). Postmodern psychology: Resonance and reflection. *American Psychologist, 50,* 394.

Gerson, E.M., & Gerson, M.S. (1976). The social framework of place perspectives. In G.T. Moore & R.G. Golledge (Eds.), *Environmental knowing: Theories, research, and methods* (pp. 196-205). Stroudsburg, PA: Dowden, Hutchinson & Ross.

Goffman, E. (1959). *The presentation of self in everyday life.* New York: The Free Press.

Goffman, E. (1967). *Interaction ritual: Essays on face-to-face behavior.* New York: Pantheon.

Goffman, E. (1973). Role distance. In A. Birnenbaum & E. Sagarin (Eds.), *People in places: The sociology of the familiar* (pp. 121-137). New York: Praeger.

Goldstein, S.J. (1964). Environmental control. In H.L. Roth (Ed.), *Planning library buildings for service* (pp. 21-27). Chicago: American Library Association.

Goodsell, C.T. (1977). Bureaucratic manipulation of physical symbols: An empirical study. *American Journal of Political Science, 21,* 79-91.

Gowans, A. (1992). *Styles and types of North American architecture: Social function and cultural expression.* New York: Icon/HarperCollins.

Gutman, R. (1969). Library architecture and people. In E.R. De Prospo, Jr. (Ed.), *The library building consultant role and responsibility* (pp. 11-29). New Brunswick, NJ: Rutgers University Press.

Hall, E.T. (1966). *The hidden dimension.* New York: Doubleday.

Jacobs, J. (1961). *The life and death of great American cities.* New York: Random House.

Jencks, C. (1980). The architectural sign. In G. Broadbent, R. Bunt, & C. Jencks (Eds.), *Signs, symbols and architecture* (pp. 70-118). New York: Wiley.

Jencks, C. (1984). *The language of post-modern architecture.* New York: Rizzoli.

Jencks, C. (1985). *Modern movements in architecture* (2nd ed.). London: Penguin.

Kuhlthau, C.C. (1993). *Seeking meaning: A process approach to library and information services.* Norwood, NJ: Ablex.

Latrobe, K.H., & Laughlin, M.K. (Compilers.). (1992). *Multicultural aspects of library media programs.* Englewood, CO: Libraries Unlimited.

Martin, D. (1994, October 2). Lobby wars: No one lives there, but everyone fights over how a building's entryway should look. *New York Times Magazine: Home Design,* pp. 14, 16.

Mead, G.H. (1934). *Mind, self, and society.* Chicago: University of Chicago Press.

Miller, E.P. (1978). Anticipating needs of users. In M.B. Steffenson & L.D. Larason (Eds.), *The user encounters the library: An interdisciplinary focus on the user/system interface.* Monroe, LA: Northeast Louisiana University. (ERIC Document Reproduction Service No. ED266791)

Mokros, H.B. (Ed.). (1996). *Interaction and identity: Information and behavior* (Vol 5). New Brunswick, NJ: Transaction.

Mokros, H.B., & Deetz, S. (1996). What counts as real? A constitutive view of communication and the disenfranchised in the context of health. In E.B. Ray (Ed.), *Communication and the disenfranchised: Social health issues and implications* (pp. 29-44). Hillsdale, NJ: Erlbaum.

Mokros, H.B., Mullins, L.S., & Saracevic, T. (1995). Practice and personhood in professional interaction: Exploring social identities in the addressing of information needs. *LISR, 17,* 237-257.

Moore, G.T. (1979). Knowing about environmental knowing: The current state of theory and research on environmental cognition. *Environment and Behavior, 11,* 33-70.

Muschamp, H. (1994, October 16). Architectural view: Ten little houses and how they grew. *The New York Times,* p. 40.

Norman, D.A. (1988). *The psychology of everyday things.* New York: Basic Books.

Ornstein, S. (1989). Impression management through office design. In R. Giacolone & P. Rosenfeld (Eds.), *Impression management in organizations* (pp. 411-426). Hillside, NJ: Erlbaum.

Ornstein, S. (1992). First impressions of the symbolic meanings connoted by reception area design. *Environment and Behavior, 24,* 85-110.

Pittenger, R.E., Hockett, C.F., & Danehy, J.J. (1960). *The first five minutes: A sample of microscopic transcription analysis.* Ithaca, NY: Martineau.

Rapoport, A. (Ed.). (1976). *The mutual interaction of people and their built environment: A cross-cultural perspective.* The Hague: Mouton Publishers.

Rapoport, A. (1977). *Human aspects of urban form: Towards a man-environment approach to urban form and design.* Oxford: Pergamon.

Rapoport, A. (1982). *The meaning of the built environment: A non-verbal communication approach.* Beverly Hills, CA: Sage.

Raskin, E. (1974). *Architecture and people.* Englewood Cliffs, NJ: Prentice-Hall.

Relph, E. (1984). Seeing, thinking, and describing landscapes. In T.F. Saarinen, D. Seamon, & J.L. Sell (Eds.), *Environmental perception and behavior: An inventory and prospect* (pp. 209-223). Chicago: University of Chicago Department of Geography Research Paper No. 209.

Ruesch, J., & Kees, W. (1970). *Nonverbal communication: Notes on the visual perception of human relations.* Berkeley: University of California Press.

Russell, R.L., & Gaubatz, M.D. (1995). Contested affinities: Reaction to Gergen's (1994) and Smith's (1994) postmodernisms. *American Psychologist, 50,* 389-390.

Scheff, T.J. (1990). *Microsociology: Discourse, emotion, and social structure.* Chicago: University of Chicago Press.

Scheff, T.J. (1996). Part/whole analysis: Towards the objective determination of meaning. In H.B. Mokros (Ed.), *Interaction and identity: Information and behavior* (Vol. 5, pp. 25-44). New Brunswick, NJ: Transaction.

Sever, I. (1987). Children and territory in a library setting. *Library and Information Science Review, 9,* 95-103.

Shannon, C., & Weaver, W. (1949). *The mathematical theory of communication.* Urbana: University of Illinois Press.

Shibutani, T. (1987). *Society & personality: An interactionist approach to social psychology.* New Brunswick, NJ: Transaction.

Sillars, M.O. (1991). *Messages, meanings, and culture: Approaches to communication criticism.* New York: HarperCollins.

Sommer, R. (1974). *Tight places: Hard architecture and how to humanize it.* Englewood Cliffs: Prentice-Hall.

Steele, F. (1986). *Making and managing high-quality workplaces: An organizational ecology.* Reading, MA: Addison-Wesley.

Thomas, W.I. (1966). *W. I. Thomas on social organization and social personality: Selected papers.* Chicago: University of Chicago Press.

Tuan, Y.-F. (1976). Literature, experience, and environmental knowing. In G. T. Moore & R.G. Golledge (Eds.), *Environmental knowing: Theories, research, and methods* (pp. 260-272). Stroudsburg, PA: Dowden, Hutchinson, & Ross.

Upah, G.D., & Fulton, J.W. (1985). Situation creation in service marketing. In J.A. Czepiel, M.R. Solomon, & C.F. Surprenant (Eds.), *The service encounter: Managing employee/customer interaction in service businesses* (pp. 255-263). Lexington, MA: Lexington Books.

Wagner, G.S. (1991). Semiotics: A tool of communication research in public libraries. *Libri, 41,* 207-215.

Wagner, G.S. (1992). *Public libraries as agents of communication : A semiotic analysis.* Metuchen, NJ: Scarecrow Press.

Watzlawick, P., Beavin, J., & Jackson, D. (1967). *Pragmatics of human communication: A study of interactional patterns, pathologies, and paradoxes.* New York: Norton.

Wener, R.E. (1985). The environmental psychology of service encounters. In J.A. Czepiel, M.R. Solomon, & C.F. Surprenant (Eds.), *The service encounter: Managing employee/customer interaction in service businesses* (pp. 101-112). Lexington, MA: Lexington Books.

Zeisel, J. (1975). *Sociology and architectural design.* New York: Russell Sage Foundation.

ENGAGEMENTS
IN MEDIATED SETTINGS

5

Support Matters
A Study of Identity in an Online Cancer Support Group

Esther Rumsey

Personal matters of identity may involve ongoing concerns such as in the case of gender or race, or they may be aroused by unexpected life events. Such is the case when individuals confront life-threatening illnesses such as AIDS or cancer. A cancer diagnosis involves the assumption of new roles for people with the illness as they suddenly find themselves to be a patient, and all that this entails, as they seek to address their illness through medical intervention. It also involves new roles for significant others, family, and friends, as they assume positions of advocacy, caregiving, and the like. For both, there is also the social stigma that results (Goffman, 1963), and more generally, the implications or impact that the illness has for these individuals' sense of self and their relationship with others (Charmaz, 1991). Indeed, Herzlick and Pierret (1985) even suggested that "sickness is an identity that must be assumed, acquired and imposed on others" (p. 147).

    This chapter concerns itself with matters of identity for individuals confronted with colon cancer as well as the significant others of such individuals. It approaches this concern through an assessment of the way that one group of such individuals made use of an online site devoted to colon cancer (Rumsey, 2001). Online sites devoted to health issues provide a

111

recently developed tool available to assist individuals confronting illness, to help them make sense of the impact it has on their lives. Such sites vary as to what they offer. Some are textually based, providing reference information about a specific health issue for those who visit the site. Other sites are interactive, offering the visitor the possibility to engage with others in online discussion. Such social support group sites are increasingly common and offer an alternative to support group options within the community. The discussion in this chapter is based on the study of this type of site, one established so as to offer colon cancer victims and their significant others a space within which to establish a social support group.

Research has shown that the availability of social support facilitates the adjustment of individuals facing a life threatening illness (Frey, Query, Flint, & Adelman, 1998; Gotcher, 1993). Additionally, research has shown that participation in a support or self-help group provides much of the same benefits as interpersonal social support (Caplan, 1982). Specifically, research has indicated that benefits of participation in a support group include access to information and validation of individual member's problems and sense of self through sharing experiences with other members (Cawyer & Smith-Dupre, 1995; Cluck & Cline, 1986; Frey et al., 1998).

Albrecht and Adelman (1987) defined *social support* as communication "that reduces uncertainty about the situation, the self, the other and the relationship and functions to enhance a perception of personal control in one's life experience" (p. 19). To these ends, social support has been conceptualized in academic research as the tangible or intangible support provided by family members, friends, neighbors, colleagues, support groups, and others (Albrecht, Burlson, & Goldsmith, 1994). Tangible forms of support include instrumental aid (e.g., providing financial or physical assistance), emotional aid (e.g., engaging in empathetic listening), information (e.g., giving directions), or appraisal support (e.g., verbal feedback). Intangible forms of support include communicative practices that contribute to feelings of security that come from the perception of being loved and cared for by others and feelings of self-worth and affirmation that come from positive communication with others (Caplan, 1976; Cutrona, Cohen, & Igram, 1990; Sarason, Sarason, Shearin, & Pierce, 1987).

Although a number of empirical studies have indicated that social support networks are important in reducing stress through advice, tangible assistance, validation, and comforting messages (Aneshensel & Stone, 1982; Bolger & Eckenrode, 1991; Kohn, 1996), research has also indicated that an individual's perception of supportive attempts ultimately determines whether such support will be useful (La Gaipa, 1990). Depending on the relationship between the individuals involved in the supportive interaction, advice and even attempts at emotional support may not be desired or perceived as supportive (Wright, 2000). However, little research has considered how and why individuals seek social support.

Specifically examined in this chapter are the first, or introductory messages of individuals who visited and participated in the site during the first 6 weeks following its establishment. Analysis of introductory messages in isolation says little about processes of social support, about what constitutes supportive communication practices. What such an analysis does offer is the opportunity to see how individuals approach such a site, how they present themselves and their current situation. An analysis based on introductory messages also provides a way to gauge why these individuals have presented themselves to others in this online context. To put this another way, this analysis of introductory messages seeks to establish how support matters to these individuals. Why, in other words, do they seek to participate? And what may be learned about the identity orientations of individuals in a crisis situation as they approach a context of purported support. What is of interest is how identity concerns surface in the context of seeking support. For it is not merely the physical dimensions of illness that motivates one to seek support, but also efforts to make sensible the psychosocial byproducts the illness has rendered.

This line of argument is developed within a constitutive view of communication, a view that argues that communication is not merely a matter of information exchange but a site within which meanings are established with identity always an aspect. From a constitutive perspective, the revelations of who one is in the context of their communication practices is not merely a matter of revealing attributes of some enduring sense of self. Instead, what is also revealed is an attitude toward self in relationship to others and the real and transferred otherness of one's self. This could be a matter of being self-absorbed and thereby seemingly not concerned with the needs of others or the impact that one's own expressed needs has on them. It could be a matter of being other-focused, attending to the needs of others, providing rather than requesting support. And, it could also be a focus on the relationship, both requesting and providing support and balancing the needs of self with the needs of others.

The discussion that follows aims to illustrate how identity matters are revealed in the context of the communication practices employed by individuals confronting a life-threatening illness (i.e., colon cancer) in their approaches to participation within an online social support group. This is approached through a systematic examination of the introductory messages posted to one online colon cancer support site.

APPROACH TO ANALYSIS

Description of the Site

The site selected for this research was designed to provide information and support to cancer victims, family members, and friends dealing with a colon cancer diagnosis through online discussion among individuals sharing the same experience. The site achieved this through what is called a *listserv*. A listserv is an e-mail-based system that provides for the distribution of messages to all those participants who subscribe to the listserv. Messages are distributed to all subscribed members whenever someone sends an e-mail message to the listserv address.

The site from which introductory messages were obtained was one of 69 active listservs developed and maintained by a nonprofit organization at the time the introductory messages discussed subsequently were posted. Through these listservs this organization sought to address the perceived needs of cancer patients, cancer survivors, family members, and friends of patients and survivors. The organization also maintained a web page with links to governmental web pages related to cancer, to web pages featuring medical information as well as to pages offering the personal experiences of cancer survivors. Additionally, the main web page also provided links to all 69 listservs, thus making it possible for anyone who might be interested to easily access and participate in multiple online support sites.

Introductory Messages[1]

Fifty-six introductory messages posted during the first 6 weeks of this site's operation were studied. As just discussed, this chapter aims to show how issues of identity are apparent within introductory messages posted to this site. This then poses the question as to how such issues of identity may be identified within these messages. The sequential organization of all messages posted to the site and content (i.e., information and themes) contained within the introductory messages were systematically analyzed in an effort to address this question. This systematic description served as the basis for subsequent interpretations and inferences about *how identity matters* within

---

[1]Examples from these messages included in the following discussion preserve what was typed by those who posted the messages including spelling or grammatical errors. This allows the reader to view these messages in the same form as participants received and read them on their computer screens.

and across these introductory messages. To put this more generally, considerations of identity discussed subsequently are anchored within a systematic exploration of the communication practices of participants at this site.

Each message was first numbered according to its placement in relation to all other messages, with "Message 1" the first message posted and "Message 56" the last posted within the time frame considered. The length of messages was then coded using a message's total number of words as an index. Thereafter, the content of each message was reviewed to gain an overall sense, across messages, of the types of information and themes they contained. This resulted in the identification of four classes of information that proved to be of focal interest for systematic analysis. They included descriptors of participant characteristics (e.g., disease status, gender, disease state); reasons for participating (e.g., problem state, expressed needs); types of expressed needs (e.g., informational, emotional/relational); and, expressions directed toward others (e.g., offering advice/information, expressions of gratitude or encouragement).

Once these classes of information were identified, individual messages were systematically coded for the presence or absence of specific features contained within each class. It quickly became clear that many individuals offered multiple reasons for participating in their introductory messages and that these reasons were embedded within needs expressions and other-directed expressions. "Reasons for participating" was therefore dropped as a coding category.

Accordingly, the final systematic coding, focused on the three remaining types of information initially identified in these introductory messages. Specifically, each message was coded as to:

1. The presence or absence of specific participant characteristics.
2. The presence or absence and frequency of specific types of need expressions.
3. The presence or absence and frequency of specific types of other-directed expressions.

This approach made it possible to generate descriptive statistics across messages and between types of messages according to these coded features.

CHARACTERISTICS OF INTRODUCTORY MESSAGES

Descriptive Characteristics of Participants

Introductory messages contained a variety of different types of information about the individuals who had posted these messages. Information about the participant's relationship to the illness, as either a cancer victim or the significant other of a cancer victim, and gender was present in each message. The 56 introductory messages contained information that identified 22 cancer victims and 34 significant others, and 25 females and 31 males as participants. The distribution of males and females did not statistically differ between those who described themselves as cancer victims or significant others nor did these participant characteristics statistically differ in relationship to the frequency or type of need expressed or other directed expressions within messages. Thus, gender and disease status are not considered further in this chapter. (For a full analysis of the relationship of gender, disease status, and expressed needs see Rumsey, 2001).

Based on geographic locations mentioned by the participants in their messages and available from their e-mail addresses, virtually all participants appeared to reside in the United States with two indicating that they were residents of Canada. Prior research has indicated that participant characteristics such as cultural, racial, and ethnic background, income, education, and age may all influence individual response to illness (Kleinman, Eisenberg, & Good, 1978; Mishler, 1981). Although information about these types of characteristics was contained in some messages, none of these characteristics could be coded across all messages and is therefore not considered further in this chapter. Readers who wish to review further these additional types of participant descriptive characteristics contained in the messages posted to the site studied may consult Rumsey (2001).

Although not recoverable for all participants, information related to the stage and duration of the illness is considered further in this chapter. Colon cancer is staged according to size and spread of the cancer ranging from Dukes A (the least invasive) to Dukes D (the most advanced). Additionally, recurrent bouts of colon cancer are considered as comparable to a Dukes D diagnosis in assessing the seriousness of the illness. Expected outcomes vary according to the stage of the disease at time of diagnosis. The American Cancer Society (1999) reports that "the 1- and 5-year relative survival rates for patients with colon and rectum cancer are 82% and 62% respectively," and that survival rates increase with detection in the early, localized stages of the illness.

The research literature suggests the relevance of such factors for the focus of discussion in this chapter. For example, Dunkel-Schetter (1984) pointed out the importance of considering illness prognosis when studying the impact of social support. Her study of cancer patients indicated that poor prognosis was related to interpersonal problems for a significant number of patients and their families. Brashers et al. (2000) also suggested that the response of individuals to the uncertainty of illness may be influenced by changes in the environment, including the receipt of new information or a change in their disease situation.

Time since diagnosis provides a crude index of the degree of uncertainty in the individual's experience. Examination of introductory messages indicated that 50% of the participants provided information regarding the stage of their disease, whereas nearly all participants (91%) provided information regarding the length of time since diagnosis. Time since diagnosis ranged from 2 weeks to 14 years across participants reporting such information. Of those individuals who reported their stage of illness, 17 had the most extreme diagnosis of Dukes D or experiences of recurrent colon cancers. None of the participants reported a Dukes A or Stage 1 (the least serious) diagnosis. Thus, at least 30% of the participants, and presumably many more, were directly experiencing the uncertainties associated with impending death.

Expression of Needs

Need statements were typically placed in the context of a problem statement. This is shown in the following example: "My doctors told me that I've gone through all possible treatment options. Is anyone out their familiar with any alternative options I might consider?" This message's author offers a problem statement in terms of her illness stage and makes an open-ended request for information that might address her problem. Also apparent in this message is the indication that this individual continues to hold out hope and does not necessarily trust her doctors' formulation, namely, that she has run out of options.

This analytic focus on motives for participating showed that most messages contained explicit reasons for posting a message to the group. Such explicit statements were treated, as in the example just given, as expressed needs. Two different general types or classes of needs were apparent across messages: informational or medical needs and emotional or personal needs. Informational or medical needs expressed a desire for knowledge that others might have about the longitudinal course and treatment of colon cancer. Emotional or personal needs expressed a direct desire for support in addressing psychosocial concomitants of colon cancer. Both of these types of expressed needs involve requests for support, although they present differing demands for those who might address them as has been discussed in the literature on social support in the context of life-threatening illness more generally (Cutrona & Suhr, 1994; Ford, Babrow, & Stohl, 1996).

Across participants, only six introductory messages contained no expression of need. Thus, 89% of the messages contained at least one expressed need. Most messages contained multiple expressions of need with 39% of messages containing three or more expressed needs, with a high of eight needs expressed in one message.

As mentioned, expressed needs consisted of two general types: informational or medical needs and emotional or personal needs. Informational needs were evident in 35 messages, whereas emotional needs were evident in 32 messages. Although 18 messages contained both informational and emotional need expressions, the majority of messages contained only one type of need. Messages containing only expressions of informational need were slightly more common (31%) than messages containing only emotional needs (25%).

Other-Directed Expressions

The coding of introductory messages also sought to systematically describe the types of communication practices employed by participants with specific focus on what are called here *other-directed expressions*. Other-directed expressions reference communication practices that speak to an individual's orientation to others. That is to say, the concern here is to identify specific practices that may be said to index the relational orientation apparent in a person's definition of the situation. Certainly, identifying one's gender and relationship to the disease, as just discussed, are examples of such practices as are the varying ways that participants expressed needs in their introductions.

The avoidance of need statements by some participants, the statement of either informational or emotional needs, but not both, by others, and the expression of both types of needs along with tendencies by still others to express multiple needs indexes a participant's orientation to others, to one's self in relationship. When assessed in this way, these differing patterns of need expression suggest some ways that matters of identity are intertwined with the pursuit of support. The aim in this section is to offer some additional types of practices that implicate an individual's relational orientation. The writings of Goffman (1959, 1967) on face-work and demeanor and deference, of Scheff (1997) on social bonds, of Brown and Levinson (1987) on politeness, and Buber's (1958) considerations of self in relationship, were central to the development of the line of argument presented here. These writings also served to guide the identification of specific other-directed practices discussed later.

Specifically, this section examines references to other participants, directness of need statement expression, expressions of gratitude and encouragement, and the offering of information or advice as examples of such practices. The practices examined thus include considerations of the manner in which specific statements were constructed as well as specific types of statements that offer insight into the relational orientation of the participants. To be sure, this is hardly an exhaustive list of such communication practices. The aim here is to provide some examples that reveal differences among participants in relational orientation, and is not meant to represent anything approaching a comprehensive investigation of this issue per se. Rumsey (2001) reported additional examples and a more extended discussion of communication practices and relational orientation than what is offered here.

References to Others. References to others within the introductory messages represents one type of communication practice that implicates an individual's orientation to others. New participants had every opportunity, and presumably all did read already posted messages prior to constructing an introductory message. The inclusion of references to others within introductory messages not only makes apparent the participant's familiarity with prior postings, but also conveys a sense of interest and involvement with the group, an awareness of, and caring about the circumstances of others. The coding of this type of practice was based on references to already posted messages, through referencing an author's name or some other component of such messages. Although not a common practice, 36% of the participants did incorporate such references to others in their introductory messages.

Directness of Need Expression. The manner by which need statements were expressed provides a second example of communication practices that index a participant's relational orientation. This coding involved the review of need statements within each introductory message and the classification of these need statements as either an example of a direct or indirect request. Need statements coded as direct requests were expressed as questions, or questions phrased as statements (e.g., Participant 48: "We are looking for information on possible treatments and clinical trials to discuss with the team."). Need statements that were not framed in such question or questionlike expressions were coded as indirect requests. Participant 9's statement, "This is really some change for a person trained as an experimental scientist" provides an example. And, because it may be assumed that all individuals engaging in this site sought to have some type of personal need addressed, those six individuals previously identified as not expressing a need were also considered to be expressing their needs indirectly. This coding of the manner in which needs were expressed was made at a message level. That is, in cases where messages contained multiple need statements, only one of these would need to be a direct request for the entire message to be counted as such. With this in mind, 63% of the participants were identified as expressing their need(s) directly.

The functional value of this type of communication practice is, to be sure, a complex issue (e.g., Spiers, 1998). For example, the framing of direct requests as either "I need," or "Would anyone know if" invoke quite different positionings of self and regard for others. Nevertheless, for the sake of the argument developed in this chapter, the distinction between direct and indirect approaches to framing requests provides one way to gauge differences in the relational orientation of participants.

Expressions of Gratitude and Encouragement. Expressions of gratitude and encouragement bear resemblance to "reference to others" practices in that these practices are also gestures of inclusion, expressions of regard and connection with others in the group. Thirty-four percent of introductory messages contained no such expressions, 10% included both expressions of gratitude and encouragement, 36% included only expressions of gratitude, and 20% included only expressions of encouragement.

Offering Information or Advice. Introductory messages not only contained expressions of need, but also offerings of information or advice that might be directed at a specific individual or the group in general. Such practices included responses to one, or multiple specific messages posted previously. Others offered information or advice to group members generally without any clear connection to specific messages posted. Such practices also differed in the manner of directness that the offering was presented. Consider, for example, the difference in directness reflected in Participant 32's offering, in concluding a detailed description of his situation, with that of Participant 38:

Participant 32: "There are probably others with similar conditions that may be interested."

Participant 38: "I have researched treatment options extensively and will be glad to point anyone in the right direction."

Although again there are notable differences in how offerings of information and advice were handled, the discussion only considers whether or not a message contained such a practice. Across introductory messages, 59% contained offers of information or advice. This again reveals differences among introductory messages, and the participants who constructed them in how they approached the situation, as a matter of inclusion through gestures of orientation to others or as a matter of personal needs, a focus primarily on the conditions and state of one's self.

Summary of the Analysis of Introductory Messages

The dicussion of introductory messages above in terms of participant characteristics, needs expression, and other-directed expressions was based on a systematic approach to the analysis of these messages. This approach aimed to not only contextualize these messages but to also offer some tangible ways to think about how considerations of identity are implicated in one's participation within a support group online. Of interest in this regard are the differences apparent between participants according to the dimensions examined within introductory messages. It is in the link at the interface of expressed personal needs for support and these individuals' relational orientations to others that the relevance of identity as a way of conceptualizing differences among participants becomes most clearly apparent. The following section addresses this as it proposes three general types of identity orientation as apparent in the introductory messages. Thereafter, the discussion again considers the dimensions of introductory messages discussed in this section as systematically related to the three relational orientation types identified next.

THREE GENERAL TYPES OF RELATIONAL ORIENTATIONS

The analysis reported in this chapter is guided by the assumption that seeking and providing information and support "does not occur in a vacuum, but is shaped and affected by the way the individuals convey regard for themselves and for each other" (Mokros, Mullins, & Saracevic, 1995, p. 238). The repeated readings of the messages in the development of an approach to the analysis of their features began to suggest the presence of a limited number of types of messages, reflecting an interface in how their authors oriented to addressing personal needs and entering into relationship with others. Drawing on Buber (1958) and Scheff's (1997) discussions and extension of his ideas, these differing types of messages were grouped according to their orientation toward self and other. This grouping indicated three general types of messages, labeled as *seeker orientation, bonder orientation,* and *giver orientation.*

Buber distinguished between two types of relational orientation, I–Thou and I–it, to describe contrasting relational orientations between people in interaction. An I–Thou orientation recognizes the humanity of both the self and the other, whereas an I–it orientation recognizes only the self and treats the other as an object. Scheff (1997) argued that Buber's explanation is limited, providing an explanation only for relationships and attitudes about the self that recognize an active self, accounting only for relationships that reflect isolation and attunement, and does not consider enmeshed relationships in which the self is objectified in relationship to the other. In response to this limitation, Scheff proposed a third relational orientation, it–Thou, in which the humanity and needs of the other are recognized and the self is objectified. These three relational orientations, I–it, I–Thou and it–Thou, provided the framework for coding and grouping introductory messages.

Additionally, Goffman's (1963) discussion of common responses to stigma suggests a link between support matters, as indicated by the frequency and type of need expressed by participants, and the three relational orientations suggested by Buber (1958) and Scheff (1997). Three responses to a stigmatizing condition discussed by Goffman suggest differing ways of identifying and addressing personal needs associated with the stigmatizing condition. The first approaches the condition as a temporary state and seeks to find a solution or cure that will return the individual to the state of "normal." The second approaches the condition as a new way of being and seeks to learn how to be in this new way through establishing a sense of belonging and identification with the group. The third approach seeks to assert control over the condition by becoming an expert and providing advice to others similarly afflicted.

Both the differing relational orientations and the differing responses to the disease implicate identity matters as they are reflected in the way participants indicate that support matters in their introductory messages. Based on the framework of relational orientations (Buber, 1958; Scheff, 1997) and approaches to stigmatizing conditions (Goffman, 1963), the messages were grouped according to three types orientations. They were called the *seeker, giver,* and *bonder* orientation and are summarized next.

Three Relational Orientations Summarized

The Seeker Orientation.   The most common type of participant orientation observed in introductory messages involved an approach to the site as a source of help, with the message emphasizing a desire or need for assistance with specific problems. These types of messages also evinced an individual or self-focused orientation in relationship. That is to say, the manner by which needs were expressed in these introductory messages reflected a focus on self without any clear expression of concern about other participants, without any reciprocal willingness to share or give information and support to others. This type of message, referred to subsequently as a seeker orientation, accounted for 46% of all introductory messages.

The following message provides an example of this seeker orientation. This message, authored by Marianne, was the third posted to the site. She wrote:

Hi, I'm Marianne James and my husband, Bert, has colon cancer with liver mets. He was diagnosed in Sept for a softball sized tumor in the colon with invasion of the bladder. He has a colostomy and a reconstructed bladder. He had 3 mow. Of 5 FU and Leucovrin, then 9mos. Of 5 FU alone which stopped being effective a few months ago. He is currently waiting for CPT11 which he is getting under compassionate need. He has done very well during treatment and looks great, is weight is back up to normal after surgery. To look at him and to ask him, you would not believe he had cancer. I'm looking for info from people who are on CPT 11 so I will know what to expect from this treatment.
If you know of anyone, please have them e-mail me. Marianne

Marianne's message illustrates a common feature of the seeker orientation, a desire for information that would bring resolution to an experienced uncertainty. Marianne's desire to "know what to expect" reflects this. Her relational orientation is embedded within her need for information, with the information she provided the group in her message offering a context for her need rather than advice for others. The self-focused nature of her message is apparent in the clear distinctions she draws between herself and others, including her husband and members of the site. This is also apparent in the expressed reason for her informational need, namely a desire to enhance her sense of control over a situation of uncertainty. Her request that anyone with information respond to her directly further underscores this self-focus and suggests that she did not consider that other participants might benefit from the information she sought.

Marianne's message suggests an individual with needs who approaches others as resources rather than as persons who may also have needs. The focus of the seeker oriented messages on informational or medical needs and emphasis on individual rather than relational concerns reflects a response to the health crisis, which views the illness as a temporary state for which a medical solution exists. The site appears then to be approached as an information center where seekers may draw on the experiences and knowledge of others in finding a medical solution. As such, participants at the site appear to be viewed as informational resources rather than as individuals confronting similar health crises.

The Giver Orientation.   Of those 30 messages not characterized as seeker-oriented, half revealed what is called a giver orientation and accounted for 27% of all introductory messages. These messages were not characterized by a desire to satisfy specific personal needs but consisted instead of offers of help and advice to others based on personal experience and knowledge of relevant research. The giver orientation was characterized by a sense of self-focus, akin to the seeker orientation although with the self presented as a resource for others rather than as a seeker of information.

The introductory message posted by "Gerald," the second participant, provides an example of a giver orientation:

> Hi Everybody! My wife Jane has metastatic colon cancer that has spread to the liver. I am the caregiver in the family and the "internetter". Do see our www page on stage IV colon cancer at http://www. We have a few other "internetters" that periodically respond from this address when appropriate: "Spot" the dog—who has metastatic cancer of the big toe (left, rear, paw) spread to the liver. (The same doe in the cartoon showing a dog typing away at his computer saying "On the internet, no one knows you're a dog.") "Nurse Bobbie, RN", Spot's full time nurse. Love from the Adams Gerald "When my time comes to leave this earth, I am banking on God's sense of humor."

Gerald's message reveals extended involvement with, and knowledge about colon cancer. Examination of the message illustrates his orientation to giving and receiving information. He makes no statement of need. Instead he offers an address that links to a web page he established to provide information to others. As only the second participant to post to the site, he was limited in his ability to link his message to prior messages. Nevertheless, his urging that others "do see our www page" underscores his orientation as an information provider, toward addressing the needs of others and suppression of his own needs. His message is thereby characteristic of the relational stance of the giver orientation.

The giver orientation represents an approach to others that seeks to affirm a new social identity, one that claims triumph over the illness by shifting the focus from the pursuit of a medical solution to gaining control over other aspects of the individual's life. This does not imply a lack of concern with medical issues, but rather the recognition of the limits of medical science and the dangers of ceding control of one's life to health professionals. Recognizing that a "cure" may not be a realistic expectation, control must be generated through other means. The giver orientation pursues this by assuming a role as expert or teacher that others who are still dealing with the uncertainty of the illness may consult.

The Bonder Orientation.   The remaining 27% of messages were classified as bonder-oriented. This type of message exhibited a relational orientation toward social connection, with emphasis placed on the development of relationships between self and other. Recognition and respect for the needs of others and of self characterized these types of messages. The bonder orientation toward others was one of both seeking and offering information and support, an attitude of sharing and collaboration, with each participant regarded as a potential contributor to, and recipient of the group's collective experience and knowledge.

The introductory message posted by "Amy," the 66th participant, illustrates this bonder orientation:

> Hello, As a new subscriber, I also wish you well. It seems this is such an up and down journey yet I continue to join my spouse in his efforts to win. And I watch him laugh and say, "We're getting better . . . I'm healing . . ." He's such an inspiration. All is 'one day at a time', uhm? I'm grateful for this group . . . a real loving troup, thanks for being there. Anyone out there with rectal cancer? Dave's is at the dentate line, about 3" tumor, and it hasn't been staged yet. He's just completed three weeks of daily does of radiation and two of chemo weeks in hospital. He chose a 'sandwich' method in hopes of shrinking the tumor to save his anal sphincter muscle. He expects surgery next month. We'll know more then. Again, our most positive thoughts for you, new friends. Amy and Dave

Amy's message illustrates an inclination toward both giving and receiving information. This sharing orientation is apparent when she writes, "All is 'one day at a time', uhm?" and subsequently when she asks "Anyone out there with rectal cancer?" In both cases she invites a sense of sharing, in the first, a sense of shared experience with the entire group, in the second, a desire for connection with specific others. That she appreciates and respects the group and sees it as a source of connection is apparent: "I'm grateful for this group . . . a real loving troup, thanks for being there." Her closing reference to "new friends" underscores a desire for connection and indeed a sense of intimacy. In these ways, Amy's message conveys a general feature of bonder-oriented messages generally, of treating the site as a social place wherein support is a matter of mutual regard and sharing.

These types of messages tended to contain a sense that their authors approached the site as a place devoted to relational support among individuals experiencing similar life circumstances. Shared experiences in struggles with cancer appeared to be regarded as a natural basis for the development of new social connections. There is, furthermore, a sense that these messages presuppose a sense of community, one that it is important to make time for, to appreciate, and to enjoy. This orientation displayed a genuine interest in the life experiences of others, treating their experiences as intrinsically supportive and valuable informationally and emotionally. The bonder-oriented messages certainly included expressions of personal needs but did so in a manner that recognized the other and saw in the sharing of experience an opportunity to address these personal needs.

RELATIONAL ORIENTATIONS AND MESSAGE CHARACTERISTICS

This section examines the relationship between those features of introductory messages discussed earlier and the three types of relational or identity orientations introduced in the prior section. Gumperz (1982) suggested one approach to the study of the relationship between individuals, and thus the reflected identity of those individuals, by examining "how a speaker by his choice of topic and his choice of linguistic variables adapts to the other participants" (p. 17). The statistical analyses presented in this section examine the distribution of specific message characteristics across the three relational orientation types, so as to consider what is done as well as what is possible, but not done in the messages. This assesses the differing needs associated with identity concerns of each orientation type as they engage others.

Relation Orientation and Participant Characteristics

Stage of Illness. Messages including information about illness stage were roughly equally distributed across the three relational orientations (seeker-oriented 13 of 26; bonder-oriented 8 of 15; and giver-oriented 7 of 15). Table 5.1 displays the frequency of specific illness stages reported by participants in their introductory messages according to the three orientation types. Among seeker-oriented messages, 70% contained reports of the most severe diagnosis, Dukes D or recurrent colon cancer. The remaining

TABLE 5.1
Frequency (%) of Illness Stages by Relational Orientation

	Stage of Disease				
	Dukes B	Dukes C	Dukes D	Recurrent	Total
Seekers	2 (15%)	2 (15%)	7 (55%)	2 (15%)	13 (100%)
Bonders	1 (12%)	4 (50%)	3 (38%)	0 (0%)	8 (100%)
Givers	1 (14%)	1 (14%)	4 (58%)	1 (14%)	7 (100%)
Total	4 (14%)	7 (25%)	14 (50%)	3 (11%)	28 (100%)

messages were equally divided between the two less severe illness stages, Dukes B and C. Similarly, among giver-oriented messages 72% reported the most severe diagnosis with the remaining 28% reporting the two less severe illness stages. Bonder-oriented messages contained less severe diagnoses, with 26% including reports of a Dukes B or C diagnosis and 38% Dukes D.

A chi-square test of independence between orientation types and illness stage indicated no significant association, although the small sample size limits the value of this test. Assuming that there is indeed no association between the stage of the disease and one's relational orientation suggests that the meanings associated with the life experience of the illness generally outweigh the significance of one's medically defined illness stage.

Although there was no association between the illness stage reported in messages and orientation type, the orientation type did reveal differences in the way the illness stage was reported. In seeker-oriented messages, the illness stage was reported as a way of specifying and emphasizing the need expressed. In contrast, bonder-oriented messages reported the illness stage as a way of establishing similarity with others in the site. Finally, giver-oriented messages reported illness stage as a way of establishing experience and knowledge about the disease.

Duration of Illness. A one-way analysis of variance (ANOVA) tested the relationship between orientation types and the time elapsed since diagnosis and showed no significant effect. However, follow-up pair-wise comparisons of differences in means between types revealed that the difference between seeker-oriented ($M = 1.34$, $SD = 2.67$) and giver-oriented ($M = 3.48$, $SD = 4.81$) messages approached significance ($p = .051$).

Prior research indicated that support needs may change over time (Reeves, 2000; Shaw, McTavish, Hawkins, Gustafson, & Pingree, 2000). This change may be due to psychosocial adjustments as well as to the accumulation of information received from health care providers and other information sources (Brashers et al., 2000). The observed difference in the reported length of time since diagnosis between seeker-oriented messages and giver-oriented messages suggests that relational and identity concerns may change in correspondence with changing support needs as the individual assimilates the impact of the disease.

Relational Orientation and Needs Expression

Frequency of need expression differed significantly [ANOVA: $F (2, 55) = 12.397$, $p = .000$] between messages grouped according to the three types of orientation. All seeker- and bonder-oriented messages contained at least one expressed need, with the seeker-oriented messages displaying a slightly higher frequency of need expression (46% one or two needs and 54% three or more needs) than bonder-oriented messages (53% one or two needs and 47% three or four needs). Indeed, 36% of seeker-oriented messages contained five or more expressed needs. In contrast, 40% of giver-oriented messages contained no expression of need. Pair-wise comparisons indicated that giver orientations differed significantly from both seeker and bonder orientations in frequency of need expression.

Differences were also identified among the three relational orientations in terms of the types of expressed needs. The distribution of the types of needs expressed by each relational type is displayed in Table 5.2. An orientation to the site as a source of information was apparent in the types of needs expressed in seeker-oriented messages. All seeker-oriented messages included at least one need statement with 92% of messages expressing informational or medical needs and 50% expressing emotional or personal needs. Similar to seeker-oriented messages, all bonder-oriented messages included a need statement. However, bonder-oriented messages differed in the distribution of informational or medical needs and emotional or personal needs with 73% of bonder-oriented messages expressing informational or medical needs and 73% expressing emotional or personal needs. Finally, unlike seeker- and bonder-oriented messages, 40% of giver-oriented messages expressed no need. When they did express a need the bonder-oriented type showed a remarkably different profile from the other two types as their messages contained only emotional or personal needs.

A chi-square test of independence of data in Table 5.2 was significant ($\chi2 = 39.29$, $df = 6$, $p = < .001$) indicating that type of need expressed and the relational orientation of the message were significantly associated.

TABLE 5.2
Frequency (%) of Need Type by Relational Orientation

	None	Informational/ Medical Only	Emotional/ Personal Only	Both	Total
Seeker	0 (0%)	13 (50%)	2 (8%)	11 (42%)	26 (100%)
Bonder	0 (0%)	4 (27%)	4 (27%)	7 (46%)	15 (100%)
Giver	6 (40%)	0 (0%)	9 (60%)	0 (0%)	15 (100%)
Total	6 (11%)	17 (30%)	15 (27%)	18 (32%)	56 (100%)

Type of Need Expressed

Frequency and type of need expressed reflected the participant's responses to the illness as well as their relational orientation to others in the site. The high overall frequency of needs and specific focus on informational or medical needs found in seeker-oriented messages reflected a response to the illness that views it as a temporary condition. Relationship to others in the site is approached as a temporary association in which the other is objectified as a source of information. The more balanced distribution of informational or medical needs and emotional or personal needs found in bonder-oriented messages reflected a response to the illness as a new way of being requiring psychosocial adjustments as well as the application of medical treatments, thus suggesting a relationship to others in the site as one of sharing and similarity. Finally, the low frequency of need expression and total absence of information or medical needs found in giver-oriented messages reflected an orientation toward the illness as a condition over which the individual has taken control. Their relational focus is on the needs of others in the site, thereby objectifying the self as a source of information and control.

Relational Orientation and Other-Directed Expressions

Other-directed expressions, such as responding or referring to other messages or participants, and directness of need expression, as well as expressions of gratitude and encouragement contained in messages reflect the relational orientation of the participant, as such expressions indicate an awareness of, and caring about other participants.

References to Others. The percentage of participants addressing or referencing another participant was 19% for seeker-oriented messages, 33% for bonder-oriented messages, and 67% for giver-oriented messages. Table 5.3 displays the frequency distribution of messages that included a reference to others by relational orientation.

TABLE 5.3
Frequency of Messages Referencing Others by Relational Orientation

Does Message Reference Another Message or Participant?			
	Yes	No	Total
Seeker	5	21	26
Giver	10	5	15
Bonder	5	10	15
Total	20	36	56

A chi-square test of independence of data in Table 5.3 was significant ($\chi2$ = 9.37, df = 2, $p < .01$) indicating that tendencies to address prior participants and individual types were associated. Giver-oriented messages differed from both bonder- and seeker-oriented messages. The probability that a message addressed another participant or message was about 3.5 times (.67/.19) more likely in a giver-oriented message than in a seeker-oriented message and roughly two times (.67/.33) more likely than in a bonder-oriented message.

The frequency of response to others associated with giver-oriented messages reflected the relational focus of this type on others and their needs to the exclusion of self and self-needs. In contrast, the low frequency of response to others associated with seeker-oriented messages reflected the relational focus on self and self needs to the exclusion of the needs of others.

Directness of Need Expression. Although some messages of all relational orientations directly expressed needs, comparison across groups indicates that directness of need expression was associated more with seeker- and bonder-oriented messages than with giver-oriented messages. Table 5.4 displays the distribution of messages directly expressing needs and indirectly expressing needs by relational orientation.

A chi-square test of independence of data in Table 5.4 was significant ($\chi2$ = 7.86, df = 2, $p = .02$) indicating a significant association between directness of need expression and relational orientation of the message. Seeker- and bonder-oriented messages were more likely to contain directly expressed messages than were giver-oriented messages, with 77% of seeker-oriented messages and 67% of bonder-oriented messages expressing needs directly in contrast to only 33% of giver-oriented messages.

The direct expression of needs in seeker-oriented messages emphasized a relational orientation that objectified the other as a source of infor-

TABLE 5.4

Frequency (%) of Direct and Indirect Expression of Needs and Relational Orientation

| | How Are Needs Expressed? | | |
	Directly	Indirectly	Total
Seeker	20 (77%)	6 (23%)	26 (100%)
Giver	5 (33%)	10 (67%)	15 (100%)
Bonder	10 (67%)	5 (33%)	15 (100%)
Total	35 (63%)	21 (37%)	56 (100%)

mation. In contrast, the indirectness of need expression in giver-oriented messages reflects an emphasis on the need of others, objectifying the self as a source of information.

Expressions of Gratitude and Encouragement. Differences among the three types of messages were also seen in the use of polite speech acts. Table 5.5 displays the frequency of use of expressions of gratitude and expressions of encouragement by orientation types. Seeker-oriented messages were more likely than giver or bonder messages to include expressions of gratitude. Of seeker messages, 22 contained expressions of gratitude, whereas only 4 bonder messages and none of the giver messages contained such expressions. In contrast, giver messages were more likely to contain expressions of encouragement than the two other types, with 8 giver messages including encouragement as compared to 5 within bonder messages and 4 observed in seeker messages

Examination of Table 5.5 indicates a marked difference between the use of polite speech acts in seeker- and giver-oriented messages, reflecting an almost polar opposite approach in use of such speech acts. This difference further illustrates the contrasting relational orientation of seeker- and giver-oriented messages. Expressions of gratitude indicate that the self has received something of worth, whereas expressions of encouragement indicate that the other needs assistance or support. The high expression of gratitude and low incidence of encouragement in seeker-oriented messages reinforces a view of the overall relational orientation as one focusing on the self and objectifying the other. In contrast, the use of encouragement and nonuse of gratitude in giver-oriented messages reinforces a view of an overall relational orientation as one focusing on the other and objectifying the self. The use of polite speech acts was lowest in bonder-oriented messages and differed from that found in both seeker- and giver-oriented messages,

TABLE 5.5

Frequency (%) of Messages Expressing Gratitude and/or Encouragement by Relational Orientation

| | *Use of Expressions of Gratitude and Encouragement* | | | | |
	Both	*Gratitude Only*	*Encourage- ment Only*	*Neither*	*Total*
Seekers	4 (15%)	18 (70%)	0 (0%)	4 (15%)	26 (100%)
Givers	0 (0%)	0 (0%)	8 (54%)	7 (46%)	15 (100%)
Bonders	2 (13%)	2 (13%)	3 (20%)	8 (54%)	15 (100%)
Total	6 (10%)	20 (36%)	11 (20%)	19 (34%)	56 (100%)

as they blended the use of both gratitude and encouragement in their messages, reflecting an orientation to connection and the mutual building of support that objectifies neither self nor other.

Offering Information and Advice. Finally, the frequency of offers of information or advice contained in messages differed among the three orientation types. Table 5.6 displays the frequency of offerings of information and advice according to relational orientation.

A chi-square test of the data in this table revealed significant association between offerings of information and the relational orientation of the message ($\chi 2$ = 38.16, df = 2, p < .001). With but one exception, giver- and bonder-oriented messages routinely contained offers of information or advice to others in the group. In contrast, only four seeker-oriented messages included such offers or advice.

Offers of information and/or advice may be seen as recognition of the other's needs and the message sender's ability to fill that need. The high frequency of offers found in giver- and bonder-oriented messages reflects a relational orientation toward the other as a person. The low frequency of offers found in seeker-oriented messages reflects a relational orientation toward the other that negates their needs, thus objectifying the other.

SUMMARY

Relational Orientations and Self-Identity

The examination of message features just presented supports the proposal of three relational orientations introduced in the prior section. The analyses of need expression and other-directed expression showed patterns of commonal-

TABLE 5.6

Frequency (%) of Messages Offering Information or Advice by Relational Orientation

	Does Message Offer Information or Advice?		
	Yes	No	Total
Seeker	4 (15%)	22 (85%)	26 (100%)
Giver	14 (93%)	1 (7%)	15 (100%)
Bonder	15 (100%)	0 (0%)	15 (100%)
Total	33 (59%)	23 (41%)	56 (100%)

ity and difference between types that were consistent with the earlier interpretive claims. In concluding this section, a framework based on Buber (1958) and Scheff (1997) is introduced to further clarify how these orientation types may be conceptualized as matters of identity in relationship. Efforts to "appropriately" construct a self and other are apparent in the ways needs were introduced and support was offered.

Scheff (1997) offered a theory of motivation for interaction that makes efforts to establish and maintain social bonds central to interactional conduct. He explained, "a secure social bond means that the individuals involved identify with and understand each other" (p. 76). Scheff linked his model to that of Buber's (1958), suggesting that an I–Thou relationship, with a balance between the needs of self and the needs of the other, represents a secure social bond while the I–it relationship, with a focus on the needs of self to the exclusion of the needs of others, reflects isolation. Scheff extended Buber's model, suggesting a third relational orientation, it–Thou, a relational orientation representing engulfment, a focus on the needs of others and not the needs of self. Implicated within this discussion of relational orientation are matters of identity, that is the establishment of self and other within relationship as this is reflected in the expression of needs and offers of support.

Within this extended framework, seeker-oriented messages reflect a self-focused orientation characteristic of an I–it relational orientation. This focus is demonstrated in the frequency and type of needs expressed as well as the infrequency of offers of information and support found in seeker-oriented messages. The use of gratitude and low use of encouragement also indicate the self-focus orientation of these messages. The seeker-oriented messages approach the site as a source of information and reflect a response to the health crisis that views the illness as a temporary state for which a solution can be found. Thus, support matters as a way of finding a solution. The identity suggested in seeker-oriented messages is one of a person in need and desiring a return to pre-disease status.

Giver-oriented messages reflect an it–Thou stance, with the role of the self as an expert offering information and advice rather than a person with needs of their own. The needs of others were acknowledged, whereas the needs of self were suppressed. The other was viewed in an almost paternalistic fashion, as someone who needs to be guided and counseled. The identity suggested in giver-oriented messages is one of a person in control, able to focus on and assist with the needs of others.

Bonder-oriented messages reflect the I–Thou relationship, recognizing both one's own needs and the needs of others as well as one's own and others' potential contribution to the process of making sense of the health crisis. The relational orientation toward the site was as a place of sharing and the relational orientation toward others was one of partnership and connection. The identity suggested in bonder-oriented messages is one of a new partner, learning and sharing a new way of being.

CONCLUSIONS

The way in which support is sought appears to be sensitive to considerations beyond simply "getting or giving social support." Considerations of self and other are apparent in the ways participants express their needs and make offers of support to others in the site. The introductory messages serve not only in notifying the group of the type of support the participant seeks, but also the roles to be taken, and the relationships proposed with others in the site.

People may have the same disease yet experience it quite differently. People bring entirely different worldviews to their illness and interactions surrounding the illness, especially in the ways they frame an etiology. When individuals interact, they implicitly manage many dimensions of the encounter. These dimensions involve individuals' identities and relationships as well as instrumental and informational concerns. This chapter has examined one particular type of speech event, the introduction of one's self to a group designed to provide information and support. The way in which an introduction is made appears to be sensitive to considerations beyond simply "seeking support." Considerations of regard for self and other, matters of identity, are apparent in the ways in which introductions are made in this online setting. Participants engaged in a broader search for meaning than just achieving informational or relational support, one that centrally concerns issues of identity.

Discussion of the characteristics and qualities of the introductory messages presented here demonstrates the differing ways participants in this online support site struggled with their illness situations and how these struggles invariably revealed the centrality of identity. The way participants entered the site, sought support, and offered support demonstrates how issues of identity are implicated in their efforts to seek relationships and address instrumental needs, and further demonstrates the complexity of individual needs in the context of health and illness. Seekers exhibited an individual orientation that negated the need of the other in an I–it relationship by treating the other as a personal resource, suggesting the identity of a person in need. Givers exhibited an orientation that submerged the needs of self in a Thou–it relationship and treated the other as an opportunity to inform and support, suggesting the identity of a person in control. Bonders exhibited an orientation to self and other that reflected the I–Thou relationship of a reciprocal social bond, recognizing both their own needs and the needs of others as well as their own and others' potential contributions to the process of support, suggesting the identity of an equal partner.

Recognizing the interrelated identity concerns and instrumental needs of the individuals may help health care providers more accurately gauge and meet the needs of their clients. Researchers and health care providers have become increasingly aware of the value of identifying the needs of critically ill patients and their families (Reider, 1994). One explanation for this need is explained by Keitel, Cramer, and Zevon (1990), who suggested that based on national cancer statistics "it is highly probable that counselors in a wide variety of settings will eventually confront clients who are struggling with issues related to the diagnosis and treatment of cancer in a close family member" (p. 163). Understanding the concerns of cancer victims and their families would be enhanced by attending to how issues of personal identity relate to the complexities of seeking and providing support. This is what the consideration of "support matters" in this chapter suggests.

REFERENCES

Albrecht, T., & Adelman, M. (1987). Communication social support: A theoretical perspective. In T. Albrecht & M. Adelman (Eds.), *Communicating social support* (pp. 18-39). Newbury Park, CA: Sage.

Albrect, T.L., Burlson, B.R., & Goldsmith, D. (1994). Supportive communication. In M.L. Knapp & G.R. Miller (Eds.), *Handbook of interpersonal communication* (2nd ed., pp. 419-449). Newbury Park, CA: Sage.

American Cancer Society. (1999). *1999 facts and figures: Graphical data* (online). Available: http://www.cancer.org/statistics/cff99/data/data-newCasSex.html.

Aneshensel, C.S., & Stone, J.D. (1982). Stress and depression: A test of the buffering model of social support. *Archives of General Psychiatry, 39,* 1392-1396.

Bolger, N., & Eckenrode, J. (1991). Social relationships, personality, and anxiety during a major stressful event. *Journal of Personality and Social Psychology, 61,* 440-449.

Brashers, D.E., Neidig, J.L., Haas, S.M., Dobbs, L.K., Cardillo, L.W., & Russell, J.A. (2000). Communication in the management of uncertainty: The case of persons living with HIV or AIDS. *Communication Monographs, 67,* 63-84.

Brown, P., & Levinson, S. C. (1987). *Politeness: Some universals in language usage.* Cambridge, UK: Cambridge University Press.

Buber, M. (1958). *I-thou.* New York: Scribners.

Caplan, G. (1982) The family as a support system. In H.I. McCubbin, A.E. Cauble, & J.M. Patterson (Eds.), *Family stress, coping, and social support* (pp. 200-238). Springfield, IL: Thomas Books.

Caplan, R.D. (1976). The family as a support system. In G. Caplan & M. Killiea (Eds.), *Support systems and mutual help* (pp. 19-36). New York: Grune & Stratton.

Cawyer, C.S., & Smith-Dupre, A. (1995). Communicating social support: Identifying supportive episodes in an HIV/AIDS support group. *Communication Quarterly 43*, 243-258.

Charmaz, K. (1991). *Good days, bad days: The self in chronic illness and time.* New Brunswick, NJ: Rutgers University Press.

Cluck, G.G., & Cline, R.J. (1986). The circle of others: Self-help groups for the bereaved. *Communication Quarterly, 34*, 306-316.

Cutrona, C., Cohen, B., & Igram, S. (1990). Contextual determinants of the perceived supportiveness of helping behaviors. *Journal of Social and Personal Relationships, 7*, 37-54.

Cutrona, C.E., & Suhr, J.A. (1994). Social support communication in the context of marriage. In B.R. Burleson, T.L. Albrecht, & I.G. Sarason (Eds.), *Communication of social support* (pp. 113-135). Thousand Oaks, CA: Sage.

Dunkel-Schetter, C. (1984). Social support and cancer: Findings based on patient interviews and their implications. *Journal of Social Issues, 40*, 77-98.

Ford, L.A., Babrow, A.S., & Stohl, C. (1996). Social support and the management of uncertainty: An application of problematic integration theory. *Communication Monographs, 63*, 189-207.

Frey, L.R., Query, J.L., Jr., Flint, L.J., & Adelman, M.B. (1998). Living together with AIDS: Social support processes in a residential facility. In V.J. Derlega & A.P. Barbee (Eds.), *HIV and social interaction* (pp. 129-146). Thousand Oaks, CA: Sage.

Goffman, E. (1959). *The presentation of self in everyday life.* New York: Anchor.

Goffman, E. (1963). *Stigma: Notes on the management of spoiled identity.* New York: Simon & Schuster.

Goffman, E. (1967). *Interaction ritual: Essays on face-to-face behavior.* Garden City, NY: Anchor Books.

Gotcher, J.M. (1993). The effects of family communication on psychosocial adjustment of cancer patients. *Journal of Applied Communication Research, 21*, 176-188.

Gumperz, J. (1982). *Discourse strategies.* Cambridge: Cambridge University Press.

Herzlick, C., & Pierret, J. (1985). The social construction of the patient: Patients and illnesses in other ages. *Social Science and Medicine, 20*, 145-151.

Keitel, M.A., Cramer, S.H., & Zevon, M.A. (1990). Spouses of cancer patients: A review of the literature. *Journal of Counseling & Development, 69*, 163-166.

Kleinman, A., Eisenberg, L., & Good, B. (1978). Culture, illness and care. *Annals of Internal Medicine, 88*, 252-258.

Kohn, P.M. (1996). On coping adaptively with daily hassles. In M. Zeidner & N.S. Endler (Eds.), *Handbook of coping* (pp. 181-201). New York: Wiley.

La Gaipa, J.J. (1990). The negative effects of informal support systems. In S. Duck & R.C. Silver (Eds.), *Personal relationships and social support* (pp. 123-139). Newbury Park, CA: Sage.

Mishler, E.G. (1981). The social construction of illness. In E.G. Misler, L.R. Amarsingham, S.D. Osherson, S.T. Hauser, N.E. Waxler, & R. Liem (Eds.), *Social contexts of health, illness, and patient care* (pp. 141-168). Cambridge: Cambridge University Press.

Mokros, H.B., Mullins, L.S., & Saracevic, T. (1995). Practice and personhood in professional interactions: Social identities and information needs. *LISR, 17*, 237-257.

Reeves, P. M. (2000). Coping in cyberspace: The impact of Internet use on the ability of HIV positive individuals to deal with their illness. *Journal of Health Communication, 5* (supplement), 47-59.

Reider, J. A. (1994). Anxiety during critical illness of a family member. *Dimensions of Critical Care Nursing, 13,* 272-279.

Rumsey, E. (2001). *Making sense of health and illness online: A study of patterns of participation and use on one computer-mediated cancer support site.* Unpublished doctoral dissertation, Rutgers, The State University of New Jersey, New Brunswick.

Sarason, L., Sarason, B., Shearin, E., & Pierce, G. (1987). A brief measure of social support: Practical and theoretical implications. *Journal of Social and Personal Relationships, 4,* 497-510.

Scheff, T.J. (1997). *Emotions, the social bond, and human reality: Part/whole analysis.* Cambridge: Cambridge University Press.

Shaw, B.R., McTavish, F., Hawkins, R., Gustafson, D.H., & Pingree, S. (2000). Experiences of women with breast cancer: Exchanging social support over the CHESS computer network. *Journal of Health Communication, 5,* 135-159.

Spiers, J.A. (1998). The use of face work and politeness theory. *Qualitative Health Research, 8,* 25-47.

Wright, K. B. (2000). Social support satisfaction, on-line communication apprehension, and perceived life stress within computer-mediated support groups. *Communication Research Reports, 17,* 139-147.

Play Matters
Playing With Identity in the MUD

Rachel D. Karetnick

A bright green cabbage wombles into the room!
A bright green cabbage noisily rustles its fronds.
A bright green cabbage ponders your existence.
The cabbage happily bounces out of the room.

I actually saw that bright green cabbage not long ago, as I was standing in a room talking with a friend about the progress of my dissertation. And "friend" may not be the right word—depending on your definition—because I've never met this particular "friend" face to face. He lives in the Baltimore area, while I'm from New Jersey, and we were both at home while we were having this conversation and watching that cabbage.

So how were we "standing in a room talking?" Both he and I were connected to a virtual environment known as a multiuser dungeon (MUD) and our characters (named Tara and Traveler) were located in the same virtual room as we typed messages to one another. During our conversation, Traveler also used the "finger <player name>" command, which allowed him to see when that particular player, identified in the <player name> slot, was last connected to the MUD. In this case, he was looking for his friend Diana.

Diana had written a computer program that caused a cabbage to enter the room when someone in that room "fingered" her. And the cabbage is not the only possible option that she has "coded"; it randomly alternates with a bogroll that stares deep into your eyes before rolling out of the room and an onion that releases fumes, making you sob uncontrollably before it exfoliates and disappears. Each of these activities is, for Diana, a means of playful self-expression that MUD programming[1] makes possible even when she is not connected to the site.

MUDs originated in 1979 when students at the University of Essex, England wrote a program for an adventuring game, and they've been used primarily for gaming purposes ever since (Curtis, 1993). More recently, however, online spaces like MUDs have emerged as places where people can play with their senses of self-identity even as they play the game. According to Bruckman (1992):

> MUDs are a workshop for the concept of identity. Many players notice that they are somehow different on the net than off, and this leads them to reflect on who they are in real life. It helps people to understand the concept of identity and the ways in which we construct ourselves.

Literature based on this perspective suggests that the online world serves as an "identity workshop" characterized by extraordinary innovation, creativity, and simulation on the part of participants (see Bruckman, 1992; Turkle, 1984, 1995). Anecdotal evidence seems to point to a view of virtual worlds as being little more than a profound "free for all" in which any and all presentations of self-identity become possible, including wombling cabbages. This chapter discusses some of the findings of a larger study (Karetnick, 2000) that investigated to what extent such virtual spaces where identity is played with are "identity workshops."

Recent years have seen an increased interest in who we are and what we do when we enter such online worlds (Baym, 1995; Bruckman, 1992; Donath, 1999; Matheson & Zanna, 1990; Turkle, 1984b, 1995; Wynn &

---

[1]It should be briefly noted here that the term programming used earlier is not in fact the term used in the MysteryMud environment. MysteryMud is written in LPC, also known as LP Code, and it is common practice to refer to the MUD code, or the act of coding (creating new areas of the MUD). However, this invites confusion between the concepts of the MUD code and the coding of the research data. In order to avoid such confusion, throughout the remainder of this chapter the term code is reserved for discussions about treatment of data, whereas the MUD code will be referred to using the computer-related term programming.

Katz, 1998). There exists a belief that the modern world, in which computers are so prevalent, "radically alters the nature of day-to-day social life and affects the most personal aspects of our experience" (Giddens, 1991, p. 1). In other words, trends toward a more computer-mediated way of life may hold implications for our senses of identity that are worthy of examination.

The issue of identity exists as a central concern in social theory. We are increasingly interested in "who participates in what ways in the social processes that construct personal identities, the social order, and codes of communication" (Craig, 1999, p. 126). Each member of society can be classified by means of some attributes that help to locate us in the world. According to Goffman (1982), the "four critical diffuse statuses: age-grade, gender, class, and race" (p. 14) that exist in our society form a grid on which individuals can be categorically identified (see also Goffman, 1971). We often rely on such classifications or statuses to help us make sense of ourselves and others in the world.

Although markers of age, gender, class and race, for example, play an important role in the definition of personal identity, such markers tap into discursive, stereotypic ways of perceiving identity without offering much insight into identity as a contingent, situational, interactive experience. The theoretical underpinnings of the discussion presented in this chapter emphasize this latter approach to identity, treating communication as a system and process as constitutive (e.g., Craig, 1999; Deetz, 1994; Mokros, 1996). From a constitutive perspective, the production and reproduction of reality arises out of communicative practice. The larger research project from which this chapter is drawn hypothesizes, along with Mokros (1996), that "how identities are constituted in lived moments of social interaction and what is entailed in an interactional analysis of identity has been largely underdeveloped" (p. 6). Such a view problematizes interaction by positioning identity as arising out of active participation with others in a process of mutual influence.

INVESTIGATING A SESSION OF PLAY ONLINE

The title of this chapter, "Play Matters," refers to two senses of play—both the playful activity taking place within the context of this gaming site and the playing out (and with) personal identity resulting from these activities. As stated earlier, the exploration of identity play within a site of game play is guided by the goal of evaluating to what extent such a site represents Bruckman's (1992) concept of the *identity workshop*. Specifically, player participation is examined within the context of a MUD, MysteryMud, an adventure-oriented game with a significant social dimension. MUDs are fictional cyberspace worlds, considered to be metaphors of real communities. Participants create a character with a name and a gender, navigate through areas of varying descriptions that approximate real space, and engage in real time with whoever else happens to be connected to the site at that time.

Mapping the Game: Microanalysis

This exploration of identity concerns within human relationships is undertaken within a research tradition focusing on the interactive process. The idea that variables exist prior to interaction (e.g., Goffman, 1982) proves problematic in light of the constitutive framework underpinning this research, which recognizes social situations as products of communication. One way to circumvent this difficulty is to consider sequential organization, what Duncan and Fiske (1985a, 1985b, 1996) called action-sequence variables. These variables emphasize the context within which interaction occurs and seek to preserve information about the ways in which activity is embedded within the natural unfolding of observable activity. To understand a particular part of a whole requires an extended context including the events before, during, and after the moment in question (Scheff, 1990).

Microanalysis is meant to capture what the environment under investigation, in this case a MUD, is like. The approach provides a view of the world by means of descriptive ethnographic accounts of the moves people make and their participatory activity. Here, this results in an empirical representation of participatory activity within the MysteryMud environment.

This chapter examines participatory activity during one session of play, in this case a meeting held within the virtual world. MysteryMud has a player-run guild system, with nine organizations fulfilling different economic functions. Each guild is allowed to have up to three Masters, people in charge of running the day-to-day activities of these player-owned and operated groups. On Sunday, April 10, 1994, a meeting was held so that the Masters could get together, along with other guild participants, and discuss the guild system. The MUD programming created a text-only transcript of the meeting as it occurred. This transcript is available online for review by MysteryMud visitors.

In order to explore the ways in which identity play emerges out of game play in the MUD world, each communicative turn contained in the transcript of the Guild Master's meeting was coded so as to preserve the sequential nature of the interactive process. A turn was defined as consisting of all text composed and sent by a participant from the start of a new line to a carriage return. Often, but not always, this consisted of a single line of text on-screen and typically started with the name of a participant. The opening nine turns of the meeting appear in Fig. 6.1.

---

1. Chris arrives
2. Storm hiccups.
3. Ghost seems to fall, but takes a step and recovers.
4. Pierre tosses out an auction ticket.
5. Spike greets Chris warmly.
6. Rob says 'Ok . . . its time to start . . . and if you don't shut up . . . I will stop.'
7. Chris hugs Autumn.
8. Ghost hiccups.
9. Spike tosses out an auction ticket.

FIG. 6.1. Text of the initial nine turns of the Guild Masters' meeting.

Each turn was then coded into categories to create a picture or map consisting of seven parts. The mapping of the initial turn, in which "Chris arrives," looked like this: 1.1.1.0.1.0.0. The first column indicated that this was the first turn in the meeting. Subsequent turns were numbered in order. Next, the second column indicates that Chris was the first participant to enter the interaction, designating him Participant 1 (P.1). The third column identifies that this was the first turn taken by Chris (P.1). The fourth column represents the patient, any object of P.1's agency from among the game features with which he could interact. The zero in this column shows that P.1 chose not to interact with any other participants. Had there been some interaction, the value in the column would reflect that individual's participant number as recorded in Column 2 on his or her first instance of participation in the gaming space. The fifth column value of "1" indicates that this is an intentional action on the part of the participant, as opposed to an unintentional byproduct of the game programming, which would have been represented in this column by a value of "0." The value of "0" in Column 6 indicates that Chris had not modified the computer-programmed default of any action. Certain actions on the MUD can be modified or personalized, laughing for example. The MUD programming includes defaults for various commands, so that if one types the command "laugh," the result is that "You fall down laughing." A participant could instead choose to type "laugh happily" or "laugh softly," and either "You laugh happily." or "You laugh softly." would appear on-screen as a modification of the standard programming (other participants would see your character name in place of "you," i.e., "Chris laughs happily."). Finally, the last column codes the participant number from Column 2 of anyone being directly addressed or engaged by the "speaker." Because Chris was not speaking, and therefore not engaging another player directly through speech, a value of "0" appears here. Chris' second turn was the seventh overall and referenced an intentional action upon another player, Autumn, who was assigned Participant 7 (P.7). The action was not modified and did not engage another player via speech. Therefore, Chris' (P.1) second turn was mapped as 7.1.2.7.1.0.0. An excerpt from the overall map (which consists of more than 1,700 participant turns) is shown in Fig. 6.2, reflecting the coding scheme just described.

Again, the purpose of this approach to transcription is to preserve the temporal structure of participation while providing a map within which issues of identity emerge and can be explored. Not all of these will be of equal importance in the subsequent discussion of identity play. Overall turn number matters only in the maintenance of the sequential nature of interaction, and participant number is simply used to identify the various participants being discussed. Columns 4 and 7, the focus of agency and object of speech, respectively, identify whether participants are in some way engaging

A	B	C	D	E	F	G	
1	1	1	0	1	0	0	Chris arrives.
2	2	1	0	0	0	0	Storm hiccups.
3	3	1	0	0	0	0	Ghost seems to fall but takes a step and recovers.
4	4	1	0	1	0	0	Pierre tosses out an auction ticket
5	5	1	1	1	0	0	Spike greets Chris warmly.
6	6	1	0	1	0	0	Rob says 'Ok . . . its time to start . . . and if you don't shutup . . . I will stop.'
7	1	2	7	1	0	0	Chris hugs Autumn.
8	3	2	0	0	0	0	Ghost hiccups.
9	5	2	0	1	0	0	Spike tosses out an auction ticket.

Legend:

A: Overall Turn Number
B: Participant Number
C: Participant's Turn Number
D: Participant or Object Being Acted Upon
E: Intent
F: Modification
G: Participant Being Addressed By Speech.

FIG. 6.2. Coding of the initial turns of the Guild Masters' meeting.

other players or computer-generated objects, a distinction that is examined later in this chapter. Intent, found in Column 5, also plays a part because only intentional actions are of interest. Finally, the value coded in Column 6 proves relevant to the forthcoming discussions of modification of computer-programmed convention, inherent in the structure and strategy framework underpinning this analysis (cf. Duncan & Fiske, 1977, 1985a).

Structure and Strategy

The transcription just discussed allows for exploration of the Guild Masters' meeting within a "contextualized framework in which to examine the interplay" of what we do and who we are (Stephenson, 1998, pp. 58-59). Such a "contextualized framework" is meant to allow for systematic examination and identification of participant activities and expectations. Furthermore, it can be assumed that consistencies in individual performance may be identified. Such consistent performances—individual strategies in the Duncan and Fiske (1977) model—are revealed through study of the structure of activity within this space.

The structured, ordered qualities of social interaction, used to coordinate action by participants is called *convention*. Convention, then, refers to shared understandings about how individuals should conduct themselves within interaction. Individuals' strategies are thus seen as "patterns of action resulting from a participant's exercising choice and initiative with respect to the options provided by convention" (Duncan & Fiske, 1977, p. 288), with the qualities of operating conventions defining the situation. For example, a multiparty conversation operating under an assumption of respect and civility will likely employ a turn-taking scheme within which only one party speaks at a time. Convention and its structure, strategy, and situation provide a vocabulary for "discussing cultural systems" (Duncan & Fiske, 1977, p. 261) such as the virtual community of a MUD.

Structure and strategy can only be effectively considered together. Structure addresses those conventions that influence one's orientation to interaction. Strategy accounts for the individual differences in the use of conventions within interaction. According to Duncan and Fiske (1977):

> [C]onventions have the effect of regularizing actions . . . but not in all respects. . . . [S]trategy is possible in part because of the degrees of freedom allowed by convention. Interaction strategies are describable in terms of the ways that individuals and/or groups actually use these degrees of freedom. (p. 247)

Within this system, identity may then be seen to be reflected in the strategies by which participants engage with one another within the contextualized framework structured by agreed-on conventions. Considering again the multiparty conversation characterized by respect and civility just mentioned, observable differences in frequency and length of speaking turns may also suggest differing dimensions in individuals' definitions of the situation. Those who rarely participate, for example, may be indicating that they view the situation as a low-interest gathering or conversely as a potentially dangerous occasion during which minimizing participation limits their exposure to possible danger. Personal identity, therefore, may be regarded as an individuals' self-other orientation as observed through the interplay among situation, structure, and strategy.

The meeting transcript was analyzed so as to reveal the ways in which MysteryMud participants played out structure and strategy within interaction. Duncan and Fiske (1985b) viewed "the relation of strategy to structure [as] simple and straightforward at the most general and intuitive level. If structure constitutes the 'rules for the game' in interaction, then strategy is the manner in which a participant or group of participants actually plays the game" (p. 31). Although they use the term *game* loosely, such a statement takes on a unique meaning in a MUD environment situationally defined as being just that—a game. Whether actively playing, or just logging in to chat socially, MysteryMud participants exhibit individual choice or strategy within a system of rules or structure, both intentionally and unintentionally. Additionally, my membership in this community as someone present during the Guild Masters' meeting provides ethnographic perspective on the rules that are being enacted, as well as those that are being set aside in favor of individual choice.

Analysis of the interplay of situation, structure, and strategy aimed at revealing identity leads to a focus on sequences of actions. Where an event occurs—its relation to other events—is as important from a microanalytic perspective as the fact that it occurs at all. The coding scheme applied defines three types of actions as being available to participants: involuntary (caused by the game programming, not the participant), voluntary (nonverbal activity initiated by the participant), and speech. A sequential analysis examines the juxtaposition of turns, characterized according to one of these three actions. Sequences may be thought of as represented in the form of a transition matrix with any given turn $[T_n]$ identified according to one of the three states of action: voluntary (V), involuntary (I), or speech (S). The transition matrix would then consist of all potential relationships between this turn $[T_n]$ and a subsequent turn $[T_{n+1}]$. Nine different combinations of turns are possible given these three actions: $[I \longrightarrow V]$, $[V \longrightarrow V]$, $[S \longrightarrow V]$, $[I \longrightarrow S]$, $[V \longrightarrow S]$, $[S \longrightarrow S]$, $[I \longrightarrow I]$, $[V \longrightarrow I]$, and $[S \longrightarrow I]$. The analysis of overall frequency with which possible sequences occur in the transition matrix provides a way to measure specific actions by specific participants within a context of normative tendencies across all participants and activity. Because participants have no control over the use or occurrence of involuntary actions, where (I) occurs at T_{n+1} [(I —> I), (V —> I), (S —> I)] is of less interest. For example, (I —> S) and (I —> V) offer an interesting glimpse at participant's reactions to involuntary actions exhibited by themselves or others, but (I —> I) merely demonstrates two instances of random, computer-generated activity in a row that tell us little about issues of participant identity.

The Guild Masters' meeting transcript consists of 1,732 turn sequences, $[T_n —> T_{n+1}]$, with (V —> V) the most common (42%) sequence and (I —> S) least common (3.6%). The complete transition matrix appears in Table 6.1. Of the 1,732 turns, 64% involve a voluntary action. Speaking turns comprise 22% of the total, with involuntary actions making up the remaining 14%.

The empirical mapping of activity just discussed also provides a systematic framework for what Mokros called interpretive microanalysis. Through vicarious engagement with the data, alternative but plausible behavioral options are developed and then contrasted with what was observed (cf. Scheff, 1990). In other words, the analysis of the Guild Master's meeting considers not only what took place—as represented in the transcript—but also what did not take place yet might have. This type of analysis involves an "ongoing process of hypothesis generation and testing" (Mokros et al., 1995, p. 242) within the data, aimed at providing a systematic approach to discussing change over time during the course of any specific interaction. Actions not used during the Guild Masters' meeting prove from this perspective to be just as relevant to this investigation as those that were. Available conventions within the game structure that were not

TABLE 6.1
Transition Matrix for Turn Units in the Analysis of Sequences

	V	S	I	Total
V	42.2%	14.0%	7.9%	64.1%
	(731)	(244)	(135)	(1,110)
S	14.1%	4.3%	3.6%	21.9%
	(245)	(74)	(62)	(381)
I	7.7%	3.6%	2.5%	14.0%
	(134)	(63)	(44)	(241)
Total	64.1%	21.9%	14.0%	100.0%
	(1,110)	(380)	(242)	(1,732)

employed, here specifically types of voluntary actions, offer future data for discussions of this space in terms of identities. For in such nonchoices, as Goffman (1967) noted, a participant "implicitly forgoes all claims to be things he does not appear to be and hence forgoes the treatment that would be appropriate for such individuals" (p. 13). These counterfactual variants in the context of actions and sequences observed offer insight into the ways in which participants did not view the definition of the situation as aspects of their performed selves.

PLAYING THE GAME

Interactional Sequences in Participatory Activity

Goffman's work serves as a major influence in my development of a constitutively based explanation of identity. A key influence throughout the remainder of this chapter is his essay on face-work (1967), in particular.

Face-work first involves an appreciation of the social situatedness of human experience:

> Every person lives in a world of social encounters, involving him either in face-to-face or mediated contact with other participants. In each of these contacts, he tends to act out what is sometimes called a *line*—that is, a pattern of verbal and nonverbal acts by which he expresses his view of the situation and through this his evaluation of the participants, especially himself. (p. 5)

Having introduced the concept of *line*, Goffman presents what he called *face*, "defined as the positive social value a person effectively claims for himself by the line others assume he has taken during a particular contact" (p. 5). The first quote positions individuals as rational and strategic agents within a social world. Of interest is how Goffman moved from such a view to one in which individual senses of self are conceptualized not as psychological entities but rather as interactionally constituted.

Line and face represent two dimensions of participant conduct and experience in contact with others within social encounters. They represent one way we can characterize the unfolding events within a particular encounter, in this case the ways in which MUD participants play with identity within the context of the gaming site. The qualities of line and face (and the related practices of deference and demeanor) reflect how individuals regard one another from the onset to the conclusion of the engagement, and therein how they expect to regard and be regarded by one another. Rituals pertaining to arrivals, greetings, farewells, and leave-taking in social relationships provide insight into line and face and, being particularly apparent, are specifically examined here. Within the single session of game play defined by the Guild Masters' meeting, individual play with identity can be observed within these types of ritual activities.

Arrivals and Greetings. The greeting of new arrivals provides participants with cues as to how the social situation into which they have entered is being defined. The transcript of the Guild Masters' meeting contains 31 arrivals. This does not translate, however, to the arrival of 31 separate participants, as several enter and leave the meeting on multiple occasions.

How participants greet new arrivals (mostly by means of hugs and "high-fives") varies during the course of the meeting. For example, two participants arriving before the meeting is called to order are greeted by those already present in the space, whereas the next eight participants to arrive with the meeting already in progress are not greeted publicly. And with the exception of one, who bows to the room at large, these "late arrivals" also do not offer greetings to those already present. This pattern changes with the 11th participant to enter the room. At this point, multiple participants greet her with hugs and "high-fives," which she reciprocates in kind with two of these participants. Thereafter, a cluster of greeting activity occurs. The next four arrivals are also publicly greeted on entering the meeting. Again, a shift occurs; overt greetings effectively stop—with two exceptions—after this point. One of these exceptions takes place when P.50 is disconnected from the MUD server and has to reconnect to the game. On her reentry, another participant greets her. The second exception occurs as the meeting is ending, after the moderator has indicated that it is almost time for closing comments.

Greeting behavior appears to be clearly permissible yet restrained and, when observed, situationally contingent. Unstated conventional rules for playing the game would seem to largely override personal inclinations in this instance. (It could of course be the case that greetings were quite commonly being expressed through "back-channels"—that is, through participant contacts not captured in the transcript of the meeting yet visible by those to whom they were directed.) It would also seem fair to say that the pattern of greetings observed in this meeting in no way deviates from what one might expect in comparable face-to-face meetings. Thus, although the meeting takes place within a play situation, it exhibits few signs of overt playfulness and playful invention.

Leaving and Farewells. Along with greetings, farewells at leave-taking "sum up the effect of the encounter upon the relationships and show what the participants may expect of one another when they next meet"

(Goffman, 1967, p. 41). Discussion of leave-taking and farewells includes two distinct considerations—how specifically a person exited the space and whether or not any farewell gestures were made by others at the time.

Leave-taking occurs 40 times during the meeting. Most (70%) of those who leave do so by means of the door to the west in the meeting room. Of those who do not approach leave-taking in this manner, 10 quit the game by merely logging off (thus not engaging in traditional face-to-face methods of leave-taking in their playing of the game). One "recalls" (a command that transports your character to the starting point of the game), and the remaining participant (a wizard named Hunter, P.16) returns to his workroom by means of a special, personalized command available only to wizard-level players (the highest status attainable by MUD participants).

Farewells by those leaving the meeting are not common, as only 23% of leavings include such gestures. Waving is involved in all nine occasions where a farewell is expressed. The finality of this farewell gesture is apparent as only one of the nine participants doing so subsequently returns, and then it is simply to give something to a still present participant. He then leaves and does not wave again when doing so.

That most individuals incorporate leave-taking into their play activity, but do so quietly and without dramatic play or fanfare, seems clear from these data. Here one does not observe hugs, speech, or more personalized gestures of intimacy. Indeed, it seems as though, for the most part, the meeting follows patterns of leave-taking and farewells quite similar to what can be observed in comparable "real world" situations. The only exception might be simply disappearing from the space (e.g., through the use of the "recall" or "quit" commands during the Guild Masters' meeting), which is not a realistic option (yet perhaps not an uncommon desire at times) in such contexts.

Turn-Taking and Related Moves. Greetings and farewells are two examples of turns taken in human encounters. They represent significant markers by which to characterize the temporal flow of social encounters and, as shown by the data, tend to be highly routinized. A more general understanding of the qualities of interaction over time can be gained through consideration of how turn-taking and exchange is conducted. Human conversation typically involves one person at a time, with minimal overlap or delay between turns. How this exchange is accomplished has motivated multiple research agendas (e.g., Duncan & Fiske, 1977; Sacks, Schegloff, & Jefferson, 1973). Goffman (1967) was quite appreciative of these interactional phenomena, as well. He wrote the following:

[a] single focus of thought and visual attention, and a single flow of talk, tends to be maintained and to be legitimated as officially repre-

sentative of the encounter. The concerted and official visual attention of the participants tends to be transferred smoothly by means of
formal or informal *clearance cues*, by which the current speaker signals that he is about to relinquish the floor, and the prospective
speaker signals a desire to be given the floor. (p. 35, italics added)

Within this context, it is of interest to ask how the participants in
an online fantasy world where playfulness may be expected handle turn-taking and turn exchange. The observed convention in face-to-face conversation of one party at a time is in some sense reinforced by technological limitations of computer-mediated communication. Online messages are displayed linearly, thereby removing from these environments observable
instances of simultaneous talk. Nevertheless, turn-taking represents an
interesting focus for inquiry into how speaker selection is accomplished.
This not only involves a search for *clearance cues,* but also a consideration of
the expected flow of conversation if participant conduct in this environment
may be said to exhibit interruptions. What is quite remarkable in the data is
that no interruptions are observed, at least not during the formal part of the
meeting during which the moderator serves as leader. Nothing prevents any
participant from speaking out of turn; the option is available to them at all
times. Instead, floor apportionment is highly scripted with the moderator
being the one to select the next speaker, making a powerful statement about
his authority. Strict sanctions guide the opportunities available to meeting
participants. Indeed, it is not until the floor is opened to general discussion
by the moderator that any participant speaks without first being given permission by him.

Regulating the Flow of Talk. Turns involving "speech" represent
an integral aspect of the Guild Masters' meeting, although only 43% of the
60 participants speak during the meeting. Those who desire to speak indicate that desire to the moderator in one way, by raising a hand. Multiple
raised hands are common at any given time. The moderator then selects
from among the raised hands and invites that individual to speak by "granti-
ng them the floor." Altogether, the moderator grants speaking turns on 39
different occasions to 25 individuals.

On six occasions where multiple participants indicate a wish to
speak, the turn is granted to the first person to have raised his or her hand,
without any additional cues or conditions apparent. On seven occasions, the
moderator selects the first person to have raised a hand following his
request that someone direct the group discussion toward a new topic. Those
whose hands had already been raised prior to such a request were not considered. The 13 remaining occasions on which multiple parties attempt to

claim a turn at talk involve the most complex type of exchange sequence observed. The person granted the floor is not simply the first person to raise his or her hand, but is instead the person who does so once the current speaker has signaled that he or she has finished speaking, either by "stepping down" or through some verbal comment of closure (e.g., "I'm done"). Again, those whose hands are already raised prior to such a *clearance cue* are not overtly considered by the moderator.

Offerings of Thanks by Selected Speakers.   Because whether or not one is granted a turn at talk is completely at the discretion of the moderator, it might be expected that individuals chosen to speak would acknowledge the privilege through some ritual offering, an expression of thanks for example. None of the first six speakers do so, and although the next two do thank the moderator the nine subsequent speakers do not. Thereafter, beginning with the 18th speaking turn, a more observable change in this practice occurs. Fourteen (64%) of these turns include offerings of thanks as compared to only 12% within the first 17 turns. The evolution of the practice of thanking as a common part of how new speakers conduct themselves may well reflect an emergent appreciation of the power that the moderator wielded over any individual's opportunity to speak.

Speaking Out of Turn.   As I mentioned previously, there are no occasions where participants speak without first being designated as the next speaker during the formal part of the meeting. This is even the case for Mike (P.9), a senior-level wizard who wanted others to stop using modified atmosphere/emote commands. Instead of just speaking out, Mike is observed to follow the apparent turn-taking protocol of raising his hand and waiting until the moderator grants him a turn.

Participants' conformity to this highly regulated pattern of turn-taking may be seen to reflect respect for the rights of others to hold the floor uninterrupted. However, this interpretation seems doubtful in the light of multiple examples where individuals manipulate the actions of others as discussed later. Instead, it would seem that the meeting is treated as a highly structured ritual occasion during which the moderator clearly exhibits enormous authority and control (at least during the formal part of the meeting). His authority is all the more evident in that he is the only participant to ever speak out of turn or interrupt others. But this authority appears to have been a matter of situated role-identity, because once he ends the formal phase of the meeting and opens the floor to discussion (turn 1718), the participants' approach to turn-taking shifts noticeably.

It becomes quickly apparent following turn 1718 that the moderator is no longer the sole determiner of speaking turn allocation. Thus, as shown in Excerpt 1, once the moderator invites "any quick comments" in turn 1723, Sam immediately asks a question without raising his hand or being selected by the moderator. Immediately thereafter, another participant, Dragon, responds to Sam's question, again without any of the prior turn exchange restrictions. Dragon just jumps right in and assumes the functional role of information provider that only the moderator had assumed prior to this point in time.

Excerpt 1: The Guild Masters' Meeting (turns 1723-1731)

1723.   Moderator says 'Any last quick comments?'
1724.   Sam says 'how many reps should be sent to the next meeting?'
1725.   Dragon says '2'
1726.   Dragon says 'only'
1727.   Storm smiles happily.
1728.   Gem says 'i have a comment on guild masters not being on active list'
1729.   Sam thanks Dragon.
1730.   Moderator says 'I'll cover that in the guild news'
1731.   Dragon says 'thats 18 people max'

Maybe it is not so much the expression of highly structured conformity in approaches to turn allocation that is of interest here, but the very fact that the 60 people who participated in the meeting made a conscious choice to "play" at an activity that many individuals loathe in their everyday organizational lives at work.

Use and Function of Voluntary Actions

Although it has been suggested that speech represents an important part of the meeting, it is a much less common activity than the use of other voluntary actions, as noted earlier. Indeed, speech is not used as a primary means by which to provide general feedback on topics, reflecting the strong constraints apparent in the use of speech. Instead, participants offer feedback and express their feelings about the meeting through nonspeech voluntary actions.

MysteryMud participants have 181 different voluntary actions available to them, all created by the MUD programmers. The MUD help files divide these actions into five major types: communication (e.g., say, tell, whisper), nonverbal expressions related to relational activity (e.g., smiling or nodding), cognitive orientations typically involving the appraisal of information (e.g., examine, look), aggressive gestures (e.g., kill, wield), and functional manipulators of the environment (e.g., drop, quit, take). Because we have already considered speech activity, the following discussion focuses on the latter four types.

Nonverbal Indicators of Agreement, Disagreement, and Social Bonds. Nonverbal indicators are used to express both positive and negative feelings, with positive expressions most often observed (in terms of frequency of use). Expressions of positive feelings include nodding (80), smiling (40), agreeing (38), and high-fiving (30). Expressions of disagreement are observed much less often, with head shakes (21 occurrences) being most common. Other indicators of disagreement used by participants include cringing in terror (2), glaring at another participant (4), and grumbling (2). Surprisingly, the most direct option for disagreement—the preprogrammed command "disagree" (which would have caused the participant using it to "disagree wholeheartedly" on-screen)—is never used during the meeting.

Overall, expressions of agreement are seven times more common than disagreement suggesting a clear preference for positive displays of emotion while playing online. This preference for agreement also suggests a general orientation toward respect and acceptance of the "line" offered by others and thereby a general valuing of relationships characterized by secure, unchallenged, social bonds. As such, MysteryMud contradicts commonly held views of such fantasy worlds as places where creative, innovative, and sometimes even aggressive activity is the norm.

Based on the notable preference for expressions of agreement, it may be said that an ongoing concern with the maintenance of face exists as a motivation for play. Nevertheless, challenges to face and needs for remedial face-work as described by Goffman are also observed. It is to these instances that the discussion now turns.

Failures in the Use of Voluntary Actions and Their Consequences. Although respect for others is clearly apparent throughout the meeting, there are several occasions when this principle gives way to challenge and ridicule. Actions that result in challenges to face often involve failures on the part of a participant to act competently within the rules guiding either the meeting in particular, or the game itself in general. Consider as an example the failure to use voluntary actions appropriately, seen in Excerpt 2.

Excerpt 2: The Guild Masters' Meeting (turns 116-132)

116.   Rob [P.6] grants the floor to Nova [P.11].
117.   Watchman [P.28] raises his hand.
118.   A rainbow shimmers across Storm's [P.2] sword and its color changes to green.
119.   Startup [P.31] hiccups.
120.   Nova [P.11] says 'Actually, I was just trying to raise an eyebrow, sorry.'
121.   Jake [P.25] leaves west.
122.   Whiskers [P.22] raises his hand.

123.   Sam [P.26] falls down laughing.
124.   Whiskers [P.31] burps.
125.   Laser [P.33] snickers.
126.   Pierre [P.4] falls down laughing.
127.   Solo [P.15] slaps his forehead.
128.   Algernon [P.34] rolls his eyes to the heavens.
129.   Shakespeare [P.13] chuckles politely.
130.   Rob [P.6] grants the floor to Gem [P.32].
131.   King [P.19] grins evilly.
132.   Dragon [P.10] falls down laughing.

The failure event itself actually occurs in turn 99, prior to the turns displayed in Excerpt 2. In that turn, "Nova [P.11] raises his hand." This voluntary move is what might be considered an incident characterized by an act of social offense within Goffman's model of face-work. As discussed in the consideration of turn-taking, this move represents a conventional signal used to indicate that an individual seeks a turn at talk. Rob, the moderator, responds to this signal when he grants Nova the floor in turn 116, the first turn shown in Excerpt 2. It is only after Nova is granted the floor that his offense becomes apparent. This is made public in turn 120, as Nova reveals that he does not want to speak after all. He had actually intended not to raise his hand but rather to raise his eyebrow in response to some comment by a previous speaker. His admission in turn 120 reveals his lack of familiarity with or knowledge of the game's conventions. Nova is what Goffman (1967) would call "out of face," a state that occurs "when [someone] participates in a contact with others without having ready a line of the kind participants in such situations are expected to take" (p. 8). His failing is not merely a technical one, but is also a matter of social consequence, an incident resulting in a variety of expressions of ridicule by eight other participants. This public shaming engaged in by these eight others includes laughs, grins, rolled eyes, slapping of foreheads, snickers, and chuckles.

Shortly after Nova's misstep, a similar failure event occurred, as shown in Excerpt 3. Here Spike (P.5) requests a turn in line 145, is granted that turn in line 150, and in response "steps down" in line 151, relinquishing the floor without speaking.

Excerpt 3: The Guild Masters' Meeting (turns 145-154)

145.   Spike [P.5] raises his hand.
150.   Rob [P.6] grants the floor to Spike [P.5].
151.   Spike [P.5] steps down.
152.   Watchman [P.28] raises his hand.
153.   Whiskers [P.22] raises his hand
154.   Rob [P.6] grants the floor to Watchman [P.28].

Whether or not this results because, like Nova earlier, Spike does not wish to speak and has misused the "raise" command cannot be determined. And it is of interest that his misstep does not result in yet another round of public ridicule, a difference from Nova's experience that invites comparison of these two examples.

What differentiates these failure events is how the individual committing the offense handles the situation. Spike steps down but never openly admits to any failing or lack of competency as a player of the game. In contrast, Nova admits his mistake by providing an account designed to make his actions understandable to others. He then follows this with an offering of apology. The dangers that such practices of self-disclosure may entail are clearly apparent. Together these examples underscore the great care required in navigating through society, a delicate and risky endeavor that requires an ongoing commitment to face-work even when at play. But then maybe what is becoming clear here is how much work aimed at addressing one's identity and relationships is actually included in our play.

Manipulating Others.   Up to this point, it appears as through the activities of participants in play hardly constitute the "identity workshop" Bruckman (1992) envisioned, wherein playful experimentation would be a common and expected feature of participation. Indeed, it is perhaps surprising how few options aimed at experimentation are observed. One option that is exercised, however, is the manipulation of others through the MUDs ventril command. Excerpt 4 below offers an example of such manipulation in practice.

Excerpt 4: The Guild Masters' Meeting (turns 906- 926)

906.   Secretary says 'Whoa, my hand is getting tired!'
907.   Laser [P.33] says 'If you want to brag about how your guild can beat another, that's ok.'
. . .
909.   Spike [P.5] falls down laughing.
910.   Powderpuff [P.17] falls down laughing.
. . .
915.   Powderpuff [P.17] gives you a high-five.
916.   Laser [P.33] says 'you are spending too much time killing and not enough on guild work.'
917.   Leaf [P. 51] comforts you.
918.   Success [P.41] pats you on the head.
919.   Storm [P.2] raises his hand.
920.   Bear [P.21] ruffles your hair playfully.
920.   Laser [P.33] says 'Also, I feel that the ability to cheat in the arena with macros'

921.   'dest Secretary' (:
922.   Secretary says 'Am I getting overtime for this?'
923.   Laser [P.33] says 'grants an unfair advantages to anyone who
       has a good link.'
924.   Powderpuff [P.17] falls down laughing
925.   Bear [P.21] smiles at Laser [P.33].
926.   Laser [P.33] says 'I feel really stupid.'

The pattern of action—or line—undertaken by Laser is that of a meeting participant discussing aspects of the MysteryMud guild system. He is an active guild member and a regular player of this game, with an investment in the success of both entities. A challenge to this line arises in the form of someone using the ventril command—discussed previously as a command enabling participants to make others involuntarily engage in a speaking turn—on the Guild Association Secretary. Laser has been speaking for some time, and someone manipulates the MUD-programmed Secretary, who is taking the minutes of the meeting, into saying that her "hand is getting tired" from transcribing Laser's lengthy comments. This leads to both laughter and some comforting of the Secretary, all of which serves to undermine Laser's position. He is no longer a respected participant, but has instead become an object of ridicule for speaking for so long. In this case, an anthropomorphized feature of the program—namely the Secretary, who is not a real participant—is manipulated using the ventril command. And as a result of this playful manipulation a social manipulation occurs as well, since Laser is consequently ridiculed.

This manipulation of the Secretary does not result in any challenges from others even though it in effect belittles Laser. In contrast, manipulation of human participants is generally regarded as unacceptable activity and consequently challenged, as shown in Excerpt 5.

Excerpt 5: The Guild Masters' Meeting (turns 1034-1042)

1034.   Solo [P.15] says 'I am a Moron.'
1035.   Piglet [P.42] raises his hand.
1036.   Salamander [P14] burps.
1037.   Solo [P.15] gasps in astonishment!
1038.   Piglet [P.42] raises his hand.
1039.   Cookie [P.50] says 'when i play reboot i have no teleport buttons
        because my characters are not in a guild and i manage'
1040.   Larry [P.47] gasps in astonishment!
1041.   Rob [P.6] says 'NO VENTRILS!'
1042.   Solo [P.15] sniffs.

In turn 1034, the first in this excerpt, Solo announces that he is "a Moron." His gasp of astonishment in turn 1037 and his sniff in turn 1042 suggest that he only appears to make this statement, when in fact he has been manipulated into doing so by another participant. Assuming the authenticity of his response, this indeed seems to be an act of possession of his online character. Someone else present in the meeting space must have typed the command "ventril Solo I am a Moron" causing Solo to then appear to utter the phrase. Rob, the moderator, certainly seems to interpret the event this way as he shouts, using capitalized speech (a common indicator of shouting in online environments): "NO VENTRILS." Nevertheless, it cannot be determined whether Solo was indeed the target of a ventril or was himself responsible for the speaking turn in question and subsequently played the role of the "victim." His reaction would suggest that someone else is the culprit. This inability to determine the source of one's activity is a common experience of life in the MUD.

What emerges from these examples is again the idea that play is as much a matter of work as it is fun. It is work to protect one's self from the potential of manipulation. The last excerpt makes apparent that although experimentation is possible the forms it takes are neither imaginative nor the primary focus of play. Manipulations of others are occasionally practiced yet remain frowned on. At a more basic level, what these last examples suggest is how thoroughly oriented these participants are to aspects of social responsibility and relationships, rather than engaging in a free-for-all fantasy opportunity.

CONCLUSION: PLAY DOES MATTER

The title of this chapter, "Play Matters," suggests that human beings actively seek out opportunities for play or amusement. Indeed, such a belief is the very underpinning of the concept of *homo ludens*, a view that human culture arises out of playful activity and can be analyzed through observation of such (Huizinga, 1967). Bruckman's (1992) "identity workshop" expresses a similar conceptualization of humans as playful. Online participants assume various personae in a series of performances aimed at investigating different modes of personal expression. Yet, what the data reported here suggest is that play is itself a form of work within which identities are constructed quite conventionally, mirroring in many ways what one observes in the face-to-face world.

Play—and work—emerge then as frameworks for examining the concept of identity. As was suggested earlier in this chapter, application of such a perspective proves particularly relevant in a MUD environment in which two types of play are available—the actual participation in the gaming site and the playing with personal identity that results from such participation. The discussion examined aspects of one episode of play within one particular site. Of interest is the restricted sense of play that seems evident in the activities of participants on MysteryMud and how that play necessitates work.

Throughout the formal phase of the Guild Masters' meeting, the moderator exercises strict control, particularly over the allocation of speaking turns. On occasions when someone manipulates the game programming to personalize some activity, the moderator asserts a desire for routinized, restricted participation. A brief glimpse of a shift in orientation to the meeting is observable thereafter. Although the majority of the meeting involves a formal discussion, it ends with a brief period of activity where the moderator's domination is replaced by a shared management of activity monitored by the group itself. Within this gaming site, a formal period of "work" (indeed, a meeting aimed at improving the conditions of the MUDs economic system) is followed by a casual period of "play."

The split between these two phases of the meeting is particularly interesting. Throughout, the ability to engage in play is available to participants, yet they choose to engage primarily in routine work characterized by restricted options for participation. As mentioned earlier, the MUD provides for 181 legitimately available commands that participants can use. Analysis of the data shows that only 78 (41%) of the available choices are ever employed, and of these more than half are used fewer than five times apiece. In other words, participants seem likely to choose from a limited set of actions despite the large number of available options.

Closer examination of the data reveals that the 78 activities used during the meeting break down into three distinct categories: nonverbal activities, vocalic activities, and substitutes for speech. Nonverbal activities include physical acts such as nodding, smiling, or giving an object to another participant. Fifty-seven of the 78 moves are in this category. Fourteen actions used are vocalic in nature, such as a laugh, snicker, or cackle. Finally, actions that would normally be spoken in face-to-face situations (e.g., an apology or a thank-you) but could, in the MUD environment, be accomplished instead by means of a programmed command, make up the remaining five activities used. Just as participants are restricted in speaking, they restrict themselves in the use of vocalic and speech activities. The majority (73%) of the activity taking place is nonverbal, further reinforcing the moderator's control over all types of spoken behavior. This world emerges as an ordered, work-oriented environment rather than a fun, playful one.

In addition to the data just discussed, the larger study (Karetnick, 2000) from which this chapter evolved also includes in-depth interviews during which four members of MysteryMud discuss their experiences in the

MUD environment. Their reflections all support the conclusions drawn here. Despite the many technological influences, which participants do admit impacts their MUD play, it appears as though no one actively believes that they engage in experimentation or identity play at the same time. The capability exists, but on reflection we find ourselves acknowledging yet not taking full advantage of the "identity workshop"—that place where we can play with identity and actively "try on" completely new senses of self free from repercussion. Instead, participants seem to work at presenting a desired face, á la Goffman.

Each participant interviewed indicates that, while engagement may be altered slightly based on the anonymity of a limited-cue environment, who they essentially present themselves to be does not change significantly. They don't overtly play with identity as they play the game. "I think my characters are pretty much like my real life self—or at least I do not seek to consciously deceive others about my true personality," says Diana. Another player, named Javelin, believes that his "character IS [him]. No differences that [he is] aware of" while Pilgrim similarly reflects that his character "is pretty close to" his real-life self.

MUD communication is, nevertheless, reflected on as being potentially different from face-to-face engagement. Participants believe that you can "hide" online, because of the cues that are filtered out. But they also seem to support a belief that, over time, we work at adapting to the medium and developing ways in which to compensate for those lost cues (Walther, 1993, 1994). "The only difference is the lack of facial expressions and tone of voice," according to Javelin, but he firmly believes that MUD participants learn to account for this and that, overall, "people [online] communicate quite similarly" to how they do so off-line.

The one time where identity play may be observed most directly in the MUD environment is in practices of gender-bending. In fact, Pilgrim discussed his creation of a second character named Sasha, the result of his "curiosity to see how often female characters really do get harassed." But, for Pilgrim, "the curiosity was just in the initial stages . . ." and wore off fairly quickly. He soon thereafter did not often think about the fact that Sasha was a female character, while he himself is biologically male. While participating as Sasha, he does not actively seek at any time to play at being female by deceiving anyone. He believes that he continues to behave in the same manner, regardless of which character he plays as. The difference in his choice of which character to log on as seems to result instead from other aspects related to playing the game, such as gendered equipment (certain equipment is programmed to be more effective when worn by characters of a certain gender) and relationship affiliations. And besides, gender-bending provides an opportunity for fun, said Pilgrim, because "it's fun to experience different

things while on a mud, and why not? it's relatively easy to get two completely different characters running." It's a game-playing opportunity for him, not
an identity-playing one.

Thus, it seems overall as though participants acknowledge but do
not in any way openly flaunt the capabilities of the medium. I have no way
of knowing for certain, other than through what they tell me, how their
identities are constructed off-line, but there is no evidence in the interview
transcripts of real play, use of unusual or inappropriate emotes, flirting, or
any of the other aspects that each participant indicated as being part of the
MUD environment. Pilgrim does lick my character, Tara, during the course
of the interview, and Xena gives Tara a french kiss, but in both cases that act
is specifically prefaced by a statement that being online made such things
possible. These interactional moves merely serve as an example of how
MUDs might encourage play through lessened inhibition on the part of participants, as opposed to activities that either participant engages in as a playful experiment. In other words, had I just been chatting with them instead
of interviewing them specifically about playing in the MUD, these activities
would not have occurred at all.

One thing that does remain the same for participants whether
online or off-line is their orientation to face and face-work as described by
Goffman. Face-work is a dimension of personhood—a person's orientation
to issues of self and other, to issues of identity. Again, face is not consciously
addressed by any participant in this research. No one says that they actively
work at maintaining social bonds and avoiding shame. One could say that,
in fact, the opposite is believed to be true. After all, both Pilgrim and Xena
mention that the Internet allows them to act in ways that they would not in
real life, because it would be considered inappropriate off-line (such as
when Xena French kisses my character during our interview, which she says
she can do online "whereas, [she] would not in RL"—that is, "Real" Life).
But further analysis reveals that as a rule, participants act in socially accepted ways. No one walks around doing things that would be considered inappropriate. The only time such actions are undertaken are as examples of
activity that could be engaged in online. Yet even though the activity can be
engaged in regularly, it is seen through analysis of interaction that it is not.
Online participants seem to be aware that in theory they can behave in certain playful ways, yet in practice they continue to be influenced by the same
structured rules for work that traditionally guide off-line participation.

The discussion of data from both the Guild Masters' meeting and
interviews shows that MysteryMud participants continue to borrow from the
outside, "real" world in conducting themselves. In the context of playing the
game in general, and participating in the meeting in particular, they simu-
late worklike activities that are hierarchically defined and strictly controlled.

The free-for-all implied by Bruckman's (1992) "identity workshop" never materializes in this environment.

The world online may be one in which play makes fantastical things possible. Cabbages can womble, and "real" people can make representations of other "real" people—even computer-generated ones—talk at will. Despite these opportunities for adventure and playfulness, this world appears in fact to be one quite reproductive of the rule-governed every day from which we enter it. In a game constructed for play, during the time focused on for this discussion, an interactionally restricted and work-oriented environment is observed. Participants do not seem to log on to the MUD and learn to take advantage of the new capabilities, thus causing engagement to differ significantly from what is experienced off-line. Rather, as I observed in a journal I kept while working on this project, "the more I [play on the MUD], the fewer of those wacky possibilities I find myself doing." And both the discussion of data from the Guild Masters' meeting and my interviews with individual participants show that others seem to agree with that orientation. For the participants, their original view might have been of the online world as a place to creatively experiment, but this view appears to be reshaped over time so as to prioritize more traditional, face-to-face guidelines for activity. In other words, although they might initially personalize their actions, flirt a little, or briefly try experiencing life as a different gender, as time passes, those things give way to structured, routinized work aimed at addressing issues of identity construction.

REFERENCES

Baym, N.K. (1995). The performance of humor in computer-mediated communication. *Journal of Computer-Mediated Communication* [Online] 1(2). Available: http://www.ascusc.org/jcmc/vol1/issue2/baym.html.

Bruckman, A. (1992). *Identity workshop: Emergent social and psychological phenomena in text-based virtual reality* [Online]. Available: ftp.cc.gatech.edu/pub/asb/papers/identity-workshop. {ps, rtf} .

Chelton, M.K. (1997). *Adult-adolescent service encounters: The library context.* Unpublished doctoral dissertation, Rutgers, The State University of New Jersey, New Brunswick.

Craig, R.T. (1999). Communication theory as a field. *Communication Theory, 9,* 119-161.

Curtis, P. (1993). *MUDs grow up: Social virtual reality in the real world* [Online]. Available: ftp.lambda.moo.mud.org/pub/MOO/papers/MUDsGrowUp. {txt} .

Deetz, S.A. (1994). Future of the discipline: The challenges, the research, and the social contribution. In S.A. Deetz (Ed.), *Communication yearbook: Vol. 17* (pp. 565-600). Thousand Oaks, CA: Sage.

Donath, J.S. (1999). Identity and deception in the virtual community. In M.A. Smith & P. Kollock (Eds.), *Communities in cyberspace* (pp. 29-59). London: Routledge.

Duncan, S., Jr., & Fiske, D.W. (1977). *Face-to-face interaction: Research, methods, and theory.* Hillsdale, NJ: Erlbaum.

Duncan, S., Jr., & Fiske, D.W. (1985a). External-variable research. In S. Duncan, Jr., D.W. Fiske, R. Denny, B. Kanki, & H.B. Mokros, *Interaction structure and strategy* (pp. 1-29). Cambridge: Cambridge University Press.

Duncan, S., Jr., & Fiske, D.W. (1985b). Structure and strategy in interaction. In S. Duncan, Jr., D.W. Fiske, R. Denny, B. Kanki, & H.B. Mokros, *Interaction structure and strategy* (pp. 30-42). Cambridge: Cambridge University Press.

Duncan, S., Jr., Kanki, B.G., Mokros, H.B., & Fiske, D.W. (1996). Pseudounilaterality, simple-rate variables, and other ills to which interaction research is heir. In H.B. Mokros (Ed.), *Interaction and identity: Information and behavior* (Vol. 5, pp. 71-96). New Brunswick, NJ: Transaction.

Giddens, A. (1991). *Modernity and self-identity: Self and society in the late modern age.* Stanford, CA: Stanford University Press.

Goffman, E. (1959). *The presentation of self in everyday life.* New York: Anchor Books.

Goffman, E. (1967). On face-work: An analysis in social interaction. In E. Goffman, *Interaction ritual* (pp. 5-45). Garden City, NY: Anchor Books.

Goffman, E. (1971). Tie-signs. In E. Goffman, *Relations in public* (pp. 188-237). New York: Harper & Row.

Goffman, E. (1982). The interaction order. *American Sociological Review, 48,* 1-17.

Huizinga, J. (1967). *Homo ludens: A study of the play-element in culture.* Boston: Beacon Press.

Karetnick, R.D. (2000). *Identity in cyberspace: An ethnographic and microanalytic study of participation in a virtual community.* Unpublished doctoral dissertation, Rutgers, The State University of New Jersey, New Brunswick.

Matheson, K., & Zanna, M.P. (1990). Computer-mediated communications: The focus is on me. *Social Science Computer Review, 8,* 1-12.

Mokros, H.B. (1996). Introduction: From information and behavior to interaction and identity. In H.B. Mokros (Ed.), *Interaction and identity: Information and behavior* (Vol. 5, pp. 1-24). New Brunswick, NJ: Transaction.

Mokros, H.B., & Deetz, S. (1996). What counts as real? A constitutive view of communication and the disenfranchised in the context of health. In E.B. Ray (Ed.), *Communication and disenfranchisement: Social health issues and implications* (pp. 29-44). Mahwah, NJ: Erlbaum.

Mokros, H.B., Mullins, L.S., & Saracevic, T. (1995). Practice and personhood in professional interaction: Social identities and information needs. *Library and Information Science Research, 17,* 237-257.

Retzinger, S.M. (1991). *Violent emotions: Shame and rage in marital quarrels.* Newbury Park, CA: Sage.

Roper, S. (1997, April). *A study on gender differences within a virtual reality.* Paper presented at the Eastern Communication Association Convention, Baltimore, MD.

Sacks, H., Schegloff, E.A., & Jefferson, G. (1974). A simplest systematics for the organization of turn-taking for conversation. *Language, 50,* 696-735.

Scheff, T.J. (1990). *Microsociology: Discourse, emotion, and social structure.* Chicago: University of Chicago Press.

Stephenson, H.C. (1998). *Guiding becoming: One instructor's approach.* Unpublished doctoral dissertation, Rutgers, The State University of New Jersey, New Brunswick.

Turkle, S. (1984). *The second self: Computers and the human spirit.* New York: Simon & Schuster.

Turkle, S. (1995). *Life on the screen: Identity in the age of the internet.* New York: Touchstone Books.

Walther, J.B. (1993). Impression development in computer-mediated communication. *Western Journal of Communication, 57,* 381-398.

Walther, J.B. (1994). Interpersonal effects in computer-mediated communication: A meta-analysis of social and antisocial communication. *Communication Research, 21,* 460-487

Wynn, E., & Katz, J. (1998). Hyperbole over cyberspace: Self-presentation & social boundaries in Internet home pages and discourse. *The Information Society, 13,* 297-328.

IV

ENGAGEMENTS IN FACE-TO-FACE SETTINGS

7

Age Matters

Encounters Between Adolescents and Staff Within One School Library

Mary K. Chelton

If identity and relationships are taken to be constituted interactively within ordinary contexts through communication, seemingly "ordinary" contexts warrant further examination, such as that of the "service encounter" which Goffman (1983) called the paradigmatic example of the sort of context available for analyzing the "interaction order," or face-to-face interactive domain. Ubiquitous in everyday life, service encounters draw on a wide cultural context involving "government protocol, traffic rules, and other formalizations of precedence" (Goffman, 1983, p. 14). That the cultural expectations within such encounters emphasize "equal treatment" is apparent in the variety of interactive resources employed to cope with different social statuses, to manage queues in some sort of temporal ordering, and to display a demeanor recognized by those served as courtesy. Underlying these rules, however, are a variety of unstated social assumptions about who can qualify as a serious candidate for service. Goffman particularly mentioned "age" as one of the situationally perceptible qualifications that has to be satisfied "before individuals are allowed to hold themselves as qualified for service " (p. 15). How "age" enters into the definition of the service situation, how age matters as an issue of identity, provides the focus of discussion in this chapter.

This issue is examined through study of staff–student encounters within one library, on one given day, over the course of three class periods. Such encounters are theoretically approached as ritual-like routinized activities choreographed by unseen, largely unconscious and taken-for-granted "rules," through which people fit their developing lines of conduct to one another. This fitting, according to Blumer (1969), is done through a dual process of interpretation and definition that both sustains patterns of joint conduct as well as opens them to transformation. The continued reflexive use of the same interpretive schemes maintains established patterns of social life and is, at the same time, maintained by them. These patterns provide ways for events to become meaningful to the participants as they provide conventional solutions to the demands faced in the coordination of communication problems (Duncan & Fiske, 1977).

Definition of the Situation

Blumer (1969) pointed out that these patterns of social life do not just "carry on by themselves but are dependent for their continuity on recurrent affirmative definition" (p. 67). The process by which the social situation comes to be defined by the participants constitutes their relationships, their behaviors, and their perceptions of what is happening. Interpretation and definition of each other's acts within a mutually agreed-on context are central to human interaction. When there is no agreement on the definition of the situation, participants may redefine each other's acts so that the meaning of the act as well as the social situation is transformed. Redefinition is common in adversarial relations, such as those that occur between adults and adolescents.

As Mokros, Mullins, and Saracevic (1995) pointed out in their study of online search interviews, the opening moments of social interactions between strangers offer researchers a window on how participants employ "framing definitions" of the situation. These moments, which are usually highly scripted, invite stereotypic and automatic solutions to the problem of how the participants should present themselves and engage with one another. These initial framings reduce uncertainty about what to do and expect, whereas at the same time giving each participant a glimpse of the other's social propriety and status. Thus, interactional frames, especially during the initial stages of interaction, become pivotal to an understanding of what is happening.

This chapter contends that the potential for a mutual framing definition of the situation is blocked in two ways: by the imposition of stereotypic expectations, or by the use of client-control routines chosen by service providers in relation to the constraints of their jobs. Through a systematic analysis of staff–student encounters within the library studied, one begins to appreciate how library service providers project a specific definition of the situation within a framework of *age matters*. Library staff, it is seen, expect to see adolescent users as irresponsible and "difficult" as evident in the extensive concern with control and surveillance observed. As each person interprets the other's acts through such stereotypic frames, whether spoken or nonverbal, a mutual definition of the service encounter becomes one of controller–controlled not one of provider–seeker. How situations are defined by their participants may be regarded as an interactional mechanism by which identity comes to matter. The deflection of the definition of the situation toward control restricts the possibilities of interaction (McHugh, 1968), and promotes the relevance of stereotypic categoric identity (i.e., age and authority) as constituting the qualities of lived experience. As Goffman (1983) suggested, "Whatever the ultimate significance of these dealings for recipients, it is clear that how they are treated in these contexts is likely to flavor their sense of place in the wider community" (p. 14).

Assuming then that social situations are interactively constructed, their investigation offers a context for examining the way in which perceptions that guide definitions of the situation arise, as produced and reproduced within it. As Mokros et al. (1995) observed, "it is fair to say that in constituting the situation, acts of communication constitute individuals, assigns them identities and possibilities, and marks them on an ongoing basis as individuals of a certain type" (p. 255). Understanding how perceptions arise and are implicated within service encounters offers a way to understand not only "what," but also "who" is being produced there.

Multiple Relational Capacities and Categoric Identity

Goffman (1967) pointed out that individuals engaged in interaction are "likely to be related to one another through more than one pair of capacities, and these additional relationships are likely to receive ceremonial expression too" (p. 61). These relational capacities are the ways in which various identity categories present themselves, evoke responses, and interactively define the social situation. These capacities may be sociodemographic or functional. Within this context, Goffman (1983) identified "four critical diffuse statuses" in society: age, gender, class, and race (p. 14). These statuses, or social categories, provide not only a cross-cutting grid on which individuals can be placed, but also offer identification markers in social situations where no other identification is available.

Such categorization commonly involves social stigma (Goffman, 1963) in that typically a discrediting attribute attached to a particular category of persons invites stereotypic expectations. These expectations in turn lead to different definitions of the situation than might otherwise occur. Stigmatized persons feel unsure of how others will identify and receive them. This may then lead them to anticipatory defensive cowering or, instead of cowering, to hostile bravado as is the case with many adolescents. Depending on the point of view of the participant, the service encounter can be defined as hostile or threatening, solely because of the imposition of social stigma. Vandergrift (1989) pointed out this process of stigmatizing children and teenagers results in staff perceptions of these types of patrons as "second-class users" in library contexts.

Adolescents themselves verify these observations in recalled perceptions of service encounters (see Chelton, 1997). For them, being adolescent is to be stereotyped and categorized as part of a group that is underestimated, suspect, watched, restricted, or ignored. Personal appearance, not only the appearance of youth, but also how expected negative behavior is "read" by adults through adolescents' clothing or their style, seems to trigger stereotypic expectations (Chelton, 1997) even though their personal appearance is a marker of their particular social world (Shibutani, 1955).

CONSTITUTIVE PRODUCTION AND REPRODUCTION OF SOCIAL REALITY

Communication can be viewed in two ways, the difference being in the perspective regarding what messages do and how joint action is produced. In the information view of communication, human interaction is an expressive information process that produces a set of knowledge claims of truthfulness, truth, propriety, and intelligibility (Deetz, 1994). Communication is conceptualized as an instrumental transmission skill that benefits the autonomous individual who can put it to the most competent use. This view of communication dominates discussions of library practice and emphasizes control. Control through communication skill resides in the hands of the expert intermediary who can use it efficiently to predict what users want, or in the hands of information-seeking users who can most effectively manipulate the information system to their own advantage.

The second view of communication, as espoused by Deetz (1992, 1994), Mokros et al. (1995), and Mokros (1996), for example, rejects the idea that meanings exist prior to communication. In contrast to the "message transmission" view just described, this perspective sees human interaction as the site of meaning construction, where personal identity is unavoidably produced and reproduced through communicative practices. These statements of identity, pervasive in everyday life, are an economical means of self-definition through which others may understand what might legitimately be expected of the person. These statements express membership and identity through social bonds (Scheff, 1990). This second, constitutive view of communication emphasizes that individual behavior is communicatively situated as a collaborative social sense-making activity, not as information that is indexical of a person's internal competencies, beliefs, and desires. The priority of events and objects are rejected in favor of the interactional system within which they are achieved "as contingent realizations" (Mokros, 1996, p. 6).

Library Practice and Communication

Although noteworthy exceptions have appeared (e.g., Frohman, 1992), the theorizing of library practice has largely been guided by a view of communication as a matter of information transfer. From the constitutive communication perspective, communication is the everyday interactive social process that creates knowledge structures through productive conversations within relationships in which identity is negotiated and meaning is coordinated. Library practice is seen therein as a context of social engagement first and foremost, within which information needs are realized. Within this perspective, the "reality" of library practice is thus both constituted and perpetuated through communication. And communication is thus not merely a phenomenon or process but a primary mode of explanation, explaining, for example, library practice as socially situated, as psychosocially consequential, and not merely a practice that assists individuals with the nuances of information retrieval and storage systems.

When library staff interact with adolescents they attempt to frame the definition of the situation according to some idea of what it is they think they are doing. In other words, they "do" or constitute their theories by enacting them. This guiding idea has two components. The first, a "theory of practice," covers concerns about their role as professional (or nonprofessional) service providers. The second component, a "theory of personhood," addresses identity concerns about actual and expected self-regard as well as how one regards others, thus simultaneously constituting the social identity of each participant within the service interaction. Mokros et al. (1995; cf. Craig & Tracy, 1995) hypothesized that these theories not only drive the definition of the situation, but some aspects of them are "explicitly statable and intentionally instantiated by interactants" (pp. 255-256). Furthermore, with regard to practice, this is particularly true if such theories are "anchored in formal institutional discipline and training," even if other types of actions reflecting theories of personhood are "largely out of awareness and unstatable" (p. 256). The ways in which these theories drive the definition of the situation for library staff will determine how staff will attempt to enact library practice through their interactions with users. Both theories (i.e., of practice and of personhood), however, are simultaneously enacted within the situational context of service encounters. How librarians interactively constitute practice and persons (i.e., themselves and users) through communication in actual service encounters with adolescents is the focus of this study.

The theory of practice (i.e., how work is to be done), embedded in nationally promulgated library service guidelines (Chelton, 1997), is idealized as a personal intermediary service available to everyone equally. Librarians/information services staff offer assistance to users in interacting with resources, help provide a link between users and resources, and guide access for users to information, services, and materials. Practice may be summarized primarily as all the ways one provides links between users and resources. Learning, understanding, interpretation of the resources, and so on, are individual assets generally expected to be already present in, or acquired by the user after staff have provided links to the right material or service. Staff providing the service should be unbiased, have good technical information retrieval skills, and good interpersonal communication skills.

The idealized theory of personhood (i.e., how users are to be regarded) embedded in these theories of practice suggest that library staff are expected to initiate contact with and relate consistently and equitably to individual and diverse users with courtesy, energy, enthusiasm, understanding, respect, and tolerance. Users are persons who bring wants and needs to staff that are then to be filled to the satisfaction of the user. Given that such institutional knowledge is typically prescriptive rather than presumptive regarding treatment of users, it thereby admits that this idealized sense of personhood is not readily achievable in practice. Ignored thereby is the suggestion by Mokros et al. (1995) that theories of personhood represent enduring orientations of individuals in how they approach and value self and other. From their perspective, theories of personhood represent the bedrock knowledge within which all theories of practice are anchored.

Here, Lipsky's (1980) discussion of the street-level bureaucrat merits consideration. These individuals, when unable to meet idealized prescriptions, commonly develop a sense of their jobs that reduces the strain between abilities and goals, thus making the job easier to manage psychologically. This means that, although street-level bureaucrats—such as direct service providers within institutional contexts generally—are ideally expected to exercise discretion in response to individual differences in clients they serve, in practice they process people in terms of "routines, stereotypes, and other mechanisms that facilitate work tasks" (p. 140). These everyday client-control routines, such as overt discrimination or special eligibility rules based on the age of the user, are often the types of service barriers being prescribed against in standards for practice.

APPROACH TO THE STUDY OF AGE MATTERS WITHIN ONE LIBRARY

The observations discussed here were developed according to principles of naturalistic, also referred to as "qualitative," or "grounded," inquiry, assuming that contextualization is necessary for understanding of what is being observed. This type of inquiry observes people in familiar, routine activities within everyday contexts, believing that through the meanings assigned to such taken-for-granted activities, larger social structure can be revealed (Giddens, 1979) as well as the experiential products and byproducts that result for individuals (e.g., Scheff, 1990). Library and information contexts provide "fertile ground" for the application of naturalistic methods of study, not only because of the highly social nature of knowledge formation, but also because of a focus in these contexts on "communities of meaning" (Sutton, 1993).

The specific approach used involves the microanalysis—analysis and interpretation grounded in transcriptions from permanent recordings—of naturally occurring, everyday library service. By microanalytically studying concrete enacted social episodes as they are understood by the actors themselves, one may glimpse not only the underlying stable organization of particular social activities, but also the intelligibility of these activities for the participants enacting them (Heritage, 1984). The emphasis here is on, "how language is situated in particular circumstances of social life, and on how it adds (or reflects) different types of meaning (expressive, instrumental) and structure (e.g., interactional, institutional) to those circumstances" (Schiffrin, 1994, p. 7).

The microanalytic approach employed may be viewed as a variant of ethnographic inquiry involving the development of detailed description of observed behavior from which interpretations of the meaning of the behavior for the participants may then be developed. This specifically involves the coding of communicative actions according to various functions identified in the activities observed, with the frequency, placement within the interactional stream, and duration of these activities recorded.

Because this is a study of enacted library practice, primarily observed in interactions between two different age and status membership categories, special attention focuses on how these categorical identities are sustained or ignored in the interactive situation. Normative structures are identified and aberrations noted, with attention to the functions they perform to alter either the definition of library practice, or the enacted conceptualization of the user.

In addition to analyses of particular exemplars that would indicate typification or changes in the framed understandings of the participants, openings and closings are specifically analyzed. Goffman (1983) suggested that there are mutually obligating, but distinct initiating and terminating rituals to service encounters depending on whether the individuals involved know each other or not. In addition to any ritual talk that may be expected to occur, whatever is first said will subsequently limit options for response. Eichman (1978, p. 212) suggested that reference librarians share similar tasks with other "professional and nonprofessional interpersonal workers outside the library" in their need to gain and keep an inquirer's confidence nonverbally while figuring out from an initial verbal query how to help a person find what it is they wanted. The lack of specificity in opening reference questions is a universal complaint of working reference librarians in this regard. Openings also may reveal control moves by providers to define the situation and to establish institutional authority within the encounter (Fisher & Todd, 1986; Mokros et al., 1995). Analysis of the first turns at talk offers a way to capture how staff exhibit "a capacity to seize and hold the initiative in the service relation" (Goffman, 1959, p. 11).

In addition to the functional analysis of turns at talk, the relational aspects of these turns are also analyzed, by attending to deference practices and face-work (Goffman, 1967) as well as attunement (Scheff, 1990), or what Watzlawick, Beavin, and Jackson (1967) called the relational rules of communication. These dimensions of communication include expressions of regard, displays of emotion, tone of voice, allocation of attention to those who may be waiting, interrupting, or eye contact. Observed relational work in interaction evidences the operation of "theories of personhood" as discussed previously.

Data-Gathering Procedures

Both audio and video recordings of actual service encounters were obtained in March 1995 from a high school library, nationally recognized as excellent (see Chelton, 1997, for a fuller account of these procedures, including ethical considerations involved in this approach to data gathering). Recordings were made on one day over the course of three consecutive classroom periods.

The data collection involved the capture of both professional and clerical encounters. Clerical encounters were targeted as it was assumed based on prior observation that these represented frequent adult–adolescent encounters in the library (e.g., borrowing and lending activities) and because many users never approach a professional librarian even though they make use of the library to check out books. If one theoretical assumption of this study is that "library practice" is produced in social interaction in library contexts, then taking the perspective of users within that context mandates the inclusion of clerical encounters in the data collection. Recordings of encounters between the one librarian who staffed the library the day the recordings were made relied on the capture of her conversations through a broadcast microphone attached to her clothing. This procedure was employed as librarians will typically move around the library when assisting users. Recordings of clerical encounters were made by placing a video-camera on a tripod and positioning so that it would capture the activity surrounding the circulation desk where library materials were checked out and returned.

The audio- and videotapes were then transcribed, and transcripts were thereafter coded for content categories and these, in turn, were grouped into activity types. The term *activity type* is suggested by Levinson (1992) as an activity-specific rule of inference that helps "participants understand what they hear, thus inextricably intertwining language use and social activity" (p. x). All content categories or activity types are grounded in the data; none were predetermined. Construction of a typology of activity types through a coding scheme developed from the data ensures that the notion of enacted library practice not only has substance, but also delineates its major forms to provide a basis for considering how practices actually work in interaction (Woods, 1992). The activity types and their components, along with specific exemplars from the transcripts, serve as a basis of the following discussion.

Encounters With Library Staff

Overall, the transcripts included 153 encounters involving the librarian and 123 clerical encounters at the circulation desk. The following discussion focuses specifically on the types, frequency, and qualities of encounters observed that involved the librarian. Encounters with staff at the circulation desk are not similarly discussed but are referenced as appropriate in discussing the librarian's encounters. A full account of these circulation desk encounters with staff is contained in Chelton (1997).

Most encounters observed involve interactions between a student and a staff member although a sizable number involve interactions among staff, with teachers and other adults. These are retained in this discussion because they offer an opportunity to contrast the qualities of the librarian's interactions with adults in comparison to those she has with students. They are also retained because they represent an aspect of the relational landscape within which librarian–student encounters were situated. Encounters with students, in particular, tended to cluster at the beginning or end of the classroom period, with only sporadic encounters in between. These clustering tendencies presumably reflect the unique usage rhythm of a school library that, despite not being a formal classroom, is captive to service traffic patterns arising from classroom scheduling.

Including both adult and student encounters, the librarian's encounters ranged in duration from 1 to 322 seconds (i.e., 5.4 minutes), with a median duration of 17 seconds, with more than four-fifths (82.4%) less than 1 minute in length. Most encounters between the librarian and students focus on single-party/task requests presented face-to-face (rather than by phone) and these account for 89% of all such in-person encounters. Those remaining encounters involved interruptions of some sort and are characteristically brief with a median duration of nine seconds. These patterns are comparable in the case of encounters at the circulation desk with staff, with no significant differences revealed in duration nor in the single-party/task orientation characterizing these encounters.

Competing Approaches in Addressing Competing Demands

The tendency for encounters to cluster at the beginnings and ends of class periods meant that the librarian was faced with multiple need requests in rapid order at these times. The demands that such a pattern of activity presented certainly required considerable mental juggling on the librarian's part to size up what students' sought and so as to keep the flow moving at these times. An example of this occurred in one of the interrupted encounters observed, best thought of as a multiparty, multitask encounter, which begins roughly 1 second after the previous encounter and lasts for 72 seconds. This is shown in two parts as Encounter with Student 16 (S16) and Encounter with Student 17 (S17).

Encounter with Student 16

[A group of students enter the library together.]

    L: You guys all with M [a specific teacher]
    S16:   Yes.
    L: Okay.
    S16:   I ??? renewal.
    L: Okay.

S16:	???.
L:	The school year's almost over.
S16:	Yeah.

[Librarian looks up student's computer record.]

L:	Okay. What's your last name?
S16:	S???, [Spells it]
L:	Okay. What does that say? It says, "No renewals as of May 15th."
S16:	Yeah.
L:	Let me see when your book is due.
S16:	I think it was the 17th or something like that.
L:	And your first name?
S16:	Stan.
L:	Okay. Okay. I show that you have three books and they're all due May 18th. Do you want them until next Friday the 26th?
S16:	Yeah.
L:	Okay. But that's the—they're all due on the 26th.
L:	Hi, M???. How are you?
S17:	Good. How about you?
L:	Good. Hold on. Okay. Let's renew these. Let's see what happens. Okay. It says you've already exceeded your maximum renewals, but I'll go ahead and renew them any . . .
S16:	Well, this one's, I've already renewed; those two I haven't.
L:	Okay, all right. I'm going to go back . . .
S16:	This one on top I can probably turn in today.

The librarian in this encounter is doing several things with one student while acknowledging another next in line for service. When Goffman (1983) said that "the notion of 'equality' or 'fair treatment' must not be understood simplistically" (p. 16), he may well have been describing something like this encounter. Here, the service provider has to juggle different activities, people, and waiting times, while also attempting to gain sufficient information to address specific requests, and all the while showing regard for all present. In this example, the primary activities are informational, with each turn at talk beginning with a query from the librarian interspersed with reporting due dates, the end of the school year, and so on, while maintaining a focus on the original student seeking information. The student attempting to renew books (S16) is greeted with a question ("you guys all with M?") that references surveillance not delivery of services. He is subsequently not referred to by name even though he provides this information to renew his books. His handling by the librarian contrasts sharply with how the second student (S17) is greeted ("Hi M???. How are you?"). This may in part serve to acknowledge him while he waits. However, as is evident in the Encounter with Student 17 shown here, their joking suggests greater familiarity than just knowing the student's name.

Encounter with Student 17

[Librarian talks to next student who has been observing previous interaction.]

L: (Laughter.) Matt. We're not going to kill him. We just want his books back by next Friday.

S17:   As soon as the book ??? missing or lost status, you try to kill them. There are these little death squads running around.

L: (Laughter.)

S17:   I know. They were after me.

L: (Laughter.) Okay. And what do you want me to do? Sign your pass? Okay.

S17:   Oh, great. Now this has just been recorded. All right.

L: That's right. You've just been recorded. Oh well.

S17:   Oh well. Don't give them my last name. Then they won't know who I am.

L: Okay. What time is it? 8:05.

S17:   I have not a clue.

L: Okay. Are you coming or going this morning?

S17:   I am coming. I just go by the bells. If some bells ring, I move.

L: Okay. Thanks, Matt.

Although this may just be the librarian's way of kidding around with a "regular" to make him feel comfortable while she finishes a prior transaction, the question arises of how such different treatment of people facilitates or impedes perceptions of "fair treatment" by users (Goffman, 1983). When combined with the clustering effect just discussed, the result of these multiply interlaced encounters is that very different relational behaviors are immediately observable by all parties present. This raises the issue of how one "standardizes" relational work in what Gutek (1995) called an "encounter" type service model, and whether this is possible or desirable. In her suggested counterpart to this model, the "relationship" model of service, the second person would normally wait outside the view of the first person or the provider and might be more likely to assume standardization because there are no other interactions to observe.

Encounters as Functional Activities

As mentioned previously, encounters are categorized according to the type of function that they addressed. Across the 153 librarian encounters, 16 types of functional encounters are identified. These are shown in Table 7.1.

The 16 functional types shown in Table 7.1 reveal four distinct clusters according to commonalities in types of functional activities. These were Service (1-7), Enforcement (8-10), Socializing (11-13), and Management (14-16) with numbers in parentheses identifying the specific

TABLE 7.1

Sixteen Types of Functions Based on 153 Librarian–Student Encounters

1. help with equipment	9. directing traffic
2. help with supplies	10. enforcing rules
3. circulation desk activities	11. chatting with people
4. offers of help	12. special events
5. work with teachers	13. greetings
6. information help	14. supervising
7. follow ups	15. scheduling
8. checking passes/sign-ins	16. locating people

functional categories included in each cluster. The frequency and qualities of encounters within each of these functional clusters are now considered, beginning with the least common, management activities. It should be noted that encounters on occasion, as in the following example, include multiple functional activities. The discussion of activities is based on data at the level of the activity, not the encounter per se.

Management Activities. Management activities are observed in 16% of the 153 encounters recorded. Although small in number, these are types of activities (e.g., supervising and scheduling of staff or student assistants) that divert the librarian's attention from students who may seek assistance (or require monitoring). And because these activities are performed in public, within proximity of students in the library, these students are thereby reminded that this individual is in charge, had authority in this space, this library.

Socializing Activities. Socializing activities are observed in 24% of the encounters recorded. These encounters are largely oriented to other adults and mainly involve greetings, more extended chatting with seemingly informal discussions of past and upcoming special events at the school a common topic. Socializing activities certainly play important functions within any organization and are not to be discounted. Nevertheless, as with management activities, these types of activities mean that the librarian is not engaged with students in addressing informational or related needs that would clearly seem to define her professional calling in the delivery of service.

Enforcement Activities. Enforcement activities are observed in 37% of all encounters and these in each case involve interactions with students. These activities consist of checking passes, getting students to sign in, directing student traffic to an assigned spot where their class is working in the media center, and reminding students of library rules. Most of these encounters are quite brief, less than 10 seconds in length. Enforcement interactions begin almost exclusively with opening questions specifically related to passes, sign-ins, and queries about what class students belong to. Although such encounters are certainly expected within a school context, they also tend to reinforce a sense of control and authority more generally, with the following example illustrating the interrogation-like qualities characteristic of many of these encounters.

Enforcement Encounter 1

[The librarian stops students entering the library.]

L:	Do you have something to do? Do you guys have passes?
S13:	We're with M???.
L:	You're with M???. Okay. Your guys are on the main floor.
S14:	I have a pass.
L:	You have a pass. Okay. Did you sign in, or are you leaving?
S14:	Yeah, I'm leaving.
L:	Okay. Bye.

In other examples, as in the following two, there is a sense that surveillance, and interrogation on some untoward noticing, represents an ongoing orientation of the librarian toward the students.

Enforcement Encounter 2

[The librarian stops students leaving the library.]

L:	You guys need to wait for the bell to ring unless you have a pass to go back to class.
S91:	There's 20 minutes left.
L:	Okay. You're right.
S91:	We'll be right back.
L:	Where are you going?
S91:	To McDonald's.
L:	No, you're not. (Laughs.) I can't let you go to McDonald's. I can't let you go . . .
S91:	Okay. I'm going to the bathroom. ???.
L:	No, you're not. Sorry, guys. You're in class.
S92:	???.

Of interest in this example is how the librarian confronts these students without being fully aware of the situation, namely "there's 20 minutes left." Rather than engage them in some productive activity, she only offers restriction. This is especially pronounced in her last utterance, admittedly situated within a climate of joking around. Assuming that S91 was joking when he says "I'm going to the bathroom," her closing response "No, you're not" is troubling in its presence, for the alternative "Do you need to go?" would certainly seem to be a quite sensible question to ask (all joking aside).

Enforcement Encounter 3

[The librarian stops a student entering the library.]

     L: Do me a favor. Don't bring juice into my . . .
     S99:   It was empty, it was empty. I was just copying down???.
     L: Okay. Thanks.

Of special interest in each case is how these encounters initially involve—from the students' perspectives—undeserved and thereby problematic challenges. Authority is invoked—authority observable in management practices is now directed at the students in direct gestures of control. These gestures of control are certainly necessary and responsible activities in the cases of checking passes, directing traffic, and enforcing rules generally. However, the pervasiveness of these encounters, along with the qualities they assume in the examples just presented suggest an orientation to students that is quite distinct from the librarian's orientation to other adults, with socializing activities providing a notable contrast. Enforcing practices could, of course, incorporate greetings, but as shown in the encounters included above they generally don't. Although the school district has a policy requiring student whereabouts to be monitored, as Lipsky (1980) pointed out, "Rules and regulations provide only a measure of guidance in determining eligibility" (p. 60). How the rules are carried out to assure faculty and student compliance is left to the discretion of the particular street-level bureaucrat who is, in this instance, the school librarian.

Service Activities. This then brings us to the final type of encounter identified, namely service encounters, the type of encounter one would expect to be the most germane and in keeping with the librarian's professional calling. Service encounters directed at students are indeed the most common type of activity, observed in 38% of all of the librarian's encounters. However, the vast majority of these service-oriented encounters are hardly of the sort one would imagine. Help with equipment and supplies account for more than half (52%) of these service encounters. The following example involves both of these most common service activities as the librarian provides not only replacement supplies, but also shows the student how to refill the paper supply hopper on the printer.

Service Encounter 1: Providing Technical Assistance

[Student approaches the librarian.]

S40:	Ms. S?
L:	Yeah.
S40:	This is ???.
L:	Hold on just a second. What do you guys need? Paper?
S40:	Yeah. It's ??? paper.
L:	Okay. Pull this off. Just kind of pull. Nope. This way. It swings. Okay. Is there any paper down there in the bottom? Okay. Grab some paper. Now pull the drawer out. Oops.
S40:	This drawer.
L:	Yup, that drawer right there. And the paper goes right there. So grab yourself a hunk of paper. It won't take the whole thing.
S40:	Oh, it won't?
L:	It'll take about maybe that much. And you can put. . . . Here, I'll hold the rest of it while you do that.
S40:	??? it right.
L:	No. It goes the other way. Straighten it up real well first, and then make sure it gets under the two little things. Okay? Yeah, you've got it. Okay. Push the drawer back in.
S40:	Put the paper away.
L:	Put the paper away. Good. You're ready.
S40:	Okay. Thank you.
L:	You're welcome.

Although such types of service are clearly of importance, they are not the types of service provision that this librarian no doubt thought she would be delivering as she prepared for her profession. The pervasiveness of these types of technical, task-oriented services is further exhibited in the third most common librarian service encounters, those coded as "circulation desk activities," a type of activity that one might assume would be relatively uncommon for her. Here she preforms tasks usually associated with clerical staff such as checking books in and out and registering students for e-mail accounts. That she is performing these at all may be explained by the continuous mobility demanded of staff within this large, three-story library.

Thus, the librarian would at times walk by the circulation desk only to find that the clerk had momentarily stepped away. If not engaged in other tasks she would routinely assist any students waiting at the desk. Through her willingness to address needs at the circulation desk, as well as in her assistance with equipment and supply needs, it is apparent that she clearly cares about the needs of students even though the tasks she undertakes were not matters of her professional charge. Nevertheless, what the data reveal is that the vast majority of her service activities are of this type— activities that by and large one would expect clerical staff to handle.

And this brings us to what may be seen as the most surprising aspect of the observations made, namely how uncommon encounters that represent the librarian's primary professional service calling were. Assistance to students in their efforts to seek information represents the least common service activity with only four such encounters observed, or 7% of all service activity encounters. These four encounters are longer in duration than others, and may be appreciated in approach through the following example, Service Encounter 2, providing assistance in seeking information.

Service Encounter 2: Assistance in Seeking Information

[The librarian approaches a student.]

L: Do you need some help?
S76:   Yeah. I need to find a picture of a baby.
L: Okay. What kind of baby?
S76:   Just like a young baby.
L: Okay. Um, let's go up and look in the baby section.
S77:   Okay.
L: You know what? I probably should have stopped downstairs first and gotten a call number. Let me just take a quick look here. Okay. You wait up here and I'll be right back.
S77:   Okay.

[interrupted by another student's request]

L   Okay, I got the number. You still here? 649. Here's some baby books. Like a picture, like that of a baby?
S77:   Yeah. I'd like a full-body picture.
L: A full body, and a photograph picture.
S77:   Mm-hmm.
L: Okay. Let's see. Oh, I know where. Let's go look in *Parents' Magazine*. That's where . . . Is it a picture that you want to take away?
S77:   I can just photocopy it.
L: Okay. Let's go down and look in *Parents' Magazine*. They have lots of pictures of babies.
Sue, he's gonna just look through some *Parents' Magazines* till he finds . . .
L: The one you want.
S79:   With the one you want ???. Report?
S77:   Actually, I'm doing—I'm drawing a baby.
L: Here's all the *Parents' Magazines*, and they often have pictures of babies in them.
S77:   Okay.
L: So you can—lots of babies. So you can just sit here and grab a stack of them and thumb through here and find the perfect baby.
S77:   Thank you.
L: You're welcome.

Limiting and Limited Encounters. One final set of observations merits consideration. Across all those service encounters observed with students, whether they involved assistance with equipment, indicating where supplies were located, or where a book might be found, only twice does the librarian follow up to evaluate the success of her intervention. The lack of follow-up may reflect the obvious time constraints and overload that competing demands in multiple areas present. It no doubt also reflects an unstated assumption of practice that, although the librarian may show someone where to find information or how to work some piece of equipment, the "real work" has to be done by the user.

This reveals an interesting paradox. At one level, students appear to be the object of ongoing scrutiny and surveillance with clearly notable indications present that they are seen as lacking common sense and that they are certainly not above suspicion. Yet, in the lack of follow-up there is also a clear sense that the librarian assumes that students will handle whatever their need may be competently, requiring in most cases only minimal instruction. And yet another way of reading this situation is that the librarian is quite careful in her monitoring practices, with "care-full" delivery of service apparently a lessor priority.

CONCLUSIONS

This chapter examines the qualities of encounters between adolescents and library staff within one school library. Video- and audiorecordings provide the basis for analysis and reveal that practices within the school studied are stilted away from helping students seek information in the library, to an emphasis on control and surveillance apparently based in attitudes of mistrust. There is no claim that the library staff in the school studied did not help students, but rather that the help provided is offered within a system of control that creates a learning environment for students that reinforces stereotypic notions about adolescents that imply untrustworthiness. The procedures enacted are ones that have implications for identity, not so much at the level of individual development of expertise and knowledge, but of a leveling of expectations, based on one's age category. For the individual this is a learning that who I am, in a real sense, does not matter, for assumptions are made about who I am and what I might do categorically. The adolescent student confronts a vision of self as someone who is presupposed to misbehave.

Ironically, these largely taken-for-granted and pervasive control systems within this and many other schools are justified as a means of ensuring student safety. Although this is a logical concern for school personnel, especially in what might be termed the post-Columbine era of secondary school administration, the effect of these systems on the construction of student identity is ignored. When Chelton (1997) asked several other groups of school librarians about the pass system, for example, the idea that this would even be of concern was considered odd. The tacit understanding within schools is that asking students to present passes to move around schools is necessary to conduct normal school business.

Van Maanen (1979) implied that the roles taken in service encounters are "minimally embraced by the participants since they evaporate as soon as the encounter is closed" because of their fleeting and routinized nature. This study in a school library suggests, however, that the membership categories communicatively produced in service encounter relationships have profound implications for the identities of the participants. If identity may be viewed as both individual–personal as well as categoric–social, communication must be seen as a powerful constitutive force in everyday professional life, with the potential to assign certain people to stereotypical and stigmatized categories. Because categories always function conceptually as a means of comparison with other categories, often invisible and out of consciousness, assigning someone routinely to a prejudicial category has consequences for both behavior and perceptions. At the least such an assignment perpetuates bias, marginalization, and unfair structures of control. By constantly communicating a negative theory of personhood to and about adolescents through various school traffic rules embodied in the pass system, not only is the librarian's time and identity usurped for nonprofessional activities, but also any claim of idealized library practice is ultimately subverted.

REFERENCES

Blumer, H. (1969). *Symbolic interactionism: Perspective and method.* Berkeley: University of California Press.

Chelton, M. K. (1997). *Adult-adolescent service encounter: The library context.* Unpublished doctoral dissertation. Rutgers, The State University of New Jersey, New Brunswick.

Craig, R.T., & Tracy, K. (1995). Grounded practical theory: The case of intellectual discussion. *Communication Theory, 5,* 248-272.

Deetz, S.A. (1992.). *Democracy in an age of corporate colonization: Developments in communication and the politics of everyday life.* Albany: State University of New York Press.

Deetz, S.A. (1994). Future of the discipline: The challenges, the research, and the social contribution. In S.A. Deetz (Ed.). *Communication yearbook 17* (pp. 565-600). Thousand Oaks, CA: Sage.

Duncan, S., Jr., & Fiske, D.W. (1977). *Face-to-face interaction: Research, methods, and theory.* Hillsdale, NJ: Erlbaum.

Eichman, T.L. (1978). Complex nature of opening reference questions. *RQ, 17,* 212-222.

Fisher, S., & Todd, A.D. (1986). Communication in institutional contexts: Social interaction and social structure. In S. Fisher & A.D. Todd (Eds.), *Discourse and institutional authority: Medicine, education, and law: Advances in discourse processes* (Vol. 19, pp. ix-xviii). Norwood, NJ: Ablex.

Frohmann, B. (1992). Knowledge and power in library and information science: Toward a discourse analysis of the cognitive viewpoint. In P. Vakkari & B. Cronin (Eds.), *Conceptions of library and information science: Historical, empirical and theoretical perspectives.* London: Taylor Graham.

Giddens, A. (1979). *Central problems in social theory.* Berkeley: University of California Press.

Goffman, E. (1959). *Presentation of self in everyday life.* New York: Doubleday.

Goffman, E. (1963). *Stigma: Notes on the management of spoiled identity.* New York: Simon & Schuster.

Goffman, E. (1967). *Interaction ritual: Essays on face-to-face behavior.* New York: Pantheon.

Goffman, E. (1983). Interaction order. *American Sociological Review, 48,* 1-17.

Heritage, J. (1984). *Garfinkel and ethnomethodology.* Cambridge, UK: Polity Press.

Levinson, S.C. (1992). Activity types and language. In P. Drew & J. Heritage (Eds.), *Talk at work: Interactions in institutional settings* (pp. 66-100). Cambridge: Cambridge University Press.

Lipsky, M. (1980). *Street-level bureaucracy: Dilemmas of the individual in public services.* New York: Russell Sage Foundation.

McHugh, P. (1968). *Defining the situation: The organization of meaning in social interaction.* Indianapolis, IN: Bobbs-Merrill.

Mokros, H.B. (1996). From information and behavior to interaction and identity. In H. B. Mokros (Ed.), *Interaction and identity: Information and behavior* (Vol. 5, pp. 1-24). New Brunswick, NJ: Transaction.

Mokros, H.B., Mullins, L.S., & Saracevic, T. (1995). Practice and personhood in professional interaction: Social identities and information needs. *Library and Information Science Research, 17,* 237-257

Scheff, T.J. (1990). *Microsociology: Discourse, emotion, and social structure.* Chicago: University of Chicago Press.

Schiffrin, D. (1994). *Approaches to discourse.* Cambridge, MA: Blackwell.

Shibutani, T. (1955). Reference groups as perspectives. *American Journal of Sociology, 60,* 562-569.

Sutton, B. (1993). Rationale for qualitative research: A review of principles and theoretical foundations. *Library Quarterly, 63,* 411-430.

Vandergrift, K. (1989) Are children and teenagers second class users? *Library Resources and Technical Services, 33,* 393-399.

Van Maanen, J. (1979). Self, situation, and the rules of interpersonal relations. In W. Benis, J. Van Maanen, E.H. Schein, & F.I. Stele (Eds.), *Essays in interpersonal dynamics* (pp. 43-101). Homewood, IL: Dorsey Press.

Watzlawick, P., Beavin, J.H., & Jackson, D. D. (1967). *Pragmatics of human communication: A study of interactional patterns, pathologies, and paradoxes.* New York: Norton.

Woods, P. (1992). Symbolic interactionism: Theory and method. In M.D. LeCompte, W.L. Millroy, & J. Preissle (Eds.), *Handbook of qualitative research in education* (pp. 337-404). San Diego, CA: Academic Press.

Gender Matters
Travails
in Becoming a Dancer

Hester Coan

The ongoing stream of communication is thus, for each individual, a continuous chain of contexts of learning and, specifically, learning about premises of communication.

—Bateson (1996, p. 61)

The first relationship, Stern (1977) suggested, between infant and mother is expressed, and can be observed, as a jointly choreographed dance. This first relationship and its choreography serve as a model or framework not only for all future relationships but also for future learning. Our first steps to language are through dance. In the coordination of arousal and pleasure between mother and child in the multiple communicative modes of rhythm, movement, touch, space, and sound, mutual assumptions about the boundaries of interaction, of relational possibilities are refined. This joint choreography of mother and child, Stern pointed out, can be seen in the infant's eliciting behaviors, the mutual anticipation and response to moves and the dynamic rhythms and levels of arousal. These interactions lead to the infant's recognition of a first relationship, which provides a model for later relationships. In addition to learning about relationships, the infant learns through this choreographic engagement—with its moments of interpersonal attunement and its moments of travail—to focus attention and create expectations based on experience. The first dance thus serves as the groundwork for all future relationships, and at the same time for cognition and theory formation.

In this chapter, I examine a different context of choreographic learning, a ballroom dancing lesson, to explore the ways in which the underlying relational work and the more obvious cognitive aspects of learning a practice or skill can be understood as interwoven in interaction. In particular, I explore the ways in which gender matters—both as a context of learning about interaction and identity, and in a particular context of learning. The ballroom dancing lesson, captured on videotape, follows an instructor and his 22 students—9 men and 13 women—in interaction over a specific form of practice—partnered ballroom dancing. The instructor's ecology of moves and his students' responses are examined in three transcribed extracts contextualized within the natural history of a 74-minute lesson (Stephenson, 1998). In these three brief interventions, moments of travail, I examine the instructor's orientations to personhood, that is, his relational expectations and rules, as they are woven through his approaches to practice, the teaching of dance. Through interpretive microanalysis, I explore issues and assumptions of gendered personhood, aroused in moments where challenges to rules of conduct, expectation, and obligation surface, and the ways in which the instructor and his students must jointly choreograph these challenges to identity and continued learning.

Feminist scholars have demonstrated that gender matters in a personal, philosophical, biological, semiotic, sociological, political, economic, geographical and scientific sense (see Bordo & Jaggar, 1989; Butler, 1990; Hanson & Pratt, 1995; Nicholson, 1990; Rhodes, 1990). Gender, like age, is an obvious marker of identity, a seemingly "natural" sign that arouses native and scholarly interests as it is inscribed into and performed through our bodies in everyday lived experience. As the pronouns "he" or "she" indicate, the possibilities of our gendered identity are discursively framed and embodied within our everyday, common sense knowledge, our *habitus* (Bourdieu, 1990). And there we are valued. We sense our place among others within the ever-present tension of social bonds. In this chapter, I examine the ways in which gender performances and senses of self are shaped, offered, evaluated, revised, accepted, and rejected in relation to assumed and generally unspoken rules of conduct, expectations, and obligations learned in our first dance and brought into each subsequent interaction.

I begin with a brief elaboration of a communicational or constitutive approach for the exploration of gender matters and the travails of becoming a dancer. Stern's first dance introduces Bateson's understanding of communication as a continual context of learning—learning not only about what it is we are trying to say but, more fundamentally, about who we are in interaction. Scheff (1990) and Retzinger (1991) built on Stern's understanding of the first relationship with an explanation of the inherent and underlying tension of the social bond as the primary motivation in interaction. Bateson (1996) and Scheff (1990) also contributed to the methodological approach I take here, the interpretive microanalysis of three interventions embedded in a natural history of the ballroom dancing lesson. These interventions are brief instructor and student interactions, all less than 60 seconds in length, that appear to be primarily over practice and yet, when approached constitutively, also reveal the relational and gendered travails of teaching and learning.

A CONSTITUTIVE APPROACH

A communicational or constitutive approach is grounded in philosophical assumptions of humans as fundamentally social, emotional, and embodied beings. In addition to the cognitive, a constitutive perspective attends to the relational and semiotic dimensions of human experience that, in their concern for mastery and individual development, education and psychology have tended to marginalize. A constitutive perspective bridges a social and individual sense of being human by exploring how, in interaction and ongoing reflection, humans produce and reproduce senses of self and of society. Senses of self are ideologically, discursively, and physiologically constrained and enabled in interaction. Interaction is understood, not as an event or an effect, but as the site within a communicative system: "within which experience achieves a sense of coherence, structure and meaning" (Mokros, 1996, p. 4).

In moving between self and society, a constitutive approach makes it possible to examine in interaction the ways in which orientations to self and personhood are interwoven with approaches to practice. These interwoven theories, understood as guides to perception and action, are cognitive/discursive/embodied ways of knowing that allow humans to define and navigate situations of being. Theories of practice address routines of work and exercises of skill and are explicitly available in an expert's discursive realm. For example, the ballroom dancing instructor's efforts are guided by his knowledge of, and experience with the steps of the specific dances and prescribed choreographic combinations. Theories of personhood, although often unacknowledged, address the underlying issues of identity active within all forms of practice—everyday as well as professional or technical practice. These orientations or expectations are revealed in everyday interaction in expressions of management or control that are in play in predictable, routinized ways as Bourdieu's (1990) concept of habitus or Goffman's (1967) elaboration of face-work suggest. In the context of the ballroom dancing lesson, gender orientations to personhood for the dance instructor and his students guide rules of conduct, expectations or senses of obligation for men and women in interaction.

Learning and Interaction

Learning in interaction is twofold. Stern (1977) suggested that the first dance, the first relationship between infant and mother serves as a framework, not only for all future relationships but also for all future learning. In Bateson's (1996) concept of communication as continual contexts of learning, this communicative coordination, or joint choreography, of arousal and pleasure remains fundamental. Bateson credited both Freud (1965) and Harry Stack Sullivan (1940) for his understanding of a continually learning, becoming self. Like Sullivan (1953), Bateson took the position that communication and interaction are of primary interest and should be the focus on social science rather than individual, internal, mental processes. From this communicational perspective, Bateson (1996) reclaimed Freud's suggestion of the meaningfulness of interaction, "but in terms of a larger interpersonal determinism. Two people cannot 'just agree' or 'just quarrel'" (p. 50). "Interpersonal determinism" highlights Bateson's commitment to an interactional perspective and the social nature of humans. He wrote, "For every human being there is an edge of uncertainty about what sort of message he is emitting, and we all need, in the final analysis, to see how our messages are received in order to discover what they are" (p. 56).

Bateson believes that much is agreed on between participants in interaction, including the rules of communication and the rules for self-perception but that many of these pacts remain unacknowledged and largely invisible. As he put it:

> This dialogue is not only between persons and about the pact that they form, it is also and more strangely a dialogue that governs what each person is. . . . In everyday language we say that a person's self-esteem is enhanced or reduced by the responses of others. . . . In communicational terms, we may translate this into a statement that the very rules of self-perception, the rules governing the formation of a self-image, are modified by the way in which others receive our messages. (p. 60)

Bateson here not only suggested that failures in and of communication are painful for interactants but that the very quality or conditions of communication impact one's being, one's identity, one's sense of self. These are the often unacknowledged travails involved in becoming.

Bateson (1996) reworked Freud's concept of the unconscious to suggest that, in fact, much of what transpires in interaction remains out of awareness. This, he pointed out, is an expected property of such a complex system. He also extended Freud's understanding of all interaction as meaningful and nonaccidental from the individual psychological realm into "the realm of interpersonal process" (p. 49). Freud's notions of transference, projection, and identification are brought into interaction, thereby recognizing between interactants the continual, shifting, unconscious premises of relationship in which instrumental activity is embedded. Relationship and practice are always interwoven.

Freud (1965) provided a broad range of examples in *The Psychopathology of Everyday Life,* of the ways in which cognitive attention is interwoven with, and can thus be distracted by, the unconscious, yet compelling, dimensions of identity and relationship. In example after example, Freud related the ways in which forgetting, misreading, slips of the tongue, bungled actions, and errors can be understood as motivated by repression, the need to avoid disturbing topics. In one example, taken from Reik, he explored the phenomenon of group forgetting. In the incident, one of two young women in a group of young men participating in a scholarly discussion introduced the fact that she had just read an excellent novel that touched on the topics of discussion. Although the young woman could remember the cover of the book, even the type of lettering, she suddenly could not remember the title of the novel. Additionally, even though the young woman provided a full description of the contents and the men in the subsequent discussion remarked that they too knew of the book, none of the men could recall the title either. In analysis, the young woman later noticed that the title of the book was *Ben Hur,* which, when spoken, sounds like the German words "bin Hure" meaning "I am a whore" (p. 60).

Freud pointed out that this collective forgetting is not unusual or unexpected. The young woman "forgot" the title because of the distressing nature of its suggestion about her character, her image of her self, whereas the young men's forgetting was part of a similar and responsive unconscious process. Freud quoted Reik's conclusion about the men's forgetting.

Their unconscious understood the real significance of the girl's forgetting and, so to speak, interpreted it. The men's forgetting shows respect for this modest behaviour. . . . It is as if the girl who was talking with them had by her sudden lapse of memory given a clear sign, which the men had unconsciously understood well enough. (p. 60)

This incident demonstrates the assumed and shared responsibility in interaction to protect the face of participants, to offer respect as required. The forgetting is an example of an unconscious avoidance ritual. Reik's identification of respect as motivating this group "forgetting" highlights the unacknowledged and largely unconscious nature of the moves of deference and demeanor within the social bond that display respect and appreciation in interaction. It also suggests the subtle ways in which issues of sexuality and gender are woven through identity and interaction, as the young woman's "modest" character, her demeanor, must be protected and maintained in the groups' shared forgetting.

The Social Bond and Learning

The recognition of the relational, participatory, cooperative nature of communication is not a new insight. Grice (1975), for example, suggested a shared fundamental assumption of cooperation underlies all conversational interactions and is experienced in the interplay of the quality, quantity, relevancy, and manner of participants' contributions. Yet, these judgments of participants and their contributions achieved in interaction imply relational risk. Cooperation is not easily or painlessly achieved. Feminist scholars such as Jaggar (1989) have called for a greater attention to and a more complex theorizing of emotions in the disciplines of the social sciences. Stern (1977), Scheff (1990), and Retzinger (1991) provided an exploration of emotions as social and semiotic signal systems that shape a sense of self in interaction and thereby inform a constitutive understanding of learning. The work of Scheff and Retzinger in many ways represents an extension of Goffman's (1967) seminal contributions to the study of social interaction, particularly his appreciation of face-work as ritual enactment that aims to protect, repair, and preserve the social integrity of self and other.

Scheff (1990) specifically focused on the social nature of humans and proposes that the achievement and maintenance of social bonds provide the primary motives for human interaction. To exist, he explained, we require a "sense of belonging, a web of secure social bonds" (p. 12). Based on this understanding of the self as fundamentally relational, Scheff argued that the myth of individualism and the discursive repression of emotions, particularly pride and shame, have obscured our awareness of social bonds and their motivating power. The social bond has been made invisible and the vocabulary for emotions limited. Although Bateson suggested that self-esteem is a crucial element at play in interaction providing an "edge of uncertainty," Scheff moved to identify self-esteem as experienced in interaction, on an emotional continuum of pride and shame, as an indicator of the value of self in relationship. He made clear the theoretical importance of emotion to identity and interaction.

Scheff (1990) relied on Goffman's work on embarrassment and most centrally on the work of the psychologist Helen Block Lewis (1971) to clarify the role of pride and shame in the "deference-emotion system" of face presentation and face-saving (p. 6). Scheff pointed out that this deference-emotion system is largely dependent on and expressed through nonverbal signals, which interact with the communication system primarily depending on linguistic symbols. Together, these semiotic systems structure and texture human interaction.

Goffman (1967) understood interaction as a sacred order in which humans engage jointly in the projection and protection of claims to social worth, to "sacred selves." As social beings, humans require the respect and appreciation of others and feel required to give respect and appreciation to others. Respect and appreciation, however, are not always displayed consistently; they may be given or withheld in symmetrical and asymmetrical ways within particular and changing social situations. For example, ballroom dance structures asymmetrical relationships between genders—men lead and women follow—additionally, classroom instruction creates asymmetrical relationships between teachers and students—teachers lead and students follow. Multiple forms of relationships and images of self are already implied in these situational definitions, and displayed in relational orientations and forms of address. *Face* is Goffman's term for the ever-present, relational identity claims and expectations in interaction and face-work points to the ongoing effort required to maintain these claims.

Although the ritual of face-work may be aggressive or cooperative, it operates according to situationally defined rules of interactional conduct. These practices assure participants a framework of possibilities to maintain face while engaged in instrumental activities. The rituals of face-work examined in this chapter assume cooperation as they reveal everyday theories of personhood in interplay with both the rules of conduct of ballroom dance and of instructor and student interactions.

Rules of conduct in interaction are not always strictly followed. In fact, it is in the infraction, sidestepping, and bending of rules—and the challenges to face that surface—that the assumption of shared rules of conduct is revealed. Goffman (1967) referred to the activities of face-work in terms of two interrelated practices, deference and demeanor. He suggested that the ceremonial moves of deference and demeanor, which are so taken for granted that they often seem empty or trivial, allow for the everyday interactional confirmation of moral order through an ongoing "ceremonial chain" of practices. In this way, these often invisible ceremonial moves provide the very "bindings of society" (p. 91).

Retzinger (1991) elaborated on the social bond as a primary human motivation in her research on marital conflict. She suggested a sense of attunement as a potential relational state in which the bond is secure, that is, not threatened by too much or too little emotional distance. But attunement is not easily achieved, between infant and mother or between participants in any other relationship. Too much or too little emotional distance can elicit a sense of shame or disconnection that, if left unaddressed, can lead to a spiral of shame and rage. In that spiral of shame and rage, the original source of conflict is never resolved until the more fundamental issues, respect and appreciation for the social bond, are addressed. Retzinger's theory and model of conflict incorporates an understanding of the interplay of identity matters and emotions into communicative moments.

Bateson, Scheff, Retzinger, and Stern provided important insights to the development of a constitutive understanding of personhood through an elaboration of the unacknowledged and often unconscious motivations that shape interaction and identity matters for participants. Stern, Scheff, and Retzinger provided an active sense of human motivation and striving from a relational interactional perspective. Scheff and Retzinger proposed the social bond as the primary motivation in all human interactions and provided a theory of emotions, particularly pride and shame, as social and communicative systems that indicate the state of the social bond. This unacknowledged aspect of communication is continuously present in all interactions and it includes a relational sense of self that is expressed in verbal and nonverbal modes.

Bateson's contribution to this chapter is both theoretical and methodological. In the next section, I discuss his natural history approach to the study of interaction that provides the framework for this exploration into three interventions between the instructor and his students. These three interventions are extracts from a larger context, the natural history of the dance lesson. Through a contextualized interpretive microanalysis, I explore the ways in which orientations to personhood, and in particular orientations to gender matters in personhood, are woven through the teaching of a specific practice—ballroom dancing.

METHODOLOGICAL ORIENTATION

Interpretive Microanalysis

This chapter is grounded in and builds on the natural history of the lesson to explore more fully the instructor's orientations to personhood, particularly in gender matters, as they are situated in the instantiations of his theories of practice. This is done through an interpretive microanalysis of three specific interactions between the instructor and both individuals and groups. The interactions discussed are moments of challenge that question participants' expectations and obligations and the acknowledgments they do or do not elicit at three points in the course of the dance lesson. The empirically grounded interpretive microanalysis also draws on 2 years of ethnographic experience in ballroom dance lessons with this same instructor and many of the same students who participated in the dance lesson recorded and transcribed.

Interpretive microanalysis of videotaped interaction provides the methodological groundwork for a systematic and structural analysis of human interaction. Interpretive microanalysis extends Bateson's suggestion for how to approach issues of meaning. Bateson was deeply influenced by Gestalt psychology's appreciation of the bracketing or framing of perception and actions into meaningful units or wholes—that is to say gestalten. He recognized the significance that a conceptualization of such frames at multiple levels of organization held for a theory of meaning. He wrote, "As we climb the hierarchic ladder of Gestalten from the most microscopic particles of vocalization toward the most macroscopic units of speech, each step on this ladder is surmounted by placing the units of the lower level in *context*" (p. 54). This concern with context, with hierarchies of contextualization, provides a grounding for the interpretive microanalytic approach employed to interrogate the instructor's interventions identified within the natural history of a dancing lesson.

Interpretive microanalysis involves a process of abduction as conceptualized by Charles Peirce and employed by Scheff (1990) in his articulation of microsociology. Abduction, according to Scheff, refers to:

the rapid shuttling back and forth between observation and imagination. . . . In effective social interaction and thought, one not only observes (induction) and imagines (deduction) but also constantly (in microseconds) checks one against the other. . . . Abduction is the process which enables participants to accomplish the incredibly complex process of understanding meanings *in context*. (p. 31)

Contextualization is primary in this approach. What makes the approach interpretive is its ongoing movement between hypothesis generation and testing. The initial stage of the research however involves the establishment of a structural account of the natural history employing categorical decisions that involve minimal interpretive work. A map or tracing of activity is rendered. Contexts or frames of interaction are then identified for analysis within the mapped or transcribed natural history. These frames are then explored through "vicariously engaging or putting oneself in the role of participants" (Mokros, Mullins, & Saracevic, 1995, p. 242). Such analytic engagement is not concerned with defining the subjective, particularly affective experience of interactants but to explore the possibilities of the interaction, to compare what happened to what might have happened. The generation of such imagined plausible alternatives to observed actions has been referred to by Scheff (1990) as counterfactual variants and more recently as hypotheticals (Scheff, 1997). The analyst's interpretive experiences when conducting the research thus add to the data while remaining anchored to the natural history transcription.

Interventions are of particular interest as they reveal an otherwise "invisible" relational dimension of the lesson. Two types of intervention are examined—group and individual. In group interventions, the instructor focuses on students in the lesson as a whole or in two gendered groups, as "ladies" or "gentlemen." In these interventions, he addresses issues of skill and reviews group performance, but he also utilizes group interventions to address issues of participation in the overall lesson. In this type of group intervention, the instructor turns away from his focus on the skills of the Foxtrot or Samba and lets the students know how the lesson will work. The first of the three interventions examined in this chapter is a group intervention that arises as the lone woman phenomenon of dance class is revealed. The "lone woman" refers to the woman not chosen by any man as a dance partner. In a class of 13 women and 9 men, this context is bound to occur. As the instructor guides the woman through this difficult moment he demonstrates to the class his position of authority and provides a definition of the situation that allows the lone woman to continue to participate.

In individual interventions, the instructor focuses his attention on a particular student and addresses issues of skill, the execution of a step or series of steps in a particular dance. The second and third coaching interventions I examine in this chapter are between the instructor and an individual. These interventions are initiated while the majority of students are occupied with the practice of dance steps in what is referred to as the practice circle. The practice circle follows each period of instruction, which takes place in separate gendered lines. This circle creates the opportunity for students to practice and demonstrate their knowledge of steps with a dance partner. A brief overview of the instructor's coaching intervention practices precedes the analysis of these two individual intervention extracts, one focusing on a male student and the other a female student. This female student is the focus of more than half of the instructor's overall intervention time during the course of the lesson, about which more is said later.

GENDER MATTERS IN MOMENTS OF CHALLENGE

The Lone Woman Intervention

The lesson begins with instruction wherein the basic steps of the Samba are taught with the men and women positioned in separate parallel lines (L1— of five such lines during the lesson), as gendered groups. The transition from instruction in lines to the first practice circle phase is signaled by the instructor with his request that men take partners and that everyone form a circle. With 13 women and 9 men in the dance lesson, the creation of the practice circle means that four women will not have male partners, with all women experiencing the possibility of no male partner in the move to the practice circle. The organization of this first practice circle is iconically represented in Fig. 8.1.

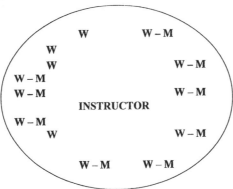

FIG. 8.1. Positioning of participants as the instructor initiates the first practice portion of the lesson in a circle (C1).

Ballroom dance requires that men and women assume complementary roles within the dance, hence mixed-gender partners represent the expected norm. And because the dance requires differing positioning and steps for men and women, women at least in this lesson were not permitted to dance with women. Figure 8.2 locates the lone woman intervention within a timeline that notes the major frames organizing the natural history of the 74-minute dance lesson. The intervention occurs roughly 2 minutes into the lesson, at the juncture between the first instructional unit on the basic dance steps of the Samba in gendered lines (L1) and the first practice circle (C1). The gentlemen are asked to "take a partner" and form a circle.

Lone woman status is for four women a structural byproduct of the composition of the class. It is an issue that requires immediate attention from

```
[L₁][C₁][L₂][C₂----][L₃-][C₃-------------------------------------- ][L₄-][C₄-------------][L₅][C₅--------]
[Samba-------------------------------------------------][Foxtrot--------------------][Samba]
   *
[0  2                                                              47              70    74]
time in minutes →
```

FIG. 8.2. Location (*) of the lone woman intervention occurs between (L1) the first instruction period in gendered lines and (C1) the first practice circle of the Samba

the instructor for the practice circle phase to begin. With 22 students in the lesson, the possibility exists for all students to be partnered throughout the lesson. Yet women stand alone. Women do not "take" other women as partners. The intimacy of the dance embrace between men and women, who may on all other levels be strangers, is made acceptable by ballroom dancing rules of conduct. This same intimacy between women is not acceptable. (Nor is the interpersonal control implied in the "taking" an option between women without violating rules of conduct and expectations of heterosexuality.) Men are not left unpartnered while there are "available" women. Additionally, women do not reject men as partners. Women then, are put in a unique position in the ballroom dancing lesson of being not only extraneous because there are too few men, but also being unwanted, because the option of choosing a partner is not under their control. For these reasons, lone woman status offers an opportunity to examine gendered personhood issues and jointly choreographed resolutions in the context of practice.

As the men "take a partner," the instructor provides no clue to the women on how to be taken or what to do if they are not chosen. In the case examined here, one woman attempts to leave the dance space and end her participation in the lesson when she encounters and cannot resolve her lone woman status. The instructor's strategies for dealing with the lone woman problem reveal his rules of conduct in the lesson and his moves of deference and demeanor. His moves suggest to the women, and the rest of the participants, his framework of possibilities for saving face in the potentially embarrassing moments that follow the identification of lone women.

As the men choose partners, four women find themselves not chosen. Three of these four lone women are grouped together in one portion of the circle (Fig. 8.1), with the other positioned between coupled partners who have already assumed the "dance position," the initial embrace of ballroom. These nine pairs of partnered students wait and watch as the instructor addresses the lone woman issue. Extract 1 provides a transcript of the instructor's talk and moves during this intervention.

Extract 1: Lone Woman Intervention

1	1:54	I need you to be a man. (The instructor addresses a female assistant coach, who moves across the circle of waiting partners.)
2	1:56	(Inaudible exchange between instructor and assistant coach.)
3	1:59	So have we got a circle? Ladies without a partner, spread out please. (Instructor looks around circle and points out empty spaces for ladies between partnered students.)
4	2:01	Will you please, spread out if you're without a partner (Two of the three grouped lone women "spread out" together to one empty space.)
5	2:05	Yeah, we should have, we should have . . . try to avoid,
6	2:06	so m [any] . . . ladies being together (The instructor is looking at the space in the circle where the two ladies are heading, one hesitates and returns to the original space as she "avoids being together." The instructor now notices the third lone woman, from this group of three, leaving the dance space.)
7	2:08	No, stay in the circle. (The third lone woman turns around and returns to the circle, the assistant coach takes her as a partner.)
8	2:12	Come on here. (The instructor directs the second lone woman to a space in the circle between partnered students, he looks around the circle once more, then he begins directing practice.)
9	2:14	Gentlemen, left leg forward,
10	2:16	just do the basic backward and forward first, before we get into any actual variations, ready?

Assumptions of Control and Rules of Conduct. In the course of roughly 20 seconds, during which the instructor addresses the lone woman problem, he limits solutions to three options. His assumption of authority and control is clearly implicated in the articulation of each. He frames ways in which ballroom rules of conduct may or may not be violated and he issues commands when his rules of conduct are threatened with violation. The instructor frames his first option (line 1 in Extract 1) as first person request, "I need you to be a man," involving both expectation and obligation for his female assistant. She moves immediately to fulfill the request indicating thereby the legitimacy of his authority and control of her participation. In so doing, she assists him in addressing expectations that the lesson will indeed flow smoothly with few interruptions over "trivial" issues.

The instructor observes three lone women standing together and offers a second option or strategy for dealing with the problem as he suggests that ladies "spread out" in the circle. The instructor's approach to conduct within the lesson, his guiding theory for practical conduct, is to "avoid" ladies grouped together. Spreading out is an alternative to groups of lone women. He shares this theory with the students, when he says (line 3) "we should have . . . try to avoid." The instructor invokes here his rules of conduct in the lesson: Unpartnered women are to dance alone, they will not take other women as partners, and they will wait for men to become available in the rotation of partners during subsequent practice circles.

The rotation of partners differs greatly from the initial coupling of partners as a circle is formed. The rotation has women remaining in place with men moving around the circle to the next available female partner. Although the lone woman problem remains, the personhood issues aroused differ as these women now alone are not alone by virtue of not having been chosen by a male partner. Thus, all women in the class will at some point be in the lone woman position but not that marked by active rejection as a partner during the transition from lines to practice circles.

Returning to the moves within the first intervention, two of the three women grouped together attempt to reposition in the circle but one lone woman begins to walk out of the dance space. Confronted with lone woman status and then the isolation and loss of support of surrounding women, she chooses withdrawal from the lesson. The instructor's voice raises to the tone of a command, "No, stay in the circle." She returns immediately, surrendering control to the instructor and allowing him to define her obligation and right to stay. The assistant coach takes her as a partner. The instructor now guides the final unsettled lone woman to a space he has chosen for her in the circle, "come on here." The instructor has demonstrated the strategy of "spread out" and voiced his authority in the circle. He begins the practice circle by addressing the men.

The command, "No, stay in the circle," transcends the effort at resolving the problem at hand in that it provides for students a context of learning the instructor's rules of conduct within the lesson. All students are obliged to follow instructions and all students will remain in the instructor's arrangements (lines and circles) and participate regardless of partner status. Generally, rules of conduct are never laid out explicitly but voiced in how situated problems are practically resolved. The instructor's rules of conduct supercede the rule of ballroom dance, which requires participants to dance in partnership. Women may dance alone. The rules of ballroom dance, more generally, are in force in other ways as they foreclose the possibility that lone women dance with each other. Although women dancing with women may certainly be observed in other ballroom dancing sessions, for this instructor such coupling is taboo as it would undermine the learning process by forcing women to learn both women's and men's parts.

Demeanor. In these early moments of the lesson, most rules of conduct are implied or assumed. The instructor does not say how to choose partners, or how to dance alone amidst partnerships or how to be a member of the lesson. When these issues arise, the tact they require suggests their importance as issues of face. Goffman identified tact, poise, and deportment as elements of demeanor, the ways that individuals communicate selves worthy of deference. The instructor maintains poise throughout the lesson, he does not suggest, through ruptures in demeanor such as hesitation or confusion, that lone women are problematic in the lesson. Instead, his presentation and avoidance moves expressed in displays of respect and appreciation, for example, as he calls one lone woman back into the circle and locates a space for another, project a demeanor of authority and consideration. He confirms the worth of participants and their membership status in the larger group by making their problem his problem.

Sexuality, Intimacy, and Avoidance. The rule that women not dance as men with other women is not discussed with the exception of the instructor's request to his assistant the she be a man, not a woman dancing as a man. It is thus unproblematic and practical for women to dance together, to be in the intimate embrace of ballroom dance, as long as one of the women is a teacher. Only coaches are considered capable of gender-switching without introducing greater challenge into the lesson. He thereby short circuits untoward byproducts that same-gendered dancing may introduce as his commitment is to honor their desire to learn to dance.

His demand that his assistant be a man is interestingly contrasted with his own conduct occasionally observed in more advanced lessons when he dances "as a woman" with male students. As this seems to invariably arouse issues of homosexuality and acceptable levels of intimacy between men, in these cases the instructor prefaces or follows up such interventions with announcements to the group—and particularly to the men—that his dancing with a man "doesn't mean . . . anything" or "it's just dancing." This accounting practice is typically met with laughter by both the instructor and his students. Of considerable interest is that he does not utter such statements or engage in such accounting practices when his female assistant, as in the example just given, dances with other women. He does not at these times remark that this kind of partnership is more fundamentally unacceptable with utterances like "it's just dancing." And there is no laughter at these times.

This extended analysis of the lone woman problem illustrates the layered complexities involved in the intertwining of practice, here matters of learning to dance, with personhood, matters of identity, of self. When the instructor's practical solutions involve gender-switching, it is only the male–male couple that leads to his further accounts. Here we see how a socially available homophobic discourse appears to ground his practices—a discourse reified in the rules of the dance. It is a discourse that suggests a hierarchy of taboos, with male coupling a much more difficult situation than female coupling. The unmarked status of the heterosexual couple, as the expected, the taken for granted, is implicated in multiple ways within these quite brief moments.

The instructor's strategies for dealing with the lone woman problem also avoids the question of social worth implied in being not chosen. Women in the lesson are exposed to the possibility of considering themselves as less desirable partners than women who are "taken." Additionally, he does not discuss or in any way influence the men's decisions in taking partners which would, of course, represent a strategic approach to short circuiting the "not chosen" byproduct of the structural configuration of the class at the outset. His failure to consider such an option seems to endorse for the men their privilege to choose, but in respecting their right to choose trouble is constituted for women

The lone woman problem appeared at each transition from instruction in gendered lines to the practice circle—C2, C3, C4, and C5. In these subsequent transitions those women who found themselves alone never walked away from the circle and spread themselves out without instruction to do so. One woman's travail, which most had only observed initially, shaped the women's sense of responsibility for handling the lone woman problem as each woman was confronted with it. The ongoing dilemma of providing partnered practice for lone women was addressed by having one or both of his assistants dance, as males, with these women. He addressed the dilemma as well by at times dancing with lone women. However, on no occasion did he rotate through all women dancing. Instead, he danced with a select few and with one woman in particular. The implications of this strategy, made possible by the lone woman problem, are discussed in detail in the third intervention examined in this chapter.

The instructor's strategy of dancing with women students to address the lone woman problem introduces a second form of intervention, direct coaching interventions with individual students, rather than with the group as a whole. Before considering how engagement with individuals and in particular the implications of such engagement with a favorite student—who is referred to as Marie—I first discuss some general characteristics of these individually directed interventions. This overview is then followed by the analysis of the first individual intervention where the instructor's focus is a male student—referred to here as Carlos.

Coaching Intervention Strategies

Coaching interventions in general are brief, mutual engagements between the instructor and individual students addressing skill and issues of performance that he introduced during the practice circle. The instructor's interventions are selective with 24 interventions distributed among only 8 of the 22 students and with significantly more time devoted to women than to men. Altogether, he made only 5 interventions with men, including 3 different men, with a total time across these interventions of 38 seconds or 8% of the time he spent in interaction with individual students altogether. Thus, more than 90% of the time he conducted interventions with individuals were directed at women and included 19 interventions in all. These 19 interventions with women were distributed among 5 of the 13 women in the class.

The difference in his intervention practices with men and women is most pronounced in how he opens each. Men are selected from a distance and addressed publicly, whereas women are approached only after the instructor has come into closer proximity and his voice is lowered thereby emphasizing intimacy and personalization. Negative evaluations of skill such as "Carlos, I can see you have your work cut out for you!" or "no movement in the arms, Ted!" are publicly voiced and a focus of attending. These public reproaches are presumably embarrassing moments for all present, not just those evaluated as Goffman suggested.

The instructor seems to assume that men, generally, can handle this more public evaluation although again only 3 of 9 males were targets of such individualized attending. The difference in approach is also apparent in his use of physical contact. His range of physical contact in male interventions includes: arms around men's shoulders initiating embrace, pats on the back or hips, and hands on a dancer's shoulders, from behind, orienting this male's dance steps to that of his female partner. Thus, although he is public in his critique of men's skills, the dance instructor is equally public in his displays of affection and attention in one-on-one efforts to promote their dancing skills. However, he does not dance with men—he dances behind them while they dance with partners. In this way his interventions with females appear remarkably different.

His interventions with women (and men) are of two general types: brief comments (verbal and/or nonverbal demonstration mirroring the comment) or more extended demonstrations of dance steps. Brief comments like "look over his shoulder," or "you want to be on his right side," and/or brief dance demonstrations that make a similar point, were directed at specific females as he monitors the progress of the students within the practice circle. He does not embrace or pat the females, nor does he dance behind them with hands on shoulders as with the men. However, as already suggested, he goes into much greater depth in his individualized interventions with females and it is evident that extended demonstrations are reserved for them—exclusively. But not all of them, for recall only 5 of the 13 women were the target of any intervention.

At the level of the individual, interventions as occurrences or events show little difference between men and women, with 33% of males attended to individually and 38% of females. However, as previously discussed and further elaborated, the frequency, duration, and quality of his interventions with males and females are remarkably different. Thus, men are critiqued in public and engaged and rewarded through physical contact, by and large briefly. Females are not engaged and rewarded through brief physical contact. They are not publicly critiqued, but advised in the case of brief interventions, and selected, physically engaged with face-to-face and treated as partners in the context of extended demonstrations.

Extended demonstrations, during the course of the lesson, were quite selective as they were directed to only 3 of the 13 women in the class, 3 of the 5 women engaged at all directly. The instructor is both partner and teacher to women in extended demonstration that is not initially apparent or appreciated until the ecology of his interventions (and noninterventions) are recovered within the natural history of the lesson. Although these extended interventions with three women appear to be simply episodes of "just dancing," there is much more here that is of interest.

He extends to women not just expertise at these times but an experience of "ideal" partnership through dance, whereas the "ideal" partnership offered to men is about dance through rebuke, assistance, and reward. In this sense, the ideal partnership offered males is an extension of the political world that constitutes male solidarity—the intimacies of the world of "guys." And what is offered women is intimacy, not intimacies. Intimacy that is in a sense divorced from the realm of the social and political, namely attunement through coactivity, an extension or analogy of the dance Stern so well described. To further illustrate these differences I now examine his interventions with two individuals: Carlos and thereafter Marie.

Coaching Carlos

Carlos was one of the nine males in the class, and 1 of 3 who received a direct intervention from the instructor, and the first student targeted for individual coaching. This first intervention is examined in detail as it nicely demonstrates how the instructor's gendered practices have the potential to create a relational unsettledness that focuses attention away from the lesson toward needs for remedial face-work.

Carlos is the focus of two interventions with the instructor, with both interventions totaling 18 seconds. Figure 8.3 locates this first coaching intervention in the natural history of the lesson.

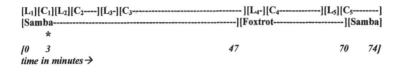

FIG. 8.3. Location (*) of the first coaching intervention with Carlos during (C1) the first practice circle of the Samba.

This intervention is located in the first practice circle just 3 minutes into the lesson, and only 13 seconds after the lone woman group intervention just examined. The instructor has just elaborated on rules of conduct, demonstrated his authority and put lone women in their place, literally. At the time of this intervention, the instructor is in the center of the circle monitoring students in practice. He is supporting the students' partnered dancing with choreographic instruction in the rhythmic pattern of the mnemonic, "1 ah-2, ball flat bum-bum, push and step, a rha-ti-da." There is no music playing. As he sweeps his gaze past Carlos, dancing with his partner, the instructor does a double take. He repeats the mnemonic once more for the group and then, in rhythm to his own mnemonic, he turns smoothly and saunters toward Carlos. The instructor is laughing as he leaves the center space and begins to talk to Carlos. He calls out to him by name as shown in line 1:

Extract 2: Coaching Carlos

1	2:39	Carlos, I can see you really have work cut out for you in this dance (The instructor laughs. Carlos drops his partner's hands; steps back and drops his head.)
2	2:43	(Inaudible talk directed to Carlos.) (Carlos lifts head, returns instructor's gaze, but does not move forward, other students stop dancing and wait for the instructor to guide them.)
3	2:46	Gentlemen, next partner please (The instructor turns to the group to direct rotation and then turns back to Carlos.)

4	2:47	(instructor's inaudible talk directed to Carlos) (Carlos steps forward and begins to move with other men around the circle to a new partner. The instructor puts his arm around Carlos' shoulder and walks him to his next partner.)
5	2:51	Instructor laughs (The instructor releases Carlos and turns toward center of circle.)
6	2:55	Left leg forward gentlemen, ladies right leg back. (The instructor returns to center of circle and directs talk to waiting partners.)

Challenges to Face. The recording of this coaching intervention was largely inaudible with the exception of line 1, where the instructor challenges Carlos' dancing skills. It might seem, therefore, that little has happened here. Yet this intervention reveals a great deal about the ways that gender matters come to command reflection through face-work, all accomplished in the fleeting moments of interaction, to address locally constituted relational byproducts of such matters.

The instructor's intervention with Carlos involves an initial challenge followed by efforts at repair or remedial face-work. This challenge begins with the instructor's reflection on expectation and performance. His comparison of these two elements, as "exhibited" in his intervention, involves his discursive, kinetically based knowledge of practice—how the dance is to be done—as a model of competence that provides the basis of evaluating Carlos' performance. While attending to the group he notes Carlos' performance and in noting, he does a "double-take," that is, looks twice at him in rapid succession. He continues to offer group instruction but now his gaze is fully oriented toward Carlos. Within a few seconds, he leaves the center, walks toward Carlos, and reveals his formulation shown in line 1 of Extract 2. The coaching intervention with a male begins with a public call for accountability.

Evaluation and Performance. Remedial face-work occurs in the context of such challenges, according to Goffman. This social repair process is set in motion when challenge is acknowledged through some form of offering on the part of the individual challenged. The challenger follows potentially with acceptance and forgiveness, and thereby mending the social consequences that challenges entail.

The instructor makes clear in a joke-cloaked manner that Carlos does not yet understand the skill requirements of the Samba. "Your work is cut out for you," suggests that the instructor has seen little evidence of skill in Carlos' performance. His challenge to some extent disconfirms the perceived skills Carlos supposed experientially. That Carlos experienced disconfirmation is apparent nonverbally. He first releases his partner and takes a step away from both the instructor and his partner. He does not engage in laughter with the instructor, and immediately avoids mutual gaze as he bows his head in response to the utterance in line 1. These actions represent an interactional marker of shame according to Retzinger and others.

Carlos appears to view the instructor's evaluation as problematic, as disconfirmation. His physical response to the instructor's challenge suggests a sense of disconnection from both the instructor and his partner in the face of their laughter and disconfirmation of his face as a dancer. The social bond is threatened. Indeed, Carlos' reaction may be viewed as a movement from shame to anger.

Thus, the first coaching intervention directed at an individual reveals something of the complexity confronted by instructors in working with students. These complexities underscore the theme of this chapter of how practice and personhood dimensions of professional conduct are intimately interwoven. The instructor's focus has been redirected in this example away from skill instruction to the need for face-work and repair. In the instructor's further attending to Carlos in lines 4 and 5 of Extract 2, we observe his sensitivity to and rapid appreciation that such must now be the focus. Yet it is fair to also infer that the instructor's challenge of Carlos in this manner suggests that he assumed a bond with Carlos that can support such teasing—he's one of the guys.

In his response to the instructor's coaching intervention, Carlos does not attempt to perform his steps with greater skill. Nor does he request specific feedback from the instructor, which might suggest that he has evaluated his own skills and also found them lacking. Carlos ignores the instructor's challenge to his skills and responds instead to his perceived personhood challenge. Carlos' moves in response to the instructor's challenge, that is, his change in demeanor—his step away and the dropping of his gaze—suggest instead a challenge directed at the instructor for his lack of respect and appreciation, the threat to face he has constituted. The instructor is now put in the position of needing to engage in face-work with Carlos, rather than engage in a repair to Carlos' skill.

Acknowledgment of the threat and repair work by the instructor is required for Carlos to re-engage in constructive practice, to learn. Carlos has the choice of offering a correction to his original misconduct, a poor performance, throughout the rest of the lesson and perhaps the remainder of the series of lessons. The instructor may accept his improved performance as an offering and Carlos may be grateful for the instructor's recognition of improved skills at his leisure. The instructor, however, is forced to make immediate repairs. Not only must he return Carlos to a sense of a secure bond, but the instructor must also work through the challenge to his own face as a competent social interactant for creating the potential conflict within the lesson and for shaming Carlos.

The instructor accepts Carlos' challenge and moves to make an offering. He spins back from his group announcement and re-engages with Carlos, offering encouragement with gestures that indicate a promise to work together with Carlos to enhance his skill. The instructor also offers, in his second round of laughter (line 5), the suggestion that his threat to Carlos' face should not be taken seriously. As Goffman (1967) put it, "an attempt can be made to show that what admittedly appeared to be a threatening expression is really a meaningless event, or an unintentional act or a joke not meant to be taken seriously" (p. 20).

Goffman also suggested that joking and embarrassment often go together as both work to deny the reality of the conflict that initiated the embarrassment. The instructor's offering continues as he embraces Carlos and walks with him to his next partner underscoring his appreciation of the significance of repairing and securing the bond between them. Carlos does little to respond immediately, but he allows the instructor to embrace him and to offer encouragement. Carlos moves on to his next partner, smiles at her, and joins in the dancing when the instructor counts off the beginning of the next round. The instructor does not look at Carlos at all during the next rounds of partnered dancing. Instead, he rotates in the opposite direction from Carlos and concentrates his monitoring on other students. The instructor does not initiate another individual coaching intervention during the remainder of the first practice circle (C1), nor does he return to Carlos in the second practice circle (C2). Carlos is, however, the focus of a second intervention in the third practice session (C3), after two interventions with other students, first a woman and then another man.

This first coaching intervention illustrates the complexities of instructional moves, of the interplay of practice and personhood. Reflections on expectations for skills and for relationships are woven together in both the instructor's moves and Carlos' responses. Challenges of performance and skill create the risk of threats to face and the social bond and bring into play—arouse for participants—issues of personhood in which approaches to practice are assumed to be embedded.

Coaching Marie

The next and final example considered in this chapter examines the instructor's intervention with a second individual named Marie, with whom he, during the course of the lesson, engages seven more times through individual interventions. Across these interventions he devotes more than half of the total individual intervention time accorded all students. In this example, I explore the impact of these eight interventions with one "favorite" student not only in terms of the instructor and student interaction, but also in terms of its implications for other women in the lesson who are not the focus of his extended attention. This intervention differs from that with Carlos, in that the instructor does not make public his reason for intervening and does not thereby arouse issues of face directly. When all eight interventions with Marie are considered they raise for others—presumably especially so for women students—generalized, that is to say, not interactionally situated as an occasion or event, personhood considerations of appreciation and respect that the desire of the other manifests through attention.

The "favorite student," Marie, is the focus of 53% of the time the instructor devotes to individual coaching interventions across eight occasions during the lesson. At these times, the instructor chooses to dance or demonstrate dance steps with Marie. The mean length of these engagements is roughly one half minute (34 seconds), but a few seconds less than the total time spent on interventions with males (38 seconds). Figure 8.4 identifies the onset point of each of the eight interventions with Marie.

The intervention with Carlos considered the instructor's strategies for initiating interventions with men and women generally and thus revealed the notable gendered differences underlying his approaches to practice and thereby personhood orientation. Examination of one intervention with Marie at this point allows an exploration into personhood issues for all participants in response to the instructor's selective approach to coaching interventions. This example of an initiation and intervention with Marie demonstrates the instructor's differing strategies for coaching women and the ways in which these strategies suggest his gendered theories of personhood. His brief intervention with Marie also illustrates how he most extensively engaged women through a combination of demonstration and discussion of their performance, an approach not made available to men and by far most commonly extended to Marie.

FIG. 8.4. Location (*) of Marie coaching intervention example at 28 minutes and the 7 additional interventions with Marie during Samba and Foxtrot practice circles

Extract 3: Coaching Marie

1	28:15	five, six, seven, and. . . .
		(The instructor moves toward the center of the circle after adjusting the music, turns, steps into Marie arms and begins dancing with her.)
2	28:40	(inaudible comments to Marie)
		(The instructor stops dancing and releases Marie from their dance frame. He talks softly and points to his leg as he demonstrates shifting weight in a Samba step. Marie stands listening and nodding, then does the step herself for the instructor.)
3	28:48	Yeah
		(The instructor thereby evaluates Marie's demonstration step. He then turns and moves to the center of the circle.)
4	28:49	Gentlemen, next partner please!
		(With the signal for partner rotation, Marie walks a few steps backwards along the line of dance, then stops, faces the inside of the circle and waits for her next partner, the female assistant coach.)

The third intervention with Marie occurs 28 minutes into the lesson, with the Samba the topic in the third practice circle (C3). The instructor moves to the sound system and adjusts the music, calling out as he returns to the circle the signal for students to begin dancing, "five, six, seven, and . . . ." He is facing the center of the circle as he gives this signal.

He now turns to Marie who at this time is a lone woman and as he completes his counting out, steps into her dance frame (arms up and open) and takes her as partner. There is no greeting. They begin dancing as he completes the signal for all participants. The instructor dances with Marie for more than 20 seconds without audible comment. He then releases his hands from the dance position with Marie and begins discussing with her a particular move within the step, the shifting of weight from one hip and leg to the other. He demonstrates the step, pointing to his own leg positions as he talks softly to Marie. His comments are inaudible for the most part. Marie nods and mirrors his demonstration of the weight shift. The instructor observes her move, comments "Yeah," and then turns, walks back into the center of the Practice Circle and signals "Gentlemen, next partner please."

Appreciation and Respect. Unlike the coaching intervention with Carlos that began with a verbal assessment and challenge, the instructor's intervention with Marie is largely nonverbal. Nothing is said as he "takes" Marie as his partner. Among students, the shift of partners is usually accompanied by some form of greeting marking this situation of intimacy. In contrast, instructor partnering with women is accomplished in silence by both. Those female students the instructor dances with are expected to be ready to dance and to accept the instructor as partner without warning, without the verbal signals marking his interventions with male students. Terminations of these interventions with females also differ. In the Marie example, he leaves at the end of the intervention and does not walk Marie to her next partner as he did with Carlos.

Women are not selected for intervention through a challenge to particular skills displayed while dancing, as men are. That is, the instructor does not tell Marie to stop moving her arms from across the room and then proceed to hold her arms steady from behind. And as already mentioned, he is consistent in this across women he targets for interventions. Nevertheless, he does challenge Marie to display a level of skill worthy of his attention and expert partnership. The instructor's trust in Marie, to meet his challenge, may be seen as a gesture of deference, a move of respect and appreciation, and a test of her skill as he suddenly assumes the role of both teacher and partner.

Women's skills are evaluated in partnership with the expert. Men's skills are evaluated as observed performances with other students. This greater context of intimacy in how he evaluates females comes with a price. If Marie fails, she cannot blame her partner. If she or any other woman does not perform well, she may indeed wonder if she will be selected again. The instructor's selectivity in interventions with lone women no doubt invites reflection by other women who wish to be noticed and tested against his expert partnership. Conversely, his failure to notice may also free these women from the threat to face they might feel if he did notice them and offer an intervention. No doubt both paths of reflection are stimulated through his intervention strategy.

The interventions with lone women are less public than interventions with men, with no public challenge to skills, no marking women by name and no laughter at what he observes. Thus, these interventions are also less likely to require remedial face-work. Yet, in the more intimate and private interventions, the quiet approach that does not call the group's attention to them, and the private space created—between the instructor's shift from public to more private talk and back—women are challenged in other ways. As dancing partners with the instructor, women are challenged to be respectful of the instructor's control of the timing, initiation and termination of interventions and of the shifting levels of intimacy within. Additionally, the selectivity of his interventions suggests reflection for all women on their desirability as dance partners.

CONCLUSIONS

I examined three instructor interventions in the context of a ballroom dancing lesson in this chapter to demonstrate how gender as one matter of identity is implicated and embedded within orientations to practice. Gendered assumptions were shown to influence the instructor's orientations to personhood and shape his rules of conduct for the ballroom dancing lesson in all three interventions examined. In the lone woman intervention, for example, a problem only because of the presence of more female than male students, gender concerns were raised in multiple ways. The instructor's expectations of women to accept dancing alone and for men to have their choice of partners were revealed. Examination of the interventions with individual students, Carlos and Marie, further highlighted ways in which gender concerns are a matter of personhood played out within the development of technical expertise. Interventions differed generally between men and women, with men receiving public critiques and displays of affection. The instructor's interventions with women were more common, less public, more intimate in some sense, but also more presupposing and thereby demanding in their ambiguity. Each of the three interventions revealed travails in becoming a dancer.

All interventions in the dancing lesson invite risk. Interventions represent a challenge of expectations and obligations in a relationship between instructor and students that is not merely a matter of skill but also of personhood. The interweaving of orientations to practice and personhood guides the instructor in his approaches to learning. Technical expertise, albeit the defined focus of the lesson is situated within a more general and very real concern with issues of self and other in relationship.

The consequences of the intervention with Carlos provided an example of how a constitutive approach reveals gender and identity matters in this context of learning. In his initiation move, the instructor intended to address the performer's skill, but Carlos' response was followed by a shift in the instructor's approach that may be said to reveal an additional focus on personhood issues, gender and identity matters. The critique of Carlos' dancing performance led not to correction of his performance as might be expected, but to a challenge for a jointly choreographed repair for Carlos, the instructor and the class. The instructor's remedial work to repair the relationship indicates his relational sensitivity and awareness. Threats to the social bond, he seems to realize require repair before attention to Carlos' missteps in the dance can be successfully addressed. He does not return to Carlos until later in the lesson. Moments of challenge suggested that what was going on between the instructor and students in this lesson was as much a matter of what was not said, or not done, as what was said and was done.

Counterfactuals, the suggestions of what might have happened at a specific moment in the interaction, examined through interpretive microanalysis, revealed ways in which avoidance as well as presentation moves were utilized to address threats to identity. For example, the instructor might have allowed the lone woman to leave the circle and thereby eliminate one "extra" woman from the group, but he did not. The instructor might have divided his individual interventions evenly between all students, but he did not. The instructor might have initiated individual interventions with women and men in the same way, but he did not. It is worth considering how the situation with Carlos would have differed had the instructor not broadcast his assessment to the entire class. The instructor might have whispered a private and simple verbal suggestion (e.g., "look of her shoulder") as he does for women, isolating one skill to work on, but he did not. He might have "taken" Carlos and danced with him as a woman, creating an ideal partnership to demonstrate his performance flaws, but he did not. At each of these choice points, the instructor was guided not only by his approach to practice but also by his orientation to personhood, his gendered sense of the obligations and expectations required to maintain the "sacred selves" continuously in play in this interaction.

I have addressed in this chapter some of the ways in which gender and identity matters were communicated in the lesson. Bateson's introduction of Freud's ideas into the interpersonal realm of interaction points to the recognition of the more subtle, unconscious tensions of arousal and pleasure in interaction as well. Freud's anecdote of group forgetting demonstrates how attention can be distracted in moments of arousal, how memory can fail temporarily on a group level to assist in the accomplishment of face-work. Freud is clear that interruptions are not unusual or unexpected in everyday activity. In Freud's example, the activity was a scholarly discussion; in this chapter, the activity is a ballroom dance lesson. Attention to the instrumental activity is distracted while threats to the bond, to face, are attended to or avoided by interactants. For example, in the lone woman intervention, the woman who attempts to leave the dance space is distracted from her goal of learning to dance by the threat of being not chosen and unpartnered. The instructor is distracted, his control and competence as a teacher threatened, by her leaving. He voices a rule of conduct for all students, "stay in the circle," and at the same time through his moves confirms her right and the right of all women to participate within his now more elaborated rules of conduct. The rest of the students stand, alone or in partnership, watching and learning as the lone woman travail is jointly choreographed.

This examination of the interplay of theories of personhood and of practice as they guide the instructor in shaping the lesson, is not intended to judge or evaluate individual strategies in interaction as problematic. Goffman illustrates how deference and demeanor moves can be contradictory and yet still satisfy the requirements of face-saving for participants. The unconscious, complex and shifting nature of theories of personhood as they weave through theories of practice in interaction, for all participants, precludes the creation of simplistic or singular solutions to the sometimes problematic relational dimensions of becoming. Instead, this chapter seeks to acknowledge the continual presence of relational dimensions in interaction and to offer ways in which these unconscious or invisible dimensions can be revealed and examined in relation to consciously motivated, rational plans. This constitutive approach may then lead to the development of a model of learning that recognizes the relational and semiotic dimensions and furthers an interactional approach to the study of practitioner conduct.

REFERENCES

Bateson, G. (1996). Communication. In H B. Mokros (Ed.), *Interaction and identity: Information and behavior* (Vol. 5, pp. 45-70). New Brunswick, NJ: Transaction.

Bordo, S., & Jaggar, A. M. (Eds.). (1989). *Gender/body/knowledge: Feminist reconstruction of being and knowing* (pp. 145-171). New Brunswick, NJ: Rutgers University Press.

Bourdieu, P. (1990). *The logic of practice* (R. Nice, Trans.). Stanford, CA: Stanford University Press.

Butler, J. (1990). *Gender trouble: Feminism and the subversion of identity*. New York: Routledge

Freud, S. (1965). The psychopathology of everyday life. In J. Strachey (Ed. & Trans.), *The standard edition of the complete psychological works of Sigmund Freud*. New York: Norton.

Goffman, E. (1967). *Interaction ritual: Essays on face-to-face behavior*. New York: Pantheon.

Grice, H.P. (1975). Logic and conversation. In P. Cole & J. Morgan (Eds.), *Syntax and semantics* (Vol. 3, pp. 41-58). New York: Academic Press.

Hanson, S., & Pratt, G. (1995). *Gender, work, and space*. New York: Routledge.

Jaggar, A.M. (1989). Love and knowledge: Emotion in feminist epistemology. In S. Bordo & A.M. Jaggar (Eds.), *Gender/body/knowledge: Feminist reconstruction of being and knowing* (pp. 145-171). New Brunswick, NJ: Rutgers University Press.

Lewis, H. B. (1971). *Shame and guilt in neurosis*. New York: International Universities Press.

Mokros, H.B. (1996). From information and behavior to interaction and identity. In H.B. Mokros (Ed.), *Interaction and identity: Information and behavior* (Vol. 5, pp. 1-22). New Brunswick, NJ: Transaction.

Mokros, H.B., Mullins, L.S., & Saracevic, T. (1995). Practice and personhood in professional interaction: Social identities and information needs. *Library and Information Science Research, 17*, 237-257.

Nicholson, L.J. (Ed.). (1990). *Feminism/postmodernism*. New York: Routledge.

Retzinger, S. M. (1991). *Violent emotions: Shame and rage in marital quarrels*. Newbury Park, CA: Sage

Rhode, D.L. (Ed.). (1990). *Theoretical perspectives on sexual difference*. New Haven, CT: Yale University Press.

Scheff, T.J. (1990). *Microsociology: discourse, emotion, and social structure*. Chicago: University of Chicago Press.

Scheff, T.J. (1997). *Emotions, the social bond, and human reality: Part/whole analysis.* Cambridge: Cambridge University Press.

Stephenson, H.C. (1998). *Guiding becoming: A microanalytic study of one instructor's approach.* Unpublished doctoral dissertation, Rutgers, The State University of New Jersey, New Brunswick.

Stern, D. (1977). *The first relationship: Mother and infant.* Cambridge, MA: Harvard University Press.

Sullivan, H.S. (1940). *Conceptions of modern psychiatry.* New York: William Alanson White Psychiatric Foundation.

Sullivan, H. S. (1953). *The interpersonal theory of psychiatry.* New York: Norton.

Authority Matters
An Examination of a Chair's Participation in a Group Decision-Making Meeting

Lynn S. Cockett

This chapter examines interactional manifestations of authority as an issue of identity through the study of one committee chair's participation in a face-to-face group decision-making meeting. In particular, this chapter considers how authority matters, how it is constituted and made situationally relevant in the course of the meeting. The chapter specifically examines the following questions: In what ways is authority situationally revealed, and what is the relationship between authority and identity?

In its investigation of authority as a matter of identity, the approach in this chapter is not only to focus on communication practices in a real-world situation, but also to aim at offering communication explanations—not sociological or psychological. Communication is theorized as a constitutive force (Mokros & Deetz, 1996) not simply a conduit for information transfer, but a process by which human beings create and recreate their social realities, situations, relationships, and identities.

WHY AUTHORITY?

This consideration of authority addresses a salient feature of organizational and professional conduct and thereby contributes to the development of theory in and for reflecting on professional practice. As corporations continue to turn toward democratic processes and work teams, issues of sharing, participation, and relationship become important for new reasons. Individuals in the workplace are learning new ways to work together, and thus, new issues emerge regarding work relationships. As Craig (1985; Craig & Tracy, 1995) suggested, through the study of communication one may contribute to the development of a practical theory of work and everyday conduct, with decision making a particularly relevant focus for consideration.

Through examination of communication practices, this research develops an interactionally grounded conceptualization of authority. Although authority has certainly been of concern for communication research, it is generally treated in rather static, role-oriented terms. For example, Stohl and Schell (1991) combined authority, rule ambiguity, and leadership uncertainty as problematic in their discussion of group dysfunction. Viggiani (1997) treated authority as one of two dimensions (the other being pay) on which organizational members measure hierarchical arrangements. Within other contexts, a similar treatment of authority is observed as, for example, Newman and Newman's (1987) suggestion that authority is what adolescents seek when attempting to resolve a decision-making conflict.

Discussions of authority, although often assuming authority to be theoretically transparent, do share similar unacknowledged assumptions. First, authority is understood in terms of organizational ideals as something to which members must especially attend if these ideals are to be achieved. Additionally, authority is typically raised as of special relevance for making sensible organizational group dysfunctions and conflicts.

RESEARCH DATA AND PROCEDURES

In contrast to this tendency to treat authority as problematic from the outset, this chapter treats authority as a feature of identity manifested in interaction and thereby as a dynamic concern for how organizational tasks such as decision making are addressed collectively. Specifically, this chapter examines the moves of, and participant responses to, a committee chair's authority within one tape-recorded group decision-making meeting roughly 25 minutes in length. Including the chair, the committee studied consisted of 11 people whose charge was the development of a set of recommendations related to educational policy. All members of the committee were active within a large national educational association, and it was the association that defined the need, membership, and purpose of such a committee. The committee worked prior to and on multiple occasions at its national convention where it sought to finalize its recommendations. The particular meeting examined in this chapter was attended by all members and focused on two specific decision-making issues. The members sought to address generally the criteria they would employ in assessing the data available to them and to examine what each perceived the salient dimensions to be addressed in developing a final set of recommendations.

As mentioned earlier, the meeting lasted for roughly 25 minutes and was audiotaped so that the talk of each committee member was discernable. The audiotape was then transcribed in multiple ways with an emphasis on capturing the organization, unitization, and content of that which occurred. The most basic unit of analysis developed from the transcript was the speaking turn. Overlapping speech was rare and brief when it did occur. Instead, a very strong preference for one party at a time, with everyone having opportunity to speak characterized the meeting. (All members did, in fact, speak.) Although nonverbal phenomena no doubt play an important role in patterns of turn exchange, these are not considered systematically as the focus here is not on the mechanics that underlie the interactive process, but to show how authority becomes meaningful within interaction.

Altogether, the meeting consisted of 29 turns, indicating that at least some, if not all, members took multiple speaking turns, as the mean turns taken is 2.6 per committee member. The organization of these speaking turns offers an initial consideration of how authority matters. In the following discussion, I specifically examine the organization of these 29 speaking turns from the perspective of the chair's participation. This involved identifying temporal and relational contexts of turns at talk. Temporal and relational contexts refer to who spoke before, and who after, any given turn. Through analysis first of the organization of speaking turns and second the content of some specific turns, I aim to show how manifestations of authority impact the group, and the personal dilemma that unfolds for the chair with respect to her position of authority.

Natural History Approach

The *Natural History of an Interview* (McQuown, 1971) established a tradition of research that has urged a foundation for the development of communication theory through microanalytic study of the processes and patterns of organization present in contexts of communication. The natural history orientation posits that it is productive to examine the properties and qualities of interaction prior to interpretive analyses of that interaction. This way, the interpretation is tied to specific communicative contexts and moves made by the participants.

The approach employed to examine the chair's participation in relation to the other committee members is guided by this natural history orientation. Instead of offering an account of the entire discussion among all 11 participants in this 25-minute meeting, the analysis here is grounded in a focus on the unfolding of participation of all members more generally. Although this discussion focuses on the chair's moves (or turns at talk), her participation is contextualized temporally and relationally, as just mentioned.

THE STRUCTURE OF THE CHAIR'S PARTICIPATION

Table 9.1 provides an overview of the organization of turn-taking observed in the meeting. It offers what may be thought of as a *map* of the meeting according to turns at talk. This map displays the manner in which the meeting unfolded and thereby offers one type of representation of the meeting's natural history. The table shows that the meeting included 29 turns. It further identifies which participant took each turn, when and for how long. Specifically, the first column of Table 9.1 identifies turns temporally, from 1 through 29, in order of occurrence. The second column identifies each participant according to her point of entry as a speaker in relation to all other members. Thus, participant 11 is assigned the "name" P11 because her first turn in turn 24 (T24) occurred after all the other 10 committee members had spoken. Finally, the third column identifies the length of each of the 29 turns in action-based units similar to the units of analysis described in the work of Duncan and Fiske (1977).

The data represented in Table 9.1 provide an initial, structural approach to examining the chair's orientation toward the meeting situation. Her orientation to the situation is assessed through her patterns of turn-taking in relation to patterns of turn-taking by other committee members, ignoring, for now, the content of her talk. In this way, this discussion offers a backdrop of participation to which the subsequently considered content of the chair's (and others') talk will be anchored, focusing therein on instantiations of authority and their interactional products and by-products. These considerations of structure and content are revisited in this chapter's conclusions where links between these analyses of structure and content of participation are discussed in relation to authority matters as an issue of identity.

TABLE 9.1
The Chair's Speaking Turns Within a Sequential Map of the Meeting by Turn Number, Participant Number, and Turn Length (in Units)

Turn Number	Participant Number	Turn Length
1	Chair	57
2	2	9
3	3	129
4	4	9
5	3	24
6	5	69
7	6	43
8	2	43
9	3	15
10	2	6
11	3	14
12	7	22
13	3	14
14	2	4
15	8	96
16	Chair	5
17	9	2
18	7	2
19	Chair	4
20	9	7
21	Chair	4
22	9	117
23	10	23
24	11	15
25	Chair	20
26	9	1
27	6	3
28	9	1
29	Chair	7

The Organization of Turns at Talk

A first notable and relevant feature of the chair's participation revealed in Table 9.1 is, of course, that she both begins and ends the discussion. She takes the first turn (T1) and the last (T29). A second feature is that she speaks on multiple occasions with four turns occurring in the course of the meeting following her first turn and prior to her last. Examination of Table 9.1 shows that after opening the discussion, the chair does not return to take a speaking turn again until T16. This turn is more than half-way into the meeting as expressed in total turns at talk, and more than two thirds of the way through the discussion when expressed as the percentage of all turn units across all turns to this point in the meeting.

Thus, the committee chair takes 6 of the 29 turns, or 21% of the total number of turns, and her turns sum to 97 units in length, or 13% of the overall discussion in terms of length. As already mentioned, the mean number of turns, if distributed proportionally across all 11 participants, would be 2.6 turns with an expected overall length of 70 units. The chair's participation, in number of turns (6) and length of total participation (97 units) show the chair to be a particularly active participant.

Consideration of the points at which the chair took her turns and how they may have impacted the group provides further structural information about her participation and her orientation to authority. Although the chair is more active than most members of the committee in total turns taken, her participation is not equally distributed throughout the discussion. In the early part of the meeting, she takes only one turn—the opening turn of the discussion. From that point on she assumes a listener role until T16. After this turn, her pattern of participation shifts. Unlike her initial approach to the situation, where she took the first turn and then ceased to talk for 14 turns, from turn 16 on, she takes 5 total turns, thus accounting for one third (5 of 15) of the turns that make up the later part of the meeting. Her approach to the situation appears to have shifted.

Social Contexts of Participation

Additional insight into the patterns of her participation may be appreciated by examining the location of the chair's turns in juxtaposition to the turns of others in the group. The representation of the chair's participation in this manner offers one way to map the social context of her participation. This makes it possible to examine a social network-based view of her participation. Such networks are represented in two different ways below. Figure 9.1 treats the chair as the center of the network and shows how others in the group are related to her or not through their turn-taking activity immediately prior to or following each of her turns at talk. Thus, this figure summarizes turn sequences, where the chair's turn is either the first or second of the sequence.

Figure 9.1 shows that the chair takes turns that follow four participants, namely P7, P8, P9 (two times), and P11. In contrast, her turns precede only two speakers, P2 and P9 (four times). Altogether, the chair's turns at talk

Does not Follow	Follows	Participant	Precedes	Does not Precede
P2			P2	
P3				P3
P4				P4
P5				P5
P6		Chair		P6
	P7			P7
	P8			P8
	P9 (2)		P9 (4)	
P10				P10
	P11			P11

FIG. 9.1. Social context of the chair's turns at talk during the discussion.

are observed in sequential relationship to five different participants with but one participant, P9, both a preceder and a follower of the chair's turns at talk. These data also reveal that she never follows the talk of six members: P2, P3, P4, P5, P6, or P10, nor does she precede the talk of eight members: P3, P4, P5, P6, P7, P8, P10, or P11. What becomes clear is that the social contexts of her talk and responses to it were selective. Selectivity was also apparent when the temporal positioning of her talk was considered.

A second way to visually represent the turn sequence network is through the representation of turn-taking sequences among all members, as displayed in Fig. 9.2. This figure shows all contingent links observed throughout the meeting. The dotted lines in Fig. 9.2 represent turn sequences that do not include the chair. The important feature of this figure, for considering issues of authority in networking terms, is the multiple links that connect the chair with P9. The chair and P9 exhibit a sequential relationship that is not only unique in regard to the chair's links to committee members as a whole, but is unique among all sequential relationships among all members of the committee.

Reflections on Structure and Authority

What may be concluded about how authority matters as an issue of identity from the admittedly limited characterization of the meeting in terms of the temporal placement and sequential organization of turns at talk? First,

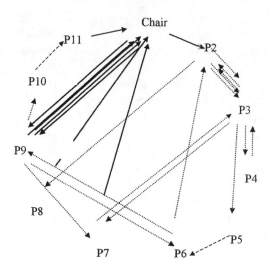

FIG. 9.2. Pattern of turn sequence links among participants.

through her initial and concluding turn the chair, and committee, mark the legitimacy of her role as chair as one with an authority, if not responsibility, to get the meeting underway and assure its timely conclusion. Second, through her level of activity as the most frequent turn-taker in the meeting, she exhibits the authority to actively engage throughout the meeting. Both of these observations suggest authority over process. Third, the temporal skewing of her turns to greater activity in the second half of the meeting suggests a change in her orientation to the situation. That is, the chair's authority relates to the process by which the meeting proceeds. Finally, sequential analysis of the relational context of the chair's turn-taking suggests an additional way authority matters are implicated. Her turns occur selectively, only in the context of some others, not all others, within the meeting. There is also evidence to suggest a privileged relationship with one participant (P9). The nature of this privileged relationship may be more fully appreciated through a consideration of the content of the talk to which I now turn. Extracts of turns at talk provide the focus of this discussion with the transcript of the entire meeting available in Cockett (2000).

CONTENT OF THE CHAIR'S CONTRIBUTIONS

Examination of the content of the chair's turns suggests that she struggles throughout with the expectations and responsibilities of her "marked" status role within the group. As chair, she is the only participating member of the committee whose status is marked by a title, yet examination of the content of her talk suggests that she acknowledges and promotes P9 as a member of privileged status and authority as well. This analysis speaks to the tensions of being "alone at the top" and illustrates how authority may be used to mark the status of others while leading. The chair struggles throughout with a dialectic tension of autonomy–togetherness, of leading–belonging as is discussed later. Through her elevation of P9, she in effect may be said to make efforts to diffuse her centrality.

The Chair's First Turn

The chair's opening of the meeting with her first turn at talk emphasizes themes of togetherness, collaboration, and codetermination in addressing the task at hand. Thus, the chair opens the meeting, as shown specifically here, with an appeal to a democratic approach as to how to proceed with the group's decision-making task. And yet, in the course of her, and the meeting's first turn, the chair moves from collaboration to control, therein suggesting that she struggles with both the position of and her attitude toward the exercise of authority.

Extract 1: The Opening Moments of the Chair's Initial Turn (T1; Lines 1-9)

1	[inaud] what's in a name
2	and are we all [inaud 3]
3	n lets just get everybody so that wr
4	we're talking a little bit about apples and apples n maybe not about apples [inaud] and cherries
5	what's our focus in this committee
6	whea [p] where do we think we're goin
7	what [p] have we defined our our audience
8	have we defined what we're looking for
9	en is everybody kind of comfortable with that

Constructing a Collaborative Space. Extract 1 captures the beginning of the chair's first turn wherein she quickly introduces her view of the problem that the committee needs to address and orients toward a collaborative discussion space. The extract contains material in brackets that identifies inaudible speech in seconds, for example [inaud 3], and notable pauses [p]. These conventions are maintained in all subsequent extracts, and therein additional bracketed materials include listener feedback, for example [back channel: laughter] (Duncan & Fiske, 1977). Parentheses are also used subsequently where a best guess is offered about a stretch of talk. The talk throughout these extracts is rendered in a way that best approximates how it was spoken as this may be expressed in standard English orthography. No additional paralinguistic qualities of the talk are reported and neither phonetic nor phonemic transcription was employed so as to facilitate ease of access for readers.

The chair's talk expresses desires for inclusion from which consensus may be derived. Her talk implies that subsequent decisions should be grounded within a shared perspective. The shared perspective that the chair advocates has a cognitive focus with the ideal that all members of the committee share a common definition of the task at hand. This common definition includes the desire to share the perceived purpose of the group, classify the target audience, and identify the types of recommendations the committee aims to make. Her suggestion, then, presupposes that if a shared perspective can be developed, the committee's practical activity can be driven by this sharing.

By overtly appealing to a sharing of personal subjectivity, the chair also would seem to reveal a personal belief or theory that human uniqueness is a more salient quality than is sharing for merely the sake of common understanding. Given the correctness of this interpretation, her talk reveals a tension between seeking the unique value of each member's input, and the pursuit of a common understanding, that would result in the identification of a singular framework to serve as a guide to the decision-making process. She thereby confronts the complexities and contradictions that efforts toward codetermination or coordination present, in the sense of Deetz's (1994) conceptualization of these communication approaches in the realm of decision practices.

The chair seems to be focused on creating a space in which individual committee members come together cognitively to achieve a shared perspective as to how to proceed in their subsequent decisions through like-minded coordinated choices. She appeals to an affective understanding of this process when she says, in line 9, "en is everybody kind of comfortable with that?"

Her question in line 9 also exhibits the qualities of her personal struggle as to how to employ her authority. It thereby references a more general problem that stems from efforts to balance membership with leadership. This would seem to reflect a desire for relatedness as against stereotypic autonomy within the group. The situated employment of authority is not merely a technical undertaking but one situated in a broad identity-based framework of relational understanding. This might be said to be a perspective on personhood, on consideration of how the relationship between self and other is understood. Thus, her utterance in line 9, considered a second time, exemplifies a spirit of codetermination, of collaboration and openness. Yet, its very articulation references her authority as it implicitly suggests that she has laid out a position with which the members of the committee could disagree. The implication is that there are alternative approaches, for she has authored only one.

After a brief pause, during which no member claims a turn in response to the question in line 9, the chair continues as shown in Extract 2.

Extract 2: Continuation of Chair's First Turn (T1; lines 10-12)

10	and um
11	what I wanted to start with
12	our charge is to p prepare this list is for recommended books appropriate for (disinterested) [p] young [p] adult [p] readers [p] ah readers

The talk in Extract 2 marks a shift in the chair's orientation as she begins to repeat the institutionally defined goal of the group that she calls the "charge" in line 12. Through this move she diffuses her authority through an appeal to a higher authority that has defined the committee's charge. This also, however, legitimates her authority, in that she is the person to whom the responsibility for following the "charge" is given. The chair opened the meeting with statements that pointed to a sharing of the discussion space and a trusting atmosphere as an ideal. To follow this articulation of group governance with her account of the institutional charge functions relationally so as to foreground a personhood perspective that values her affiliation with the group rather than her separateness as chair. In effect, when she cites the committee's institutionally defined charge (line 12) the chair also communicates to the group her relational orientation that although she is the chair, she is just as much subject to the demands of the organization as the rest of the group, and she seeks a collaborative rather than a controlling role for herself as chair.

Shifting Communication Strategies in Matters of Authority. To this point I have discussed how the content of the chair's opening turn at talk implicates a clear orientation as to how the meeting, and subsequent decision processes, should proceed. The chair advocates collaborative processes. I have also suggested that she therein also reveals a tension, for her, as to the qualities of membership she desires and the potential threats that her role as chair present to the realization of such qualities. What becomes of interest when subsequent content of her talk is examined is how the qualities of this tension itself begin to shift.

Extract 3 offers the continuation of her presentation of the institutional charge to the committee.

Extract 3: Continuation of the Chair's First Turn (T1; lines 11-16)

11	and um what I wanted to start with
12	our charge is to p prepare this list is for recommended books appropriate for (disinterested) [p] young [p] adult [p] readers [p] ah readers
13	and the purpose is listed fr
14	for young adults ages twelve to eighteen who for whatever reason
15	do not like to read
16	and [p] I take that to mean

Line 16 suggests a shift in her orientation, one that privileges her personal interpretation of the problem. It could have been the case that the chair extended an invitation to speak to other members either directly, by asking for others' opinions, or indirectly, by pausing long enough to open up the discussion space prior to asserting her interpretation of the charge. Instead, she offers an authoritative position to the group. In line 9, the last in Extract 1, she had said "en is everybody comfortable with that" followed by only a brief pause, an apparent first invitation for others to participate. Her invitation was, however, met with no takers. She then shifted focus immediately thereafter to a recitation of the committee's charge and concludes, in line 16, that she has a clear opinion to offer in response to her initial invitation to the group.

This assertion of personal authority following her opening statements—with its focus on collaboration—seems incongruous. During the remainder of her first turn, there were additional moments when the chair directly asked committee members to "jump in" to the discussion but at each point she continued to speak without any notable pause and no members were observed to claim a turn at talk in response. Thus, although she opened her turn with an orientation toward collaboration, the lack of participation by others within a context inviting collaboration may offer a possible reason for the chair's progressively controlling orientation in the remainder of her first turn. There we see the collaborative orientation giving way to a more controlling orientation.

Within this shift in orientation she continued to express a concern over a struggle to balance the dialectics of control and collaboration. This is quite apparent in the next stretch of talk, Extract 4.

Extract 4: Continuation of the Chair's First Turn (T1; lines 17-19)

```
17      n ah I'm gonna just start the discussion so
18      everybody feel free to jump in
19      this is not the gospel according to [me] at this point
```

Here she states her plan to begin the formal discussion of the problem, but that "everybody" should "feel free" to take a turn at talk (line 18), thereby directly signaling to the group that what she is about to say is not "gospel," that she is not the authority, and she is simply a member with an opinion or perspective. Her "gospel" statement is relationally deferential as she makes clear a view that sees her opinion as open to question and alternatives. That as chair she uttered this statement (line 19), as a preface to her own personal interpretation of an important issue, before other participants' opinions were solicited, is important. It may be the case that she imagines the possibility that "start[ing] the discussion" might itself be regarded as more than opinion. Thus, within the opening moments of her turn she dominates by maintaining the floor, but at the same time, she depreciates her own participation by drawing attention away from it, and yet also marking her authority through deprecation.

After an initial self-deprecating move, the chair continues to elaborate and clarify the charge that was delivered in lines 12-15. In Extract 5 (lines 19-24) she introduces ways of framing the problem that are inadequate, and concludes with a direct statement as to what the institutional charge does mean.

Extract 5: Continuation of the Chair's First Turn (T1; lines 19-24)

```
19      this is not the gospel according to (P1) at this point
20      um [p] this is not kids who can't read necessarily
21      um [p] it might be kids who don't read at grade level
22      or whatever
23      an they may have learning disabilities of one kind or another
24      but its kids who choose not to read
```

Although expressions of qualification are apparent in lines 20 to 23 (as underlined), the talk captured in this extract may be considered not so much expressions of insecurity as to the confidence she had for her own perspective but as indicators of the certainty and the complexity of the reasoning that has led her to hold this perspective. She continues her interpretation of the charge but now does so as if she were summarizing the charge itself and concludes as if this is not merely hers, but "theirs," as she and the committee are both responsible to a shared institutional charge. This is suggested in her choice of the inclusive pronoun "we" in Extract 6 (line 25).

Extract 6: Continuation of Chair's First Turn (T1; lines 25-26)

```
25      and so we're sposed to identify recreational reading
26      not for curricular or remedial use
```

The chair's "we're sposed to" (line 25) seems to reaffirm or re-establish her position as one of the group rather than one who controls the group. She places herself in a position to be thought of simply as a messenger, and not an authority. That lines 25 and 26, however, indeed reveal her perspective is apparent in Extract 7 (lines 27-32) and is made explicit therein in line 31 when she says, "[this] is the way I read it."

Extract 7: Continuation of Chair's First Turn (T1; lines 27-32)

```
27      so we're looking for things that can hook kids
28      who for whatever reason just choose to go play basketball as
        opposed to
29      um
30      that may mean we find some really high quality books
31      is the way I read it
32      but it also may mean some of those books that we think "oh
        this is really great" [p] really [p] don't [p] fit [p] this
```

Because her talk in lines 27 and 28 continues with a "supposed to" orientation she herein veils her interpretation, embeds it within, blurs it with the institutional charge, and thereby appeals to her commonality with the group rather than her authoritative stance. It is in lines 30 and 31, however, that the group learns that this is the chair's interpretation: "that may mean we find some really high quality books is the way I read it." Thus, within a brief course of time, from lines 25 through 32, we see quite differing orientations toward collaboration and control, toward a position of and articulation of authority. She has created a context for other members to treat her interpretation as a matter of institutional authority. This again shows her approach to the situation as one confounded by a personal tension within a dialectic of control–collaboration related to a desire for "we-ness" and a belief in her personal (and received) authority.

Although the chair tells the group, in line 31, that this is indeed her interpretation ("[that] is the way I read it") she continues in line 32 with an admonishing statement. She thereby reminds the group that decisions about which books to choose are not to be based on personal criteria. Thus, she anticipates that members may feel that a book "is really great" that such assessments may not be sufficiently policy guided. Thus, while inviting everyone's perspective and thereby valuing uniqueness of perspectives, her invitation aims not at a multiplicity of perspectives but instead as a way of gauging the potential lack of common understanding of the committee's charge (as she has interpreted it).

She follows in lines 33 and 34 with "I'm gonna just open it and let um people jump in and speak to this because." This phrase is an appeal to openness and collaboration, and it is another explicit offer for others to "jump in." However, she again continues to direct the group in a more serious and authoritative way, making clear that a cavalier attitude toward this process is unacceptable. Lines 35 through 46 (Extract 8) reflect the chair's progressively serious orientation within her first speaking turn.

Extract 8: Continuation of Chair's First Turn (T1; lines 35-46)

35	um I really wanna start
36	everybody to be able to look at themselves when you go home tonight
37	tch you're going to be looking at your lists
38	deciding which ones you wanna vote
39	because when we're here tomorrow morning
40	that's it
41	there will be no revote
42	[back channel: mmm hmmm]
43	n the choices will stand
44	[inaud 1] decisions [inaud 1.5]
45	so [p] I want you to really search your souls
46	because we don't want a list of a hundred and fifty titles

It is in this portion of her turn that she most clearly moves from facilitator to leader in her role, and from an authoritative to an authoritarian stance in her relationship to the group. Previously, the chair shifted back and forth between expressions of inclusion and personal assertion suggesting a struggle with the autonomy–togetherness dialectic. By line 45 she seems clearly positioned as separate from the rest of the group—so separate in fact that she not only admonishes them but invokes a "soul-searching" metaphor emphasizing the need of each member to take this exercise more seriously than she projects they have.

This shift, from wavering back and forth between authority and belonging is also reflected in how she invites others to participate. During her first attempt to invite participation, her talk was oriented toward deference through the qualification of her statement. By the time of her second such appeal (line 34), stating that she wants "people [to] jump in and speak to this," she shifts from deferential talk to an indirect accusation that the committee has not fully comprehended the seriousness of its work and that unless consensual understandings, as she articulates them, are achieved that members of the committee will have to bear responsibility for their collective failure.

The progressively control-oriented development is evident in multiple ways including how she invited others to participate in the discussion. Both of her invitations to this point include "jumping in" as a metaphor for inviting others to speak. To "jump in" also metaphorically appeals to taking a risk. Jumping in conjures up images of jumping rope—of timing one's entrance just right so as not to trip or fall, or lose face in Goffman's (1967) sense. By inviting members to "jump in" and then quickly continuing to talk, the chair, in a sense, assumes a parental authority role of protecting others in her charge from potential loss of face. For members of her committee her invitations and rapid continuations create a risky environment indeed—one that would be difficult to find footing in because it might mean interrupting the chair's talk.

The chair's reference that subsequent discussions will be made based on voting (lines 38-41) contradicts a spirit of collaboration and consensus building. This appeal to voting references a technical/rational decision-making process, not a relational or codetermining approach.

She concludes her first turn by again requesting "please jump in here." This invitation for others to participate is offered following a short stretch of talk where she elaborates on why "we don't want a list of 150 titles" (introduced in line 46). Once she concludes this turn, she does not speak again until 7 of the 10 committee members have had turns at talk, taking 14 turns. Ironically, then, although her first turn at talk has been argued to increasingly forefront her authority, and increasingly emphasized control, once it is over, the meeting subsequently displays an orientation to collaboration. In refraining from talk she certainly supports a climate of sharing and participation.

The Chair–P9 Dyad

Unlike the chair's first turn, all of her other turns were relatively short and interactively responsive to the group in many senses. Each of her remaining turns is examined as to how matters of identity are implicated therein as discussed below. In particular, the discussion focuses on the interactional relationship between the chair and P9 that had been shown in Fig. 9.2 to be structurally unique relative to all others during the meeting.

The Chair's Second Turn: Summing Up and Inviting P9's Perspective. The chair's second turn (T16 overall) is shown in Extract 9. It begins (line 555) by acknowledging the relevance of the committee members' contributions over the course of the 14 turns since her charge to them in the first turn of the meeting. She continues (line 557), after a brief

moment of laughter, to indicate that their contributions were not only relevant but that everyone had "real good ideas" (to paraphrase her talk). These utterances would appear to signal her wish to shift the course of the meeting, to refocus it in a direction wherein the committee would develop a statement of criteria based on the perspectives voiced during the prior 14 turns (15 if we include the chair's first turn). This is suggested in line 558.

Extract 9: The Chair's Second Turn (T16; lines 555-559)

555	you're all hittin on all the problems
556	[back channel: simultaneous laughter]
557	everybody's got got real good good ah ideas
558	and somehow we're gonna have to put all of those together
559	[inaud] (P9) did you wanna say anything

The chair's wish to shift the course of the meeting is apparent in the juxtaposition of her "summary evaluation" of the committee's accomplishments to this point (lines 555, 557), with the formulation of a new task before them, one that suggests "summing up the meeting" itself (line 558). She concludes the turn by directly addressing another participant, asking whether she had something to say. This other participant is P9, who had moments before entered the room, who, in other words, had not been previously present in the meeting. That the chair directs this question to her is made clear as P9 begins to speak (and was presumably clear as the chair was speaking—in context—to all present). It is worth noting that the chair's invitations to P9, here and following, are the only times that she singled out a committee member to speak next (in so far as this is observable through talk).

It is unclear whether the chair's concluding utterance, "do you wanna say anything" (line 559), is an invitation to speak to her formulation for how to proceed (line 558), or if it invites a re-opening of the perspective-offering talk that she had seemingly summed up in her previous utterances (lines 555-558). This ambiguity remains as P9 responds (line 560) to the chair's invitation in line 559 with "I don't know wha" (followed by a brief moment of simultaneous laughter in line 561). The incompleteness of P9's uttterance is left on hold, interactionally, as P7, who had last spoken in turn 12, interjects at this point (turn 18), "but I wanna back up to me later" (line 562). Through this utterance, P7 requests the floor again, but not at this moment. She continues and concludes her brief turn with "cause mine was just off the cuff" (line 563), thus offering a reason for wanting to speak again. P7's brief turn appears to respond to the chair's proposed shift of focus for the meeting which would then suggest that P7 treated the chair's invitation to P9 as but a momentary amendment to her proposal, one that would allow P9's perspective to also be heard.

The chair now has before her requests from two interactants. As shown in Extract 10, the chair apparently handles this situation by first responding to P7 with "Okay" (line 564). Assuming that this is indeed a response to P7, it is quite minimal as she does not specifically refer to the nature of her request. Instead, the chair moves to immediately signal that she ("we") wishes to hear from P9 and attempts thereupon to clarify what it is she wants to hear (from P9), thus addressing the ambiguity(s) resulting from her prior turn (lines 565-566).

Extract 10: The Chair's Third Turn and P9's Response (T19-20; lines 564-568)

```
564      Okay [inaud] why don't we go to (P9)
565      we're talkin about uh what is a (name of material)
566      uh [inaud] everybody [inaud]
                             [       ]
567      P9:           oh I would like to talk about that
                       [           ]
568      P1:                [inaud]defining where we are
```

P9 quickly interjects, overlapping the chair's clarifying talk, that she "would like to talk about that" (line 567) as the chair concludes her turn. Both are speaking simultaneously from line 566 to 568, the brackets between lines meant to indicate this overlap. Although the chair relinquishes the floor, P9's turn (T20), begun in overlapping speech (line 567), indicates, as it unfolds, that she is unclear as to what the chair wants. This is evident in the sequence of false starts that make up her turn from 570 to 573 and publicly stated in line 574 of Extract 11.

Extract 11: P9's First Full Turn at Talk (T20; lines 569-574)

```
569      do you mind
570      because I've thought about it
571      cause you had said last night
572      that was one of the things
573      I think a (name of material) is
574      are you talking about name or what the book itself [inaud]
```

In line 574, P9 again requests clarification in her attempt to size up the situation. The chair responds, adding to her prior clarification with a brief statement that reintroduces the salient concerns of her opening turn, namely, the coordination of subsequent decisions around a shared set of criteria with each individual extended the opportunity to share their personal perspective. This is shown in Extract 12.

Extract 12: The Chair's Second Clarification in Response to P9 (T21; lines 575-578)

575 just what goes into what we're gonna do
576 in that final decision making
577 uh [p] basically that's so that everybody gets a chance t to hear
     what we're all talking about
578 n to see if we can't refine our ideas a little bit more

Missing from this clarification is any reference to the specific ideas that other participants had raised in sharing their thoughts. Again, it would seem, it is her perspective that dominates, albeit presented as if it represents the group's. Also, the chair's offer of clarification, both here and in her earlier attempt in T19 (Extract 10, lines 565-566 and 568), stands in marked contrast to what she offered to the group in the first turn of the meeting. Specifically, P9 is not admonished; she is not given instructions about how to proceed; and, she is not warned about selecting inappropriate materials as was the case for the nine members in attendance at the beginning of the meeting. Additionally, P9's lateness is not raised as an issue.

These contrasts suggest an attitude of collegiality and recognition toward P9 that differs in kind from the attitude the chair holds in relation to the other committee members. Her deference to, and focus on P9 in these turns is of interest given a quite notable shift past this point in the dynamics of the meeting as only one of the seven members who had previously spoken again claims a turn at talk after this point, and then only briefly (i.e., P6, T27). It might be suggested that these earlier participants, indeed, chose not to participate in response to the contrast in how the chair approached them as compared to P9. Given that she subsequently "forgets" the explicit request to speak again (T17) offers yet another experience of contrast for the group and especially P7 who quite clearly expressed that she wanted to participate further.

The chair could have invited prior speakers to give brief summaries of their comments to address P9's request for clarification. The chair could also have chosen not to select P9 and to instead let her find her own way into the discussion. The chair's apparent strategy to move toward collaboration and consensus expressed in her opening turn certainly seems to have shifted as is apparent by what she does, and what she doesn't do subsequently in the meeting. Her framework for how to proceed endures as a matter of authority. Although she may modify her framework in deference to the authority of another, namely P9, she gives no hint that the group as a whole will contribute to such modification.

CONCLUSION

This chapter examined *authority matters*, as a type of identity issue within the context of one 11-member committee meeting. Specifically, the chapter focused on the committee chair's participation, with her participation contextualized in relation to the participation of other members of the committee. As a dimension or manifestation of identity, authority matters may invoke considerations of how institutionalized authority (such as the designation of someone to lead a committee as in this case) is exhibited by a designated authority figure as well as the responses of others to this authority. This of course then invokes issues of governance.

Was the chair, for example, clear on her approach to governance? Do members of the committee respect the chair's approach to governance? How is this observed in their communication practices? Within a group decision-making context, how does the chair champion her own perspectives and those of others?

The manner in which matters of authority come to influence the directions of processes and types of outcomes has great relevance for the further understanding of organizational life. Attending to expressions of, and responses to authority reveals how pervasive manifestations of, and responses to authority are.

Although outcomes were not directly considered in this chapter, the analyses reported here suggest multiple local outcomes—outcomes that seem to shift the course of the meeting. These outcomes exhibited differing senses of appreciation of some members and not others. These are constitutive relational byproducts that at first glance seem irrelevant to the task at hand.

There is a second sense in which matters of authority represent issues of identity. This sense considers how someone in a position of authority reflects upon his or her obligations and relations to others. The focus on the chair in this discussion treated this as a central concern. Reflection— that is to say the deliberate mental engagement with how to approach, respond to, evaluate, and reconceptualize activities in the here and now of experience—was treated as it is reflected in the polysemic and often contradictory patterns and themes of communication conduct observed.

The analysis of the chair's participation in this setting suggests that orientations to authority are hardly matters of technical license or institutional privilege. Orientations to authority are enmeshed within participants' orientations to conceptualizations of self and other and the expectations, obligations, and responsibilities that hold between self and other.

REFERENCES

Cockett, L.S. (2000). *Self, other, and situation in collaborative contexts: A study of personhood in a group decision-making meeting.* Unpublished doctoral dissertation, Rutgers, The State University of New Jersey, New Brunswick.

Craig, R. (1985). Communication as a practical discipline. In B. Dervin, L. Grossberg, B.J. O'Keefe, & E. Wartella (Eds.), *Rethinking communication, Vol. 1: Paradigm issues* (pp. 97-122). Newbury Park, CA: Sage.

Craig, R.T., & Tracy, K. (1995). Grounded practical theory: The case of intellectual discussion. *Communication Theory, 5,* 248-272.

Deetz, S.A. (1994). Future of the discipline: The challenges, the research, and the social contribution. In S. A. Deetz (Ed.), *Communication yearbook 17* (pp. 565-600). Thousand Oaks, CA: Sage.

Duncan, S.D., & Fiske, D.W. (1977). *Face-to-face interaction: Research, methods, and theory.* Hillsdale, NJ: Erlbaum.

Goffman, E. (1967). *Interaction ritual: Essays on face-to-face behavior.* New York: Doubleday.

McQuown, N.A. (Ed.). (1971). *The natural history of an interview* (microfilm collection of Manuscripts on Cultural Anthropology, No. 95, series XV). Chicago: University of Chicago Press.

Mokros, H.B., & Deetz, S. (1996). What counts as real?: A constitutive view of communication and the disenfranchised in the context of health. In E.B. Ray (Ed.), *Communication and disenfranchisement: Social health issues and implications* (pp. 29-44). Mahwah, NJ: Erlbaum.

Newman, B.M., & Newman, P.R. (1987). The impact of high school on social development. *Adolescence, 22,* 525-534.

Stohl, C., & Schell, S.E. (1991). A communication-based model of small-group dysfunction. *Management Communication Quarterly, 5,* 90-110.

Viggiani, F.A. (1997). Democratic hierarchies in the workplace: Structural dilemmas and organizational action. *Economic and Industrial Democracy, 18,* 231-260.

10

Other Matters
The Achievement of Identity Through Otherness

Hartmut B. Mokros

Vin and Sly are salesmen at a wholesale produce market located in a large U.S. city. They work at one of the multiple businesses or "houses" that make up this market. These salesmen work on "the floor" of a house where sales are made from roughly 2 a.m. until 10 a.m. each day. Their house is one of the largest and most successful at the market according to its owner, employees, and customers. The owner is highly respected by employees and customers alike and this is true of the house in general. It is regarded as a fair and friendly place by buyers, many of whom spend considerable time visiting members of the house with long-term and quite intimate relationships common.

This house consists of three levels. The floor is the main level, with large storage coolers located in the levels above and below providing space for hundreds of pallets of crated or boxed produce. Overhead doors open the floor to front and back walkways that run the length of the entire building that the house shares with six others. The floor consists of a large open space with a large enclosed structure in the middle that, among other things, houses an elevator. This structure has two levels, with stairs going up to offices that have windows overlooking the floor or sales area. At floor level, this structure contains lavatories, a small "lounge," and an elevator entrance large enough to accommodate a forklift holding a pallet of produce. The lounge is more accurately a locker room, with always available coffee, where employees on the floor place personal belongings. This space is rarely used for socializing or conducting business. These activities occur on "the floor," the place where "the action is." The floor is the place where one is expected to be ("Jimmy here?" "He's on the floor somewhere. Have him paged and stop bothering me.") and is typically referenced when seeking someone out ("Is Vinny on the floor?").

Business peaks between roughly 3 a.m. to 7 a.m. each day. During these hours, Vin and Sly are mostly at their sales desk, one of a dozen located on the floor. Each desk represents a "department" that sells a specific line (e.g., assorted greens) or a single kind (e.g., tomatoes) of produce. Although Vin and Sal frequently wander elsewhere in the house, as do other salesmen, they conduct business, as we usually think of it, mostly around this desk. The sales desk represents for them a home base. Here they write up orders placed by the hundreds of buyers who each day either stop by while cruising through the market or check in by phone.

The sales desk abuts a 2-foot square structural support column on its east side. Vin is routinely positioned northeast when at the desk where he repeatedly examines his inventory ledger, which sits on an angled lectern facing him. In this ledger he records sales or "orders" that he and Sly make on any given day and wherein he maintains a running total of orders placed against the total counts of each type of produce that their department has available that day. Sly is positioned on the south side of the desk, facing Vin. Each has a phone next to him. Vin and Sly typically place their hand-sized sales pads, with carbon copies of customers' orders folded over the tops, on the desk when nearby. Otherwise, when they are elsewhere in the house they take them with them, because orders are also placed away from the desk. Extra sales pads are routinely atop the desk, along with cups of coffee. Both keep their "lunches" in drawers below the countertop. They eat lunch at roughly 7 a.m. each day as business is dying down.

Buyers, salesmen, and other workers—some driving forklifts or pushing hand trucks—are constantly moving along two paths that form a T-intersection at this sales desk. One path runs east–west immediately behind the desk with the wall of the office structure here defining its border. The other path runs north–south and is immediately to the west where it ends as it meets the east–west path. The path south leads toward the front walkway and loading docks immediately outside the house. Parallel to the desk, on the other side of this path, Sly constructs a terraced structure of crates and boxes with the top boxes opened and angled forward to display the types and quality of produce available in this department any given day. This display includes such vegetables as cabbage, carrots, celery, green onions, parsley, radishes, and various greens. Pallets of produce frame the display. Pallets of fruits and vegetables are everywhere on the floor of the house, surrounding each of the dozen departments with the particular items available there. These displays and pallets define the borders of the paths that maze the floor allowing buyers ease of access to all departments and a constant view of what is available.

Physically, their desk is nothing more than a roughly 4-foot square, waist-high cabinet with a flat laminated countertop. During business hours, this is not just a physical place but a "social oasis" where members of the house, members of the market, and members from the world at large meet to do the business of meaning-making that includes, of course, business as one usually thinks of it. Socializing is a significant aspect of activity at the desk. It is part of doing business and it is also a break from the routine functions of doing business. At any time, the selling of produce may be put on hold in order to catch up, hear a good story, or the like. Who one is in relationship to others, and how one's activities are meaningful, in a general sense, represents the bedrock within which work at the oasis, and house at large, is situated.

The Oasis as a Research Site[1]

The description just given is located in the past. It is based on a 6-month field study conducted during the spring and summer of 1980. This study sought to explore how the work of everyday interaction, the demands of social responsibility and accountability, relate to the conduct of doing work such as the buying and selling of produce. Methodologically, the study integrated the recording of videotapes within an ethnographic study of the market, and house in particular, as a community. In this way, the study sought to develop a systematic approach to research of social interaction, what Goffman (1953, 1983) called "the interaction order," within a meaningful real-world setting.

The field study was conducted in the context of an ongoing program of research of interaction structure and strategy developed by Duncan (e.g., Duncan & Fiske, 1977; Duncan, Fiske, Denny, Kanki, & Mokros, 1985; Mokros, 1984). This program of research evolved a systematic approach to the study of the interaction order, with particular focus on the coordination of activity in dyadic conversations between strangers through

---

[1]This chapter presents the first publication developed from these data. Three conference papers (Mokros, 1990a, 1990b, 1993) examined some of the data reported here.

the microanalysis of transcribed interaction. Application of this systematic approach to more complex real-world contexts was the key motive for conducting this field study. Ethnographic study embedded the development of videotapes for two reasons: to define a systematic approach to recording interaction in this context, and to contextualize these recorded interactions within the social and meaning systems that defined this community.

A tripod-mounted video camera recorded the activities at the social oasis for an hour each day at roughly the same time over 30 days altogether. Typically, the camera was located on a small landing roughly 8 feet above the floor and some 50 feet to the southwest of the oasis. The decision to record from this spot was based on technical considerations and led to the selection of Vin and Sly's sales desk as a focus for recording. Placement of the camera on the floor was ruled out because the ever-shifting arrangement of pallets on the floor made unobstructed views of any sales desk within even one recording session difficult and impossible over the course of multiple sessions. The raised positioning of the camera on this landing represented a practical solution to this problem with the sales desk manned by Vin and Sly selected as it was the only one that could be put in full view from this vantage point.

Before each recording session, a broadcast microphone was clipped to Vin's phone to capture talk at the desk. The camera's zoom lens was then adjusted to frame the desk and the immediately adjoining paths. Recording proceeded thereafter without interference, unless the view of the desk was obstructed for any extended time in the course of each session. Recordings were made for 30 minutes, the capacity of each reel of videotape, with a new reel then placed in the recorder. The total recording time of one hour each day (two reels) reflects the battery life of the then "state of the art" Sony Portable Video Recorder used to make these tapes. The general logic of recording activities at one desk, without interference, was influenced by the pioneering efforts of Bateson and Mead (1942) in their study of Balinese culture. The development of a systematic approach to recording activities in the field was also informed by the "focal animal sampling" technique in ethological study of primates (Altmann, 1974) and Barker's (1963) observational study of situated behavior.

The Achievement of Identity Through Otherness

Data from this field study orient the discussion of "other matters," the focus of this chapter, that considers the representation of, and emergent interactional relevance of identity as achieved through appeals to "otherness." Otherness refers to characteristics of another or group that provides a basis by which individuals, groups, and communities articulate a sense of who they are by referencing that which they are not. Specifically examined in this chapter are the qualities of self, group, and community identity as these are achieved in relationship to otherness, through the analysis of specific recorded happenings or events at the social oasis. These events are grounded in ethnographic description and interpretation of the social and cultural organization of this community.

The concern with identity in this chapter addresses the fundamental question "Who am I?" (Carbaugh, 1996) as this relates to one community's sense of identity as constituted through otherness. The relevance of the other for addressing the question "Who am I?" has guided scholarly inquiry of identity within a variety of traditions. Philosophical consideration of identity treats the very possibility of an experiencing self as inseparable from the experience of one's own sense of otherness (e.g., Ricoeur, 1992). The relationship between self and other has long represented a way to conceptualize the links between psychological reality and the perception of one's being, and social experience (e.g., Goffman, 1963; Laing, 1969; Mead, 1934) in the social sciences. Differentiation from and identification with the other represents an enduring framework for thinking about the emergence of self in many studies of infant development (e.g., Stern, 1985). Finally, recent postmodernist considerations position the identity of the "subject" within the context of knowledge production, the operation of power, and the semiotic basis of meaning as achieved through binary oppositions like "self–other." In this literature, identity is approached as a matter of difference, whereby what self is—be the focus personal, institutional, or categorical—is achieved in contrast to the other. Self is made visible through the illumination that otherness provides, through semiotic distinctions that in the case of gender, for example, come to mat(t)er through systematic worldly practices (e.g., Kristeva, 1981). These scholarly traditions support a focus on otherness for systematic inquiry of identity, albeit from differing perspectives.

The analyses presented in this chapter examine how otherness conditions the sense of community and self-identity among its members within the house studied. It approaches this issue by examining first, the idealized view members of this community express as they provide accounts about the qualities of life at the market. Specific social encounters or happenings at the oasis are considered next. Analyses of these happenings illustrate features of social interaction that reflect this idealized sense of communal identity. Finally, the chapter provides an in-depth look at how otherness functions as a resource within interaction through the analysis of a transcribed multiparty set of linked conversations among five individuals at the oasis. This last analysis demonstrates how the otherness of multiple nonpresent others is interactionally employed to ascribe blame for misconduct and to deflect a threat to individual relationships and group solidarity that results from these charges of wrongdoing.

Before specifically examining identity in relation to otherness through these examples, the chapter first considers background information about produce markets in general, and the physical and social make-up of the market and house where the oasis is situated.

THE OASIS IN CONTEXT

General Characteristics of Wholesale Produce Markets

Wholesale produce markets, like the one where Vin and Sly conduct business, receive rail, truck, and air shipments on consignment or through outright purchase from growers and shippers within the United States and abroad. Some houses specialize in specific commodities (e.g., bananas, potatoes and onions, tropical fruits), others offer a full range of fruits and vegetables available at any given time, with "Vin's house" being a token of this type. Sales activity peaks during night time and early morning hours across these markets. Retailers and wholesalers, whose buyers represent them at the market, make purchases from houses at these markets. Retailers include chain-store, single-operator farm stands, and stores of varying size in between. Wholesalers cater to end-user outlets such as grocery stores, institutions, and restaurants, and also redistribute to smaller wholesalers within the geographic region served by the market. Sometimes called terminal markets because they are receiving hubs for a large geographic region, not just the immediate metropolitan area, houses like Vin's daily draw customers from well over a 100-mile radius.

Salesmen at the market see customers and buyers in more varied terms. Some of the distinctions that Vin and Sly treat as meaningful are big order–little order, daily customer–occasional buyer, comparison shopper–over-the-phone purchaser, good friend–pain in the ass, real character–ordinary guy, must be covered–don't sell to him no matter what, and similar to me–other than me. Most buyers frequent the market and place orders only after comparing quality and price across multiple houses, although sight unseen phone sales are not uncommon particularly among chain-store buyers. Comparing price and quality during the course of visits protects the buyer from "being gouged." Larger buyers, especially, establish relationships with specific houses and salesmen to ensure that their customers' needs are covered at times of short supply. Although prices vary daily, predictability of supply is more important than cost. This encourages the establishment of firm social bonds (Scheff, 1990) between regular buyers and specific houses and sales-men. To protect against market volatility and potential difficulties that any sin-gle house's shipments may encounter, larger buyers establish stable relation-ships with several houses and salesmen and take care to distribute their orders across these multiple relationships.

The Physical Context of the House

The "house" occupies more than one third of the western end of a block-long warehouse building, with six other houses neighboring to the east. The market consists of four such warehouse structures. Each house occupies an area running the entire width (roughly 100 feet) of one of these rectangular structures. Bay doors at the front and rear open to concrete walkways that stretch the length of the building. Rail tracks along the rear of these build-ings hold refrigerated boxcars of produce. These are unloaded directly into customer's trucks. The tracks do not run along the rear walkway such that their content must first be loaded into trucks if the produce is to be stored in the house.

The front walkways, also called "the walk," "front," or simply "out-side" are raised to a height above the ground that allows the direct loading and unloading, by forklift and hand truck, of trucks "docked" at the walk-way. "The walk" also serves as a pathway for pedestrians who come to check out "the action" on their tour of the market. Stairways leading down to the ground are located at the four corners of each building and at several points along the front walkways. Cars park along these walkways wherever trucks are not backed in.

The front walk faces an identical building several hundred feet away. An east–west city street runs through the middle of the space between and meets north–south streets shortly past either end of the market. Further to the east, this street crosses two main north–south streets and leads within a mile to a "spaghetti bowl" of intersecting interstate highways. Immediately surrounding the market, particularly to the west and north, are tens of blocks of largely open space once lined with houses whose shards are mixed among the dirt and weeds. Few people live in this area and those who do are among the poorest in the city. Rundown houses dot this landscape along with make-shift shelters whose designs reflect the pronounced resourceful-ness of people lacking financial means whom we typically discuss as "home-less." On Sundays the area is abuzz with hundreds of thousands of people, mostly poor immigrants with English but one language among many that fill the air. These people are drawn each week by the hundreds of tables and displays offering every imaginable kind of stuff—cheap.

The Social Context of the House

The social make-up of the market divides most basically into members and visitors. Members include those who work in the market and those who come to do business at the market. Those who work at the house include the owner, salesmen, workers who unload and load produce, and day-time staff who handle paperwork. Those who come to the house include buyers (the customer's representative) and their truckers (who pick up each day's purchases); two police officers who regularly patrol this beat; a U.S. government agricultural agent who monitors and reports daily market conditions; and long-distance truckers who deliver shipments from various growing areas around the country.

The market allows public access as no gate or security check point restricts would-be visitors. Among visitors, curious "thrill-seekers," politicians, researchers, television crews, and troublemakers (by profession) are routinely witnessed at the market checking out the action, although typically no more than a few are likely to appear on any given day. "Neighbors" patrol the fringes scavenging spilled or discarded produce. Visitors are not discouraged from walking around and through houses with the exception of "neighbors" and suspected troublemakers who are kept at a distance, sometimes through physical force. As a rule, anonymity is impossible at the market (cf. Philipsen, 1976), for knowing who is who is critical to the conduct of business. Strangers are quickly noted and sized up by members who typically ask each other, in the visitor's presence, "Who is that guy?," or directly approach the visitor with "Need help?" or "Need something?" usually in a quite friendly manner.

Strong friendships are evident among members working in the house and among those who come to the house, especially between salesmen and buyers. Indeed, buyers and sellers are generally quite intimate in their greeting behaviors and commonly express genuine concern and interest about each other's lives. This makes sense because long-term buyers are very likely related to someone at the market, and, even if not, have in a real sense grown up (and old) together in the dark early morning that sets the market apart from the life of the city.

Familial relations are quite common within houses including Vin's house. Why? "They're the only ones stupid enough to get up at this hour" suggests one salesman as a group nearby offers enthusiastic support for his claim. Family ties are also evident over time, with most salesmen (and many workers) having worked alongside their fathers or uncles for some period in the past. Only one father and son sales team works in the house currently (i.e., 1980), an illustration of how this pattern is breaking down. Most salesmen's sons are, these days, likely to pursue other careers. For example, one of Vin's two sons is a surgeon and the other an accountant for a major corporation. His daughter does, however, work in the house as an employee among the clerical staff. Multiple cousins and nephews are also employed, and indeed "Vin is the boss' cousin," as Sly let me know the first time I visited with him. Nevertheless, the decrease in recruitment of family members is also reflected in the age of the members of the house, with salesmen typically in their 50s or older.

This aging of the workforce relates to a quite pronounced characteristic of the social scape of the market. Although considerable ethnic diversity is continuously evident at the market during business hours, the houses are systematically stratified by ethnicity as the family links just noted suggest. Membership within a house tends to display ethnic homogeneity, particularly among owners and salesmen. Most larger houses, and many others as well, are Italian American, with Greek, Jewish, and Latino houses making up the rest. Chinese, Danish, French, Korean, Portuguese, Russian, and Zulu houses, to suggest just some possibilities, are not represented. One prominent exception to within house homogeneity is the employment of African Americans who work across the various ethnically defined houses at the market. However, no house employs any of these individuals as salesmen (or as office staff at Vin's house). It is also rare to see an African-American worker driving a forklift. The tools of their trade, as well as most other workers, are the pallet jack, the two-wheeler or hand truck and, of course, their bodies.

The owner, most salesmen, and workers in the house are Italian Americans with roughly a dozen African Americans among the workers. Two Irish Americans work as salesmen at the entrance to the house, a department that offers green peppers, cucumbers, and eggplant. A Jewish salesman, partnered with an Italian American, runs the tomato department located on the other side of Sly's produce display.

Long-term buyers are also predominantly Italian American although buyers of more recent vintage, all small-scale buyers, include individuals of Asian, North African, and Latino descent. The ethnicity of these individuals is commonly a source of ridicule and insult, almost as habit, for many workers and some salesmen, even as they are in the process of writing up orders placed by these individuals. Ridicule and insult are hardly reserved for these individuals as such acts are not uncommonly expressed toward buyers who match the member's ethnicity, although mutuality of insult tends to be the rule on these occasions. Ethnic others, with the exception of a Puerto Rican duo, avoid responding in kind to such verbal assaults. This in part explains the lack of physical violence between house members and these individuals. When violence erupts it typically begins with vicious bouts of ridicule and insult and most commonly involves Italian-American workers and truckers picking up customer orders, with house members noting "bad blood between them" as an explanation for such conflicts.

Finally, the social membership of the market is clearly stratified by gender. There is no house where women work on the floor. The larger houses employ many women who work day-time hours handling purchase and billing records. At "the house," one woman arrives in the early morning hours and handles phone calls and pages members on the floor. Thus, although the floor is a man's world, this woman's voice is heard repeatedly over the loudspeaker through the course of the working hours each day. Occasionally, a female over-the-road trucker delivers a shipment to the market although this is rare. There are a handful of women customers, usually small buyers, who frequent the house, but only one female buyer—Mattie—makes daily appearances. In contrast, and maybe not unexpectedly, "the neighbors" at the fringes and "thrill-seeking" visitors are more likely women than men.

The adventure of two such "thrill-seekers" who visited the market, house, and oasis one morning is described next. This follows a look at some of Mattie's experiences at the oasis as examples of the relevance of otherness for understanding the unique qualities of identity in this community. The interactional experience of these women at the oasis is preceded by an ethnographically based account of the idealized sense of the community's identity as revealed by its members. This idealized sense of identity is notably defined through otherness—the otherness of female. Mattie's experiences and the visitors' adventures in the course of their interactions with members of the community illustrate the link between this idealized sense of identity and everyday practice at times when "the other," that underpins this idealized identity, is physically present in the house. The final analysis examines a different kind of appeal to otherness than is the case in these examples. Specifically, a case where nonpresent others are used to preserve group solidarity in the context of emergent troubles within a sequence of conversations at the oasis is examined.

IDENTITY THROUGH OTHERNESS IN CONTEXT

Otherness and the Idealized Sense of a Community's Identity

Members of the house commonly employ spatial terms. "House," "floor," and "outside" are prominent examples. In use, these spatial terms do not just point to physical locations. They also index situated expectations and, in the case of "place" and "house," ideals of community and membership. "Place," as in "this place" is especially interesting in that its use tends to occur in metapragmatic contexts, where talk is about the meaning of everyday practices. In such contexts, "place" references the interface between house and market as a symbolic space, with unique meaningful characteristics that sets it apart from other places in the social world. In referencing "place," particularly on such occasions when members reflect on the qualities of their work lives, they reveal an idealized sense of the community's identity. Through their talk about "place" they reveal what Carbaugh (1996) called "sociocultural radiants of identity."

Phrases like "This place is a zoo," "This is a crazy place," or "This place has some real characters" are expressed among members when discussing specific events that catch their attention. These phrases popped up repeatedly in my initial visits with individual members, and were returned to in subsequent encounters when, upon witnessing some seemingly bizarre event, someone might say to me: "What did I tell you about the characters in this place? Wasn't I right?" The members of the house are not unique in their characterization of the market as "a crazy place," for as Carbaugh (1994) noted, this type of view is widely expressed about work life across a broad range of organizations. This would suggest a general tendency for members across organizations to think of their organizational culture as unique—in the sense of uniquely dysfunctional.

Calling this place a crazy, zoolike habitat is related to the stress of their working hours, frenetic pace, unpredictability, and common social tensions. "They're all crazy here. You've got to be crazy to get up at two every day and do this" states a salesman. A buyer passing by adds, "The hours are sure to head toward a divorce." It would, however, be in error to see these expressions as indicating that members viewed the house as dysfunctional. To the contrary, it is precisely the sense that this is a zoo, a crazy place with some real characters, that excited these men about their world of work, that made coming to work each day some time after midnight rewarding. And whereas the market may be viewed as a topsy-turvy, always active world it is also a place of enormous redundancy. Although specifics may change, and each new day brings novel problems to solve, the roles and tasks that individuals take on are fundamentally simple, practical routines: move produce in and move it out, and in the process make sure to do so at a profit. Most of the men I got to know had been working at the market, performing roughly the same functions for more than 30 years. In this light, the conditions and activities that enable a view of craziness serve as an antidote to the mundane aspects of the work they do day in and day out (cf. Handelman, 1975; Roy, 1959/1960).

Additionally, these characterizations of "place" are not merely descriptive statements about activities and lifestyle that create stress, give meaning, or serve as antidotes to the sameness of existence. For these characterizations of "place" position individual and community identity through contrast with otherness—that which is not this place.

House, Not Home. This sense of place is particularly apparent in how members contrasted "house" with "home," in describing their lives and sense of being more generally. They made quite clear that "a house is not a home," with this opposition engaging a whole hierarchy of significations within and through which they understood themselves to be selves of a specific kind. House is a place of work, home is a place of rest. House is where the action is, home is a place of order and civility. House is a crazy place, home is a place of sanity. House is a place of uncertainty and unpredictability, home is just the opposite. Of considerable interest is how they understood themselves through distinctions in communication practices related to the opposition of house and home. Practical jokes, nonverbal greeting behavior (e.g., "goosing"), and especially the use of swearing are member practices at the house, but certainly not practices carried out at home (as idealized; cf. Philipsen, 1975). Swearing was constant. As one salesman put it, he spoke two languages, one at work and the other at home with the key distinction being that one did not swear at home but did at work. Another salesman offered: "You can call a guy a mother fucker in here and not worry. You can't do that on the street [in the world outside] or at home." Thus, for many, swearing came with the territory, with activity in the house, although Vin and Sly, for example, tended not to swear.

Finally, as has been implied, the house was a place of men, home a place of women. Within this context it is of interest to consider how this idealized sense of community revealed itself, played itself out as it were, when house and home confronted each other through the presence of women in the house, through the presence of "the other."

In the Presence of "The Other"

Mattie Does House Talk. As noted earlier, no women work on the floor and very few women enter the house as buyers. Among them, Mattie is the only one who comes to the market daily. She regularly hangs out with Vin and Sly, tells them what's going on and they very much welcome her company. Mattie always seems to enjoy hanging out and being one of the guys. She freely shares with them what many male buyers also do, namely accounts of how things are going at home. Vin and Sly especially look forward to updates on her kids' softball season. Sly is more active in this respect and regularly asks about the kids and appears prideful when she reports their successes.

However, on one occasion Sly became quite distressed at what Mattie had to say. On this day she appeared upset and Sly picked up on this and said, "Mattie Mae what's with you today?" He and Vin both listened attentively, as did a male buyer present before she arrived, as she expressed her frustrations with trying to manage the needs of her kids and her job. She was getting worn down she confided. In the course of her story, she swore, although hardly with the gusto and bravado typical of the men. "Well, I'll see you tomorrow" she said rather dejectedly as she left the oasis.

Sly turned to watch her moving toward the front walk for a few moments and then turned back, lowered his upper torso almost across the desk, and with a quiet and concerned voice said: "She swore. Did you hear that? She swore." She became the focus of an extended discussion involving all three men. Each expressed disapproval that she swore, and voiced additional concern for Mattie's children, the difficulties that her divided roles presented for her, in the context of their general perspectives on family, women, and home. "She shouldn't be working" was clearly their conclusion, not because they didn't enjoy her presence, but because she was unable to adequately address the responsibilities of her place in the world: home. Mattie's visits at the oasis were recorded on at least 10 of the 30 days tapes were made. This was the only time I am aware of that Vin or Sly raised questions about Mattie's presence at the market. Her "doing house talk," namely swearing, apparently stimulated this open review of Mattie and brought to the fore the foundational, if not sacred sense of meaning that the distinction between house and home, men and women held for Sly in particular.

Touching Matters for Mattie. A few days after Mattie "talked like a man," Mac the cop appeared and passed behind her as she was standing next to Vin at the desk. As Mac approached, he took out his nightstick and feigned tapping Mattie's behind several times as he passed her. Mattie was oblivious to what was happening as she and several other buyers were trying to place orders with Vin. Mac moved next to her at the desk and slapped down his withdrawn nightstick and ticket pad in front of her. Mac is a very large man who patrols this beat with a partner each day. He enjoys picking on Sly, who, if forewarned that Mac has entered the house, as he was this day, slips away quickly. Mac likes to inflict pain.

Mac moved away from Mattie behind a small-time male buyer and began massaging the buyer's neck. This attracted others to the oasis who chatted and giggled as they watched, seemingly in the know that Mac would soon go too far. He did, causing the buyer to yell and, through mild struggle, break away. Mac then moved in back of Vin and began to massage him. As Vin asked Mac to stop, Mattie uttered "death of a salesman" and this aroused some laughter. A male buyer assumed the spot next to Mattie, and as she looked at him he reached out and pinched (with a twist) her cheek. She had unsuccessfully tried to pull away before he touched her, and subsequently said nothing as if she was used to this (which she was). By this point, Mac had gone too far yet again. Vin screamed "Stop it," clearly angered, and Mac let go immediately. The owner came over just as Mac was letting go, as Vin then said: "Get this guy off me boss." Mac almost immediately laid his hands on the owner. The owner, much more quickly than the other two victims, yelled "Stop it, ow." Again Mac complied once his complaint was uttered. As the owner yelled, the crowd, including Mattie, dispersed. The owner appeared to head off but returned in Mac's direction and said to him, with laughter, "I guess we got rid of her." Mac also laughed as the owner, without stopping and still laughing, headed for the stairs to his office.

Touch is quite common among the men, and Mattie is also touched albeit differently. The men are gentler with her but, as in the two examples on this occasion, had a tendency to either sexualize through pseudo-touch, always performed out of Mattie's view, or to perform infantalizing gestures, the buyer's cheek pinch an example of this. The events surrounding Mac's visit illustrate something else. Mattie is integrated into the happenings around the oasis. She makes efforts to be one of the guys ("death of a salesman") and is appreciated for contributing a sense of humor. However, she is always noted in distinct ways. In this example, the owner after all does not reference anyone other than Mattie, and in what he says, it is fair to assume that he wishes she was elsewhere: at home not in the house.

Female Visitors and the Mouse in the House. The approach of unfamiliar women visitors (typically observed in pairs) creates a stir along the walk and requires that Vin be notified ("go tell Vin"). Indeed, the excitement on the walk is not so much about these women's presence as it is of possibly witnessing Vin, a noted and admired master prankster, perform his magic.

Once notified that female visitors are nearby, Vin prepares himself. He scans the floor by moving his head quickly from side to side, presumably to determine if the women are already approaching. He then reaches into his drawer, withdraws a rubber mouse and places it in his hand or into the large pocket of the gray smock that he and most salesmen wear while on the floor. Multiple men engage and greet these women and encourage them to enter the house and meet some people who will be glad to show them around. The men then escort the pair straightaway to the oasis. Men from outside and within the house follow, as Vin waits down the aisle. By the time this party reaches the oasis many others within the house have abandoned their activities so that once the women arrive, a group of 40 to 50 men has gathered in the vicinity. Vin's preparations and the gathering congregation of soon to be onlookers happens quickly, within the time it takes to casually walk 50 to 75 feet, although on this occasion the older of the two women stops the entourage momentarily so that she can take a picture of one of the produce displays en route. The younger woman bears a somewhat anxious grin as she appears to have noted the large flow of men that follow and the building congregation awaiting them on the path ahead.

The community's ability to quickly transmit information that something of interest is about to happen or has occurred is itself quite remarkable. That members additionally seem to understand what will happen next, and feel the desire to be part of the scene suggests its importance to their working world. Even the owner has descended the stairs of the office and is approaching the oasis. Vin has moved from his normal position facing the ledger to the outside corner of the desk.

The entourage arrives and all stop with the exception of the older woman who with camera in hand takes a picture of Sly's display and then moves toward Vin as he greets her saying, "Beautiful morning. Let me show you something." With the younger woman a few steps behind her, she approaches the desk and Vin immediately deposits the rubber mouse on the desk in front of her. She now seems quite curious as to what exactly is going on, as she scans the gathered crowd, and either does not notice the mouse or chooses to ignore it. The younger woman "appears to get it" as Vin would like. She cups her hands over her mouth, this in consort with Vin's response to the older woman's "failure to get it."

Vin scrunches his shoulders as he moves his hands together up along the side of his face and shrieks in high pitched voice, "Eek, Eek," an apparent invitation for mimicry, the response that, in other words, the older woman ought to have already produced. He ends this display of fright by picking up the mouse and dangling it in front of the woman's face by its tail and again shrieks, thrusts it forward a couple of times and now she gets it. The woman shrieks and raises her hands to her face in similar manner to the younger woman's response a moment earlier. Vin returns the mouse to the desk, pokes it, and again acts as if frightened. The older woman does not mirror Vin's performance. Instead, she touches the mouse and, as she does, he again shrieks. Not in the least frightened, she continues to probe the mouse with a look of curiosity that a butterfly collector might have coming upon an interesting and unexpected specimen. Vin laughs loudly as he slaps his legs, and all around him laughter and talk fill the air. The women too are smiling and Vin shakes both their hands, taking his hat off as he does, says something to the older woman and both laugh briefly.

The owner now comes over and shakes each visitor's hand, and Vin's hand too accompanied by a slap on the back. The older woman asks Vin and the owner to stand together. Vin puts his hat back on, as these two place their arms around each other's shoulders and pose as the woman takes the shot. She then motions to Sly, and positions him with Vin in front of the produce display. They pose together with their faces showing a sense of pride and joy. Vin and Sly now shake hands with both women and both laugh, leaning their heads back as they do so, and are suddenly back at their desk with big smiles on their faces. The congregation of members has largely dispersed already as the owner now talks to the women and escorts them through the house, pointing to various things while laughing repeatedly along the way, as he leads them out of the house and waves good bye. Sly is still giggling at the desk although looking down and writing something in his order book as Vin has already put the mouse in storage again, and is busily checking his ledger. This all took place within no more than 5 minutes from the time the women were first noticed on the walk.

I witnessed this "ritual without a name," the mouse game as it were, four times with two of these recorded on videotape and was told about other performances on multiple occasions. Two salesmen asked me several days before I met Vin if I had seen his mouse. They brought this up in the context of discussing the enjoyable craziness of this place. At the time, I had no sense what they meant, other than that he performed some kind of practical joke with women that involved a rubber mouse. Vin was invariably mentioned as one of the "real characters" at this place. He did things that were fun and funny, a guy that everyone seemed to like. He could be counted on, and in many ways was counted on to make special things happen. This in part explains why the oasis attracted as many travelers as it did. Interesting things happened there—from the perspective of members.

I only observed Vin "bring out his mouse" with women visitors and it was always discussed with me as performed in the context of women. However, there was at least one occasion where a group of children were the target. Mac the cop one day brought in a stack of pictures of a group of children taken at the oasis days earlier. He volunteered time, when off duty, to work with a group of mentally disadvantaged youngsters and had brought these youngsters to the market, introduced them to Vin, and Vin had presented the mouse. While looking through the pictures, Sly, Vin, and Mac recollected how everyone had such a wonderful time. Mac's caring and affiliative attitude on this occasion contradicts profoundly with the sadism observed but a few days earlier. The juxtaposition of these two sides of Mac suggest how one's own otherness relates to one's sense of self-identity, namely its quite contradictory, dialectic tendencies.

Otherness as an Interactional Resource

The examples in the prior section examined otherness and its relationship to the representation of the identity of a community and its members. This is one focus for discussing identity suggested by the title "other matters." The second is contextual relevance, specifically how otherness is employed to resolve practical problems of identity within interaction. Appeals to otherness in the context of troubles that arise within a series of chained conversations over the course of roughly 3 minutes are examined to discuss this issue. These conversations include five individuals, with the appeal to nonpresent others the specific analytic interest. A transcript of these chained or linked conversations guides the discussion. The transcript is divided into a series of extracts that mark salient junctures or shifts as events unfold. These extracts display talk roughly as it was spoken, with only minimal paralinguistic notation added. Punctuation is used to identify discrete units of speech production marked by brief breaks or pauses. Words placed in CAPS are prominently stressed or overloud in relation to the ongoing pattern of the individual's talk. Material in parentheses identifies stretches of inaudible talk (inaud), best guesses as to the content of talk, and stand-alone paralinguistic activities (e.g., laughter, notable pauses). Brackets contain relevant contextual information, including arrivals, departures, and noteworthy nonverbal adjustments or bodily reorientation. Stretches of overlapping talk are also identified in brackets. Selected segments of talk are referred to by line numbers (e.g., L1 identifies the first line in Extract 1) with portions of the transcribed material that figure prominently in the discussion underlined.

Extract 1, Lines 1-5

1	Ben:	spinach Vin? [Ben reports on market activity for the U.S. government.]
2	Vin:	no. no spinach of any kind. [Vin is looking at and writing in his ledger as he has throughout the time Ben has posed questions to him.]
3		[Sal, a buyer, walking by, stops, and approaches the desk as Sly begins talking on the phone, his talk overlapping with L4/5.]
4	Ben:	okay. (several second pause) I guess that's it. thanks Vin. [Ben departs.]
5	Vin:	okay buddy. [Sal moves to Ben's spot at the desk.]

Extract 1 begins with Ben, Vin, and Sly at the desk. Ben stopped by a few minutes before to obtain information from Vin on items available, their growing area, and price so that he can prepare his market report for that day. Vin reports he has no spinach (L2) in response to Ben's last question (L1). As he leaves, Sal, a daily buyer, moves to the spot Ben has just vacated (L5). Business is dying down and Vin has been preoccupied, as he is at this time each day, figuring out what has and has not been sold, while Sly places a phone call to attract a taker for some "merchandise" deserving a home. (His talk is not represented here or at the other times he speaks, at each point only briefly, before hanging up in L26.) Sal placed an order with Vin more than an hour before and appears to be "heading out" when he suddenly stops (L3) and moves to the desk. Why he stops is unclear at this point, but second visits are hardly unusual once buyers have taken care of their daily needs.

The interactional activities presented in Extract 1 are typical of how the business part of business at the oasis is conducted, even though, in this case, the "customer" (Ben) only seeks information. Talk is brief and to the point when making a sale and often combined with other activities involved in moving produce in and out of the house (e.g., balancing the daily ledger). At moments like this, role performance defines activities (and identities) at the desk. Nevertheless, even when preoccupied with instrumental tasks, Vin and Sly are consistently courteous and "straight" with customers. There are no irrelevant questions, for both understand their success as salesmen is based on the relationships they develop with their customers, and both approach this not as a strategy for success but as a more fundamental appreciation of how "others" engender the quality of their lives. In this light, Vin made time for Ben and will now make time for Sal. For who knows, maybe Sal has a good story to tell, one that will make him laugh.

Extract 2, Lines 6-14

6	Sal:	you know what spinach is pretty good. I hear yesterday Vin? was out of. New York. Canada. from the (top corner) I got some. clipped spinach. th. really was nice.
7	Vin:	BUSHELS? [Sly overlaps here and into L8 as he talks on the phone.]
8	Sal:	bushel boxes. cardboard boxes.
9	Vin:	oh loose.
10	Sal:	yeah. seven and a half I paid him.
11	Vin:	not bad if it was good.
12	Sal:	I bagged up. I got twenty pounds out of a bag.
13		[Ned, one of the workers in the house, parks and gets off his pallet-loaded forklift. Paper bag in hand, he hurries over and positions himself at the desk between Sal and Vin while Sal is speaking in L12.] .
14		[Sal looks up at Ned and appears angry as he is forced to slide over.]

The space and time Vin makes available to others is repaid through mutual concern and respect as Sal demonstrates as he provides Vin information about spinach (L6). Sal, thereby, makes sensible why he suddenly stopped on the path to elsewhere—he overheard Ben and Vin's brief question/response sequence (L1/L2) while passing by. Vin is immediately interested as he looks at Sal, removing his gaze from the ledger where it has been fixed for quite some time. Although appreciative of the information, Vin reveals no particular urgency to "score" some spinach, at least not the kind that Sal describes (L9). Although the talk represented in this extract is about business, that it happened at all says much more about Sal's commitment to his relationship with Vin. Voluntary practices, such as Sal performs here, encourage mutual trust and respect between self and other and serve to secure their social bond.

Sal is also respectful of Ben, waiting until he has concluded with Vin before approaching the desk. This is not the case with Ned, a worker in the house, who barges between Sal and Vin as Sal is still "speaking spinach" (L12/13). Sal's nonverbal response makes apparent his displeasure at being forced to slide over (L14). As was the case for Sal, Ned also interrupts his travels, as his hurrying to the desk and pallet-containing forklift suggest, but he interrupts business at the oasis as well and appears oblivious to the disrespect his actions produce. Identity has, we might say, become interactionally relevant at this moment through Ned's hurried demeanor and lack of deference (Goffman, 1967).

Extract 3, Lines 15-18

15	Vin:	well it's about time NED. long time. [Spoken as Ned takes a tomato from his paper bag and hands it to Vin, as Vin removes a paper bag from the drawer of his desk—his lunch.]
16	Ned:	I. [overlaps with Vin's "long" in L15.]
17	Ned:	I don't. I'm not OUTSIDE no more Vin.
18	Vin:	well you've GOTTA BE. if you'd walk in the FRONT there once in a while.

Life at the oasis becomes testy quickly following Ned's appearance. He has upset Sal, and Vin immediately reveals that he also is upset with him, but for different reasons. Indeed, Ned's hurried approach and disregard likely relate to the expectation that Vin will indeed be upset with his tardiness (L15). Ned's attempt to account for and excuse this (L17) is treated by Vin as unacceptable (L18). This interchange is quite distinct from Vin's two previous engagements with Ben and Sal. Vin treats Ned as a subordinate, in a much more condescending manner than might be expected based on organizational position alone. And his reproaches (L15,18) certainly contradict his demeanor with others generally.

What exactly is the problem that explains Vin's ire? Vin is hungry! As noted at the beginning of the chapter, he eats "lunch" around 7 each morning and it is now nearly 30 minutes later than this. Vin enjoys a tomato with his lunch and Ned routinely supplies these and other items Vin might desire. Ned does this for several other salesmen also, at least some of whom have not yet received their tomatoes this morning as his bag is not yet empty.

Vin's ire certainly seems excessive especially because he is but 15 feet away from the tomato department which is located on the other side of Sly's produce display. It would seem reasonable and easier for Vin to just go get a tomato from the department "next door."

Extract 4, Lines 19-25

19	Ned:	I'm not OUTSIDE no more. you know. I can't help it. I need some tomatoes. for cryen (inaud). <u>I had to STEAL</u>. <u>they</u> won't even give YA a tomato.
20	Vin:	<u>they</u> won't?
21	Ned:	HELL NO. the mother fuckers. I'm telling you <u>they're</u> a FUCKING BUNCH of cocksuckers over there (inaud). GET THE FUCK OUT OF HERE.
22	Vin:	they're dumpen em. why can't they give em to you?
23	Ned:	hu?
24	Vin:	I sez they're dumpen em. why can't they give you half a dozen? (chuckles)
25	Ned:	fucken (inaud). three little fucken tomatoes I need. <u>gotta wait til their backs' turned and steal three tomatoes</u>. isn't that SOMETHEN? fucken department. the <u>WORST OF EVERYBODY</u>. you ask anybody in this place where they'll give you anything you want.

Ned again repeats his reason for being late (L19), "I'm not outside no more," which, when accepted as the reality of his situation, makes Vin's latest rebuke and suggested solution (L18) out of touch with Ned's current work assignment. However, rather than pushing this point further and noting that he risks getting into trouble with "the boss" should he heed Vin's suggestion, Ned instead reshapes his defense (L19). In what he now says, he commits a rather strategic error in judgment that raises quite profoundly the extent that identity achieves relevance within the subsequent moments of this interaction. The reason for his tardiness is not so much that he isn't "outside no more," but that the tomato department will not give him tomatoes, *gratis*. "I had to steal," he confides, not a smart thing to say in front of a customer, particularly one already bothered by how Ned has treated him but a few moments ago. It is not so much that Ned admits to theft that marks the increasing relevance of identity at the oasis, although this too will soon become an issue. It is instead how Ned positions blame for his inability to satisfy Vin's need. "They," namely the tomato salesmen, are to blame. "They" are manifest as scapegoats. In other words, nonpresent others are responsible for Vin's frustration and the infelicity that has momentarily colored his relationship with Vin. Ned's claim, that he had to steal, is not raised in Vin's subsequent response (L20) as he instead acts surprised about the collegiality "they" (the tomato salesmen) lack.

To fully appreciate the complexity beginning to unfold requires that one reconsider Vin's early suggestion that Ned "walk in the front" and also his resistance to personally ask for a tomato from the salesmen located within shouting distance of the oasis. Vin's proposal to "walk in the front" is an indirect way of saying to Ned that he should "take" tomatoes from boxes about to be loaded onto customers' trucks. That is after all what is located "outside"—customer orders awaiting pickup. And this, of course, is a proposal that Ned steal from customers, one of whom is standing at the desk at this very moment. Why go outside to do this? Because Vin knows the tomato salesmen will not give tomatoes to Ned and he personally has nothing to do with them, nor they with him.

Vin's two subsequent turns (L22, 24) that follow his surprise (L20) on learning that the tomato salesmen won't give Ned tomatoes are ironic in this light. He begins each with an observation, a statement of fact. "They" are dumping tomatoes (because of oversupply). He follows this with a question, namely why in this context they won't give Ned any tomatoes. Ned responds to the first of these turns with puzzlement ("hu?" L23) and seems not to respond to the second at all. This is quite likely not "a failure to communicate," but a manipulation of the situation on Vin's part. He and Ned both know "they" would dump every single tomato they had before giving one to either of them or anyone else in the house. This suggests that these two turns (L22, 24) are intended to function quite differently than would appear on the surface. These turns subtly disengage Vin from the crime confessed to by Ned. Through his talk (L20, 22, 24) Vin differentiates himself from Ned's thieving even though he supported and encouraged theft, albeit not explicitly, as the solution to his needs. Vin's approach does not just function to differentiate himself from Ned (and theft). Through these turns he backs away from challenging Ned through the resource "they" offers, and thereby defuses the tensions his earlier expressed ire might create within their relationship. And in drawing on "they" as a resource he furthers the constitution of a scapegoat, a nonpresent other as culpable for misconduct.

There are of course alternative interpretations of his talk (as is true of the discussion of the talk and activities at the oasis throughout this chapter). Nevertheless, it is a quite plausible interpretation given the context of Sal's presence. And it is a plausible interpretation given the general contempt that Vin and everyone in the house have for the tomato salesmen, especially "the other" tomato salesman, the head of the department and lone Jewish salesman in the house. He never comes to the oasis to visit or watch the action. He is obnoxious with others, including his partner, and especially vicious in how he treats small buyers, particularly recent immigrants. He doesn't wear smocks like the other salesmen. He is different—an easy target for scapegoating. And this is what Ned notes in his two scalding characterizations of the tomato department (L21, 23). "They" are different from everybody else in the house he argues (L23), and this is why he had to steal. Others, "they'll give you anything you want," says Ned to end L23. "They" are not other but "otherness" it seems, totally distinct from members of the community. If there is a problem here, it is "they."

No matter how accurate Ned's ranting about the tomato department might be, he has, nonetheless, constituted himself as a thief, repeating his confession in L23 ("gotta wait til their backs turned and steal three tomatoes"). His ranting, in context, is easily interpreted (from Sal's perspective) as an effort to defend himself in the face of Vin's ire. Ned was not wise to introduce, and then repeat again (L25), that he stole. However, he further compounds the potential for trouble (L25) as he adds that other members of the house will "give you anything you want" (from boxes ultimately delivered to customers as Sal well knows). What he adds furthers the constitution of "they," the tomato department, as scapegoats by noting their difference from everyone else. Yet, he now exposes to view, for Sal the buyer, not an isolated incident but an institutionalized practice within the house.

Extract 5, Lines 26-35

26		[Sly speaks briefly and concludes his phone call as Vin begins eating while eyeing his ledger, and Ned turns to leave, paper bag in hand. Ned stops as Sal begins to speak (L27) and breaks the momentary silence.]
27	Sal:	you know what's happened over there. and I've complained about it a lot of times. somebody will buy a pallet of tomatoes. and you ge. you find a box that's HALF FULL. (inaud). REALLY. I tell you. you. you can NOT. and IF I WERE in. if I was this place. I would not break ONE PACKAGE. you go by Angelo's. somebody lifts a lid he throws em OUT.
28	Vin:	no kidding.
29	Sal:	you wanna buy it. YOU BUY IT.

30	Sly:	for cash.
31	Sal:	when the CUSTOMER gets that package its gotta be in good shape.
32	Sly:	you know when a customer
33	Sal:	I tell ya (overlaps Sly's utterance)
34	Sal:	this is the ONLY PLACE that I find. PILFERAGE. in my merchandise. that's no SHIT. and I TELL YA. people won't like it Ned. [Sal turns and looks directly at Ned as he says "people."]
35	Ned:	oh sure. I (know that).

A momentary quiet settles at the desk as Sly concludes his phone call and Vin begins to eat while studying his ledger. Ned at this point, seemingly convinced that he has reestablished "face" (Goffman, 1967), turns and begins to move toward his forklift. Ned aborts this trajectory as Sal, who has not been heard from since Ned's arrival, rejoins the conversation. Immediately, Sal makes quite clear that he has a much different take on the problem at hand (L27). Neither Ned's tardiness, nor the lack of cooperation that the tomato department offers are at issue for him. Quite to the contrary, he challenges the very conduct being discussed as it affects him and other customers. From Sal's perspective Ned is not stealing from the tomato department but from customers who, like him, discover tomatoes missing from the orders they purchase. Indeed, this is something he's "complained about a lot of times."

Of interest is how Sal positions his "challenge" to this "incident" (Goffman, 1967, pp. 19-20). He does not initially challenge Ned's conduct, and he does not approach the problem of shortage in merchandise as characteristic of other departments in the house. It is instead a problem "over there." He, thereby, engages the appeal to otherness ("they") introduced by Ned and picked up by Vin in Extract 4 as the source of the problem, but only superficially. He, after all identifies the site of a problem, not the source of the problem—"over there." Ned may read Sal's initial statement in L27 as vindicating him, but is quickly made aware that the complexity of the situation is about to increase (and that he should probably have continued on his way when he turned to leave a moment ago). Sal is, and has been in the past, the victim, and this is not acceptable according to his account (L27). He aborts what would appear to be a direct challenge ("I tell you. you can not."), and shifts to the realm of the hypothetical, of how he would approach this situation ("If I was this place") and specifies "his rules of conduct for the house" in two subsequent turns (L29, 31). Sly, endorses the first (L30) and follows the second with a question (L32) that Sal interrupts, not yet finished with what he has to say in reaction to what he has witnessed. By L34, he drops the hypothetical approach and shifts to direct challenge. This first implicates the house in general, and concludes by focusing on Ned's culpability: "people won't like it Ned."

What began as a problem "over there" is now a problem that differentiates the house from others at the market. And yet Sal qualifies this in conclusion by implicating only Ned's conduct, and does so in a manner that reduces his culpability as Ned's accuser. For as he says when he "fingers" Ned, it is "people" who "won't like it." Here then is a quite different kind of appeal to nonpresent others, generalized others as judging the situation, that in a sense protect Sal from being perceived as the accuser. Sal never implicates Vin who is, after all, the motivator of the crime, whether because of Vin's approach to Ned's revelation (L20, 22, 24) or simply because he needs Vin for supplies on a daily basis. Ned is the scapegoat—through self-identification.

Sal finds himself with a rather profound dilemma. How might he express his anger and the threat he perceives in the wrong doing of these significant others? For to confront significant others has implications for his relationship with them and thereby the possibilities of a different kind of threat to him—alienation from these individuals. This is a dilemma for Ned and Vin as well. Each of them perceives that he has been the target of wrong doing. The sheer complexity of this quite ordinary situation is no doubt faced by individuals on an everyday basis. One of the ways individuals bypass threats to social solidarity and yet get their point across in the context of being wronged is revealed in the further development of Sal's talk, as shown in Extract 6.

Extract 6, Lines 36-42

36   Sal: I mean. if you guys want tomatoes you could get a. a three four. [Three four refers to a size of tomato defined by its fit within a standard shipping box, namely three rows of four per layer.]

37   Vin: BREAK A BOX. break a box.

38   Sal: AND SPLIT IT UP. that's all there is to it. if I catch somebody in the store doing that. I'd. you know what happened the other day. this JEW comes in. he makes. uh. CHEESECAKES. and I had bout forty cases of Driscoll berries. and I sez (inaud). go (try) to pick out a case of strawberries. I went in the cooler about fifteen minutes later. THIS JEW was going through ten cases of berries. MY BROTHER. everybody got (inaud). PICKED THAT JEW UP and threw him against the wall. I was gonna KILL HIM. you know I got a temper. (inaud). I go WILD. (he) turned white and ran out of that store like a deer. and I ha. I haven't seen him since.

39   (Vin laughs.)

40   Sal: I. I was gonna KILL the son of a bitch.

41   [Ned closes his paperbag and <u>quickly walks to his forklift</u>]

42   Sal: fucken JEW. <u>he'uz trying to take advantage of me</u>. NO WAY. [Throughout the time he says this, <u>Sal turns and follows Ned with his eyes, grabs his pants at the belt-line and pulls them up</u>, then reorients toward Vin.]

Sal moves away from accusation (L36) and again offers a solution he introduced earlier (L29) to address the practical problems he, Ned, and Vin confront with respect to tomatoes and merchandise generally. This is a solution that Vin whole-heartedly endorses (L37) before Sal has even completed stating it. Sal finishes his thought (L38) and now the talk moves in another direction. His offer of a solution appears to be an effort to diffuse the situation and reestablish solidarity. Yet, Sal has apparently not resolved his anger over what he witnessed and the threat this represents to him. Rather than focusing on the accusation of those present he begins to position these events within a hypothetical situation, by suggesting what he would do if he caught someone stealing ("doing that") at his business.

However, he also aborts this hypothetical approach and instead opts to relate a recent experience to make his point. Sal tells a brief story that identifies a nonpresent other, a Jewish customer who makes cheesecakes, as a wrong doer and relates in his story how he handled this. He tells everyone that he was mad enough to kill the customer simply because the customer had hand selected a case of strawberries from among 40 cases in Sal's cooler. He equates the actions of this customer with Ned's theft and indeed equates Ned with the customer. As he repeats again that he was mad enough to kill the customer (L40), Ned finally exits and quickly returns to his forklift. Sal continues to speak, again referencing the customer in derogatory terms, and again asserts his clear intolerance for anyone "trying to take advantage" of him, with the stealing of his merchandise (before he ever receives it) certainly of this ilk (L42). His talk is not directed toward the desk but toward Ned. Sal tracks Ned with his eyes and as he finishes speaking, pulls up and adjusts his pants while still facing Ned. This gesture certainly does not seem to be just about adjusting his shorts. He has succeeded in making his point, by identifying and reprimanding the villain, and has done so in a manner that made Vin laugh (L39). And yet, he has no doubt profoundly humiliated Ned, albeit indirectly, through the telling of his story with the timing of Ned's exit likely not just about getting back to work.

In protecting his self (interest) Sal moves to also protect his relationship with Vin. He does so through the appeal to a scapegoat, a nonpresent other, and a member of one group that has been rather profoundly exploited as a scapegoat for the sake of maintaining group solidarity within the Western tradition. His multiple articulations of "Jew" are in each case loaded with signification. He has thus also reproduced a rather historically pernicious practice—scapegoating—that Frazier (1949) noted to be a remarkably common practice pan-culturally, one that involves the sacrifice of innocent individuals "to effect a total clearance of all the ills that have been infesting a people" (p. 575). The appeal to a scapegoat offers a way of cleansing the disharmony through a sacrifice of otherness. A nonpresent other is positioned as blame-worthy for the offense encountered at the oasis. Notable, of course, is that Ned made a similar appeal to otherness earlier to defend himself from blame. He too chose a nonpresent other as a scapegoat, that although not explicitly stated, included the lone Jew in the house, the head of the tomato department.

Extract 7, Line 43

43   Sly: well that's merchandise. now when Angelo? let me ask you a question. you know. when Angelo? does he mer? uh. does he display the mer? I mean like you say when lift. a ba. a box. I mean. aren't you allowed to look?

Once Ned leaves Sly reorients the conversation back in time, asking the question he had attempted earlier (L32) in reference to Sal's comparison of practice at the house in relation to another house (L27). The difficulty Sly exhibits in asking his question certainly suggests that the events that have taken place have been unsettling for him. Sly, Vin, and Sal continue to talk for another 2 minutes with Sly, during this time, quite focused on undoing Sal's image of the house as a den of thieves. This line of talk ends as Sal directly implicates Ned, a now nonpresent other, as the source of the trouble in the house. He is the scapegoat that absolves the house of wrongdoing. Immediately, thereafter the conversation concludes where it began—about spinach. Sal and Vin agree that they will talk on the phone later to discuss spinach. As Sal leaves, so do Vin and Sly, each in different directions and each voicing farewells as if nothing out of the ordinary has happened. The social oasis has closed for a moment with only a desk that is nothing more than a roughly 4-foot square, waist-high cabinet with a flat laminated countertop in view.

CONCLUSION

The oasis is a place of constant activity. Buyers come to place their orders, workers come to receive their orders of what to do next, and visitors stop by. Among these frequenters of the oasis, many not only aim to do business but to also hang out or just take a break for a moment in the company of others. The oasis is rarely empty. Even when Vin and Sly are not around, people are observed standing at the desk scanning the action on the floor. During the more active sales hours multiple buyers await placing their orders. Others come by periodically to check if Vin is available and, if not, proceed to other departments to take care of other needs. The positioning of the oasis in the center of the house, where the north–south path merges with the main east–west passage, means that people continuously flow by.

This constant human presence makes events at the oasis quite public. Even individuals who did not plan to do so, may stop at the oasis as they see an acquaintance or overhear something that matters to them. The physical placement of, and action at the oasis foster this serendipity of social engagement. Serendipity is also characteristic of the natural history of talk at the oasis. Someone overhears something being said and joins in, and not uncommonly that something is quite secondary to the talk at hand. Workers interrupt ongoing conversations to update the salesmen. These updates, as is true of other unexpected interjections, provide new material that those already present may now comment on or elaborate. And indeed interlopers who had not planned to hang out, but only offer news may suddenly find themselves furthering their stay as such comment and elaboration unfolds. This type of climate is not unlike life in a house that is a home, although certainly on a smaller scale. It is no doubt not unlike activities across many social settings where people engage with one another with explicit intentions and reasons only to discover that they have entered into something quite other.

This it seems to me is what communication is most fundamentally like in the world. It is interactive and emergent. What emerges is of course not just limited to more talk. Issues of identity emerge continuously in such a climate as the examples presented in this chapter suggest. Individuals find themselves affirmed, attended to, attracted, challenged, liked, ridiculed, slandered, and stereotyped without expecting that this would happen to them. And they find themselves to be the otherness that gives members a sense of who they are.

Such is the climate within which individuals are developmentally constituted and constituted in the moment—when viewed from the perspective of communication. It is in such a climate that social meaning and individual experience is constituted. It is a climate of roughness and contradictions, with identities themselves maybe best thought of as contradictions. It is a climate that quite frankly cannot be grasped in the way we have attempted to grasp it, through either system-based or psychologically based accounts.

It is a climate that communication scholarship can have much to say about if it can manage to not reduce the roughness and contradictions to merely bad practices, to sexism and anti-Semitism as the examples in this chapter most easily suggest. This type of characterization is ironically the only space typically given to such practices in our textbooks, and then but a few pages at best. Treated as such, the members of the market are reduced to prejudiced individuals. Their identities are thereby fixed, accounted for through traits that describe such individuals (as other). Quite possibly they are just individuals who struggle to define who they are in climates of contradiction that through time and across cultures give rise to a surprising sameness of injustice in resolving questions of "Who am I?"

REFERENCES

Altmann, J. (1974). Observational study of behavior: Sampling methods. *Behaviour, 49,* 227-265.

Barker, R. (1963). *The stream of behavior.* New York: Appleton-Century-Crofts.

Bateson, G., & Mead, M. (1942). *Balinese character: A photographic analysis.* New York: New York Academy of Sciences.

Carbaugh, D. (1994). Personhood, positioning, and cultural pragmatics: American dignity in cross-cultural perspective. In S.A. Deetz (Ed.), *Communication yearbook 17* (pp. 159-186). Thousand Oaks, CA: Sage.

Carbaugh, D. (1996). *Situating selves: The communication of social identities in American scenes.* Albany: State University of New York Press.

Duncan, S., & Fiske, D. (1977). *Face-to-face interaction: Research, methods, and theory.* Hillsdale, NJ: Erlbaum.

Duncan, S., Fiske, D., Denny, R., Kanki, B., & Mokros, H.B. (1985). *Interaction structure and strategy.* Cambridge: Cambridge University Press.

Frazier, J.G.F. (1949). *The golden bough: A study in magic and religion.* New York: MacMillan.

Goffman, E. (1953). The interaction order. In E. Goffman, *Communication conduct in an island community.* Unpublished doctoral dissertation, University of Chicago.

Goffman, E. (1963). The self and its other. In E. Goffman, *Stigma* (pp. 126-139). Englewood Cliffs, NJ: Prentice-Hall.

Goffman, E. (1967). *Interaction ritual: Essays on face-to-face behavior.* Garden City, NY: Anchor.

Goffman, E. (1983). The interaction order. *American Sociological Review, 48,* 1-17.

Handelman, D. (1975). Expressive interaction and social structure: Play and emergent game forms in an Israeli social setting. In A. Kendon, R.M. Harris, & M.R. Key (Eds.), *Organization of behavior in face-to-face interaction* (pp. 389-414). The Hague: Mouton.

Kristeva, J. (1981). Women's time. *Signs, 7,* 13-35.

Laing, R.D. (1969). *Self and others.* London: Penguin.

Mead, G.H. (1934). *Mind, self and society.* Chicago: University of Chicago Press.

Mokros, H.B. (1984). *Patterns of persistence and change in the sequencing of nonverbal actions.* Unpublished doctoral dissertation, University of Chicago.

Mokros, H.B. (1990a, June). *The centrality of concerns with equality in definitions of the situation at a traditional work setting.* Paper presented at the annual meeting of the International Communication Association, Dublin, Ireland.

Mokros, H.B. (1990b, November). *Women in a man's world of work: What the structure of female-male interaction reveals about the social definition of the situation.* Paper presented at the annual meeting of the Speech Communication Association, Chicago, IL.

Mokros, H.B. (1993, November). *The everyday residue of correcting others.* Paper presented at the annual meeting of the Speech Communication Association, Miami, FL.

Philipsen, G. (1975). Speaking "like a man" in Teamsterville: Cultural patterns of role enactment in an urban neighborhood. *Quarterly Journal of Speech, 61,* 13-22.

Philipsen, G. (1976). Places for speaking in Teamsterville. *Quarterly Journal of Speech, 62,* 15-25.

Ricoeur, P. (1992). *Oneself as another.* Chicago: University of Chicago Press.

Roy, D.F. (1959/1960). "Banana time": Job satisfaction and informal interaction. *Human Organization, 18,* 158-168.

Scheff, T.J. (1990). *Microsociology: Discourse, emotion and social structure.* Chicago: University of Chicago Press.

Stern, D.N. (1985). *The interpersonal world of the infant: A view from psychoanalysis and developmental psychology.* New York: Basic Books.

Epilogue

Christine A. Lemesianou

Identity is an ever-relevant aspect of all human activity constituted as products and byproducts in communicative moments. Simply put, the contributing authors to this volume take communication seriously. They don't see communication as the assumed backdrop against which identity theorizing is built, and they don't treat communication as a mundane and predictable activity that, if carefully engineered or managed makes "good" communication practices and outcomes possible. Rather, communication is not only a site of study but also an explanatory approach to questions of identity across a wide array of pertinent everyday contexts.

This is what contributors consistently expressed in response to Mokros' invitation that they construct an epilogue to *Identity Matters* based on an online discussion once everyone had the opportunity to read the entire manuscript. Specifically, he posed the following question: "Reflecting on your own work and that of other contributors, how do you view the claim I make in the introduction that the chapters in this book represent efforts developed within a coherent program of research?" My colleagues suggested that I elaborate on the tenor of this discussion. In the following pages I consider three things: first, the complexity introduced by the constitutive approach; second, going beyond dualisms; and third, the relevance of communication-based explanations to a broader range of enduring issues.

In chapter 1, Mokros identified multiple themes that guided the research of "identity matters" reported in this book, particularly its ontological and epistemological assumptions. These assumptions range from the recognition of language as a powerful system of organizing and reorganizing experience; an orientation to human "being" as relational; methodological systematicity and flexibility capable of revealing the organizational complexity of communicative moments; and the pursuit and privileging of communicational explanations of identity. These assumptions are foundational to a constitutive perspective or view. Theorizing and empirical study of human experience within this perspective might be said to involve matters of "scaling." In terms of theory, this scaling is achieved by considering the intricate interdependency of discursive, interactive, and reflexive levels of abstraction implicated in the shape of observable communication moments. In terms of methodology, scaling is achieved through the interplay of the macro-structural examination of communication and the grounded micro-analytical interpretive work that follows. The further juxtaposition of detailed quantitative and qualitative maps of an empirical landscape are particularly useful in examining the same site from multiple angles.

Coan (chap. 8) explicates the theoretical complexity well when she elaborates on the challenges presented by the constitutive approach to understanding the professional practices of one dance instructor that inadvertently enact discursive understandings of gender. She writes:

Like many of the other chapter authors I am indebted to *The Natural History of the Interview* collaboration, particularly Bateson for his explication of interpersonal determinism, and to the foundational works of Goffman, Duncan, Stern, Scheff, and Retzinger. A constitutive approach has allowed me to talk about the complexity of interaction and to address the unconscious, relational, and embodied undercurrents I sensed as communicative when I began my studies but could not explore without this theoretical framework. . . . One of the most difficult aspects of my examination of the instructor's moves in the dance lesson was to let go of my need to portray him positively, that is to have all of his moments of interaction be problem free lest he seem problematic. It was, after all, the assessment of these lessons as positive learning experiences and of this instructor as a good teacher that led me to select this site for an exploration of the concept of guided becoming. The student–instructor interactions discussed in my chapter illustrate types of problems that arise when an individual's expectations are not met as made apparent when the instructor interrupts the flow of practice. I have come to see these moments as highlighting not the failures of this instructor to maintain "best practices," that is, his slipping away from some idealized script. Instead, I see them as highlighting inevitable moments in interaction wherein the expectations and obligations to relational understanding, to an individual's orientations to the social bond are aroused. These are moments that may be handled with creativity and poise or that may be allowed to spiral into doubt, shame and anger. A constitutive approach does not prescribe best practices because it recognizes the relational and largely unconscious or invisible complexity of the communicative moment. It thus allows for a broad range of possibilities in negotiating this complexity including, but not limited to, avoidance and repair.

Similarly, Maynard (chap. 3) highlights the theoretical complexity of the constitutive perspective when he explores the juxtaposition of competing discursive realms, those of a host and foreign culture, in Japanese advertising and the various ways identity matters very much in today's globalized world. He writes:

My work is premised on Babba's (1995) assumption that one can only see culture at moments of negotiation, not at the boundaries of the Culture's own self-sufficiency and shows that those moments of negotiation, the give and take of foreign and domestic icons and text within the discursive, and globalized, space of the advertisement are controlled by the host culture, Japan. The two nostalgic representations of a bygone America, as seen through the lens of an appreciative Japanese cultural industry (i.e., the advertising professionals who specify the Other on behalf of the nation's collective imagination), portray an Other constructed exclusively, and, as it turns out, fondly, for Japanese consumption.

In my own chapter (chap. 2), I also emphasize the interconnections between the discursive and interactive realms for Generation X-ers. Specifically, my work focuses primarily on the constitutivity of discourses as diachronic realizations of competing forces and interests, discourses that do not remain on an abstract level of linguistic expression but have very pragmatic "identity" implications for those they speak for, to, and about.

The methodological orientation of the constitutive perspective with its emphasis on the scrutiny of both the macro- and micro-levels of communicative activity, is a common thread binding all chapters. This scaling between macro- and micro-levels is an issue that has forced most authors to re-examine basic assumptions about the research process, its scope, and the reach of potential "findings." This is clearly articulated in Thomas' (chap. 4) reflections where she elaborates on the usefulness of the ethnographic methods and natural history techniques employed in multiple chapters:

> Especially important in this regard are explanations of approach, method, and interpretation that will allow readers of this book to "think" along with the researcher as they enter each observational setting and engage each data set. I am thinking here specifically of the explanation of coding techniques, the relation of structure and content in analysis and interpretation, the consideration of counterfactuals, and the explanation and use of descriptive statistics. All other values aside, as a demonstration and explanation of a research methodology, the chapters in this book make a valuable contribution to discussion of contemporary social science research.

Along similar lines, Cockett (chap. 9) raises the thorny issue of interpretive relativism in social science research and the grounding that the scaled examination of empirical data provides:

> First, I am interested in everyone's approach to the very broad concern of the social sciences—that social science is an interpretive science. Although we did not all address this issue overtly, I see a common thread of methodological argument that runs through all of our work. In thinking about my own work, I remember struggling to make interpretive claims about the interactive moments that I was paying close attention to. However, by examining the constitutivity of communication systematically, I was able to place a stake in the ground and decide that from that spot I would make my interpretive claims. Thus, the research (and here I reflect on all of our work) is not only grounded in actual lived moments and texts but also brings into relief systems of meaning that organize these moments and texts.

Coan also reflects that she grappled with the demands of scaling the empirical world in attempts to preserve the complexity with which human interaction presents itself:

> I see the constitutive approach addressed in *Identity Matters* as a coherent program of research because it offers a consistent perspective of humans as relational beings and a consistent method of exploration that relies on careful examination of contextualized, everyday interactions. What I find in each of the chapters, including my own, is an effort to address a "simple" question that leads not to a simple answer, but to an empirical exploration and then interpretive analysis that explodes the myth of simple explanations and accounts and offers

appreciation for the complex and contradictory qualities of communication practices. I know from experience with my own data, that one dancing lesson carefully transcribed and examined led me to new discoveries as to the complexity of each moment of interaction and its sequential implication for all moments before and after. After 2 years of applying traditional ethnographic approaches I thought I "understood" something about the dance lessons. In capturing one lesson on videotape and examining that 74-minute period carefully on a second-by-second basis I was forced to confront the sweeping assumptions I had made and surrender to the complexity of micromoments and re-examine my achieved understanding in their light. I gained tremendous appreciation for transcription as a tool for exploration and reflection as it lays bare invisible structure. Indeed, I found in these moments the intricate and fleeting elements of face-work that reveal the ever-present tension of the social bond and relational being I sought to understand.

Beyond the theoretical and methodological complexity discussed above, another commonality that provides a backdrop across research efforts reported is the initial affirmation and eventual negation of dualisms that have so dominated Western philosophy and scientific inquiry. Some of the dualisms that highlight the ongoing relevance of issues of identity in each chapter are the following:

Local–Global (Lemesianou)
Sameness–Otherness (Maynard)
Form–Function (Thomas)
Process–Outcome (Rumsey)
Work–Play (Karetnick)
Structure–Agency (Chelton)
Theory–Practice (Coan)
Control–Collaboration (Cockett)
Harmony–Discord (Mokros)

A constitutive approach to communication offers the ability to examine these dualisms in an empirically grounded and reflexive manner that moves away from essentializing practices and provides a deepened appreciation for the complexity of human social, cultural, professional, and recreational practices. Their import for identity claims is evident throughout *Identity Matters* as humans struggle to make sense of their world through interaction and reflection, through creative invention and habitual reproduction of senses of being in the world. The relationality of the self, that is constantly at issue, is highlighted in the routine interactions and practices explored in a number of contexts in *Identity Matters* such as Japanese maga-zines in chapter 3, "Culture Matters"; the MUD in chapter 6, "Play Matters"; or the committee meeting in chapter 9, "Authority Matters." In our work, however, these dualisms are not viewed as separate and independent realms that define humans and their practices but as situated dialectical tensions that come to be constituted in communicational practices. As Karetnick (chap. 6) points out reflecting on the inescapable tensions in her research:

> Seeing *Identity Matters* as a coherent body of research despite the great differences in our subject matter becomes much simpler for me when viewed in terms of the dualism. It points out the fact that if identity is relational, negotiated, and situationally contingent, then multiple realities become not only possible but inevitable. I know that my own chapter did not start out as a discussion of work versus play, but that the research became much more coherent and inter-esting once Harty suggested that I explore those issues in relation to one another. The dualism also resonates with me because of my own research . . . the split between RL ("real life") and the MUD so inherent in much MUD research. My research shows that the split is not quite as pronounced as many in the field have suggested. Appeal to the duality of work and play provided a productive approach to probe participants' motivations for both their identity work and their identity play.

The ongoing struggle of communication research guided by a con-stitutive approach is the profound temptation to provide solutions or answers to situated occasions wherein enduring questions of identity arise. Rumsey (chap. 5) indicates this when she writes:

> One of the things I find interesting is that in each of the contexts we looked at, establishing a personal identity was not an overt goal of the individuals interacting and yet within the interactions studied issues of identity are clearly evident throughout. In my own study, I was not initially concerned with questions of identity; rather I was looking at how people used online sites to make sense of their health issues. What very quickly emerged in that examination was evidence of quite distinct approaches to the site and to interaction with others in the site that show how identity, as revealed through behavioral patterns, was an inescapable aspect of overt goals relat-ed to quite specific health issues.

The tendency to explain what a person meant to say or did say is quite pro-found and profoundly challenged when one is forced to "stick to the data" and their representation through analysis. Although the chapters presented in *Identity Matters* diverge considerably in terms of the empirical contexts and data examined and analytical approaches employed, they preserve a committed theoretical accountability to the empirical realm.

The chapters in this book represent examples of an increasingly notable constitutive turn in communication scholarship. Their engagement with communication directly as the site and process whereby identity may be productively explored and explained opens up the possibility that other timeless human concerns, such as mind and society, may be explored and explained communicationally. This is what Mokros would seem to have in mind when he writes in chapter 1: "Suppose instead for a moment that identity is an historically enduring practical problem relevant within all moments of lived experience and that communication might offer explanations why this is so." This broader calling appears to be the core of the research program offered in *Identity Matters*.

About the Contributors

Mary K. Chelton (Rutgers, 1997) is associate professor in the Graduate School of Library and Information Studies, Queens College, City University of New York, and previously on the faculty of the School of Library and Information Management at Emporia State University. Her research focuses on how categoric identity is produced though communicative activity in library contexts, particularly in terms of "age."

Hester Coan (Rutgers, 1998) is assistant professor in the Department of English, Communication and Philosophy at Fairleigh Dickinson University. Prior to this, she was a National Research Council associate and senior research associate with the San Jose State University Foundation working at NASA Ames Research Center, Moffett Field, California. Her research is concerned with an empirical approach to the study of interaction and a constitutive understanding of personhood and practices.

Lynn Cockett (Rutgers, 2000) is assistant professor in the Department of Communication at Juniata College. Before joining the faculty at Juniata College, she was assistant professor and director of undergraduate studies in the Department of Communication at Rutgers University. Her research interests include the development of appropriate methods for examining interaction, and she studies interaction as the site of professional practice and identity/personhood issues.

Rachel Karetnick (Rutgers, 2000) is visiting professor in the Department of Communication at Monmouth University. Her research is concerned with issues of identity in mediated environments.

Christine Lemesianou (Rutgers, 1999) is assistant professor and director of the basic course in the Department of Communication at Montclair State University. Her research examines the production of discourse and how it subsequently serves as a resource for the construction and expression of identity and a sense of place.

Michael Maynard (Rutgers, 2001) is associate professor in the Department of Journalism, Public Relations and Advertising at Temple University. Prior to joining the Temple faculty, he was vice president, senior writer at Backer Spielvogel Bates Advertising, in New York City; copy supervisor at Leo Burnett Advertising in Chicago; and copywriter at Ketchum, Japan. His research is concerned with a textual analysis approach to the study of image production in mass media, particularly, cultural and gender images in Japanese advertisements.

Hartmut Mokros (Chicago, 1984) is director of the Master's Program in Communication and Information Studies and associate professor in the School of Communication, Information and Library Studies at Rutgers University where he is the immediate past chair (1996/2000) of the Department of Communication. Prior to joining the Rutgers faculty, he was assistant professor of psychiatry and psychology at Rush Medical College, and director of research in child psychiatry at Rush-Presbyterian-St. Luke's Medical Center. His current research is concerned with work and its relationship to one's sense of self and orientation to society.

Esther Rumsey (Rutgers, 2001) is assistant professor in the Department of Communication at Sul Ross State University. Her research is concerned with personal meanings of illness experience.

Nancy Thomas (Rutgers, 1996) is associate professor in the School of Library and Information Management at Emporia State University. Her research interests concern the social and interactive nature of information seeking and issues related to information access, equity, and diversity.

Author Index

A

Adelman, M.B., 112, *135, 136*
Albrecht, T.L., 112, *135*
Altman, 78, *105*
Altmann, J., 242, *266*
American Cancer Society, 116, *135*
Aneshensel, C.S., 116, *135*
Austin, J.L., 10, *25*

B

Babrow, A.S., 117, *136*
Bakhtin, M.M., 13, *25,* 32, *51*
Barber, B.R., 55, *74*
Barker, R., 242, *266*
Barthes, R., 57, *74*
Bateson, G., 4, 14, 16, *25,* 38, *51,*
  187, 189, 190, 191, *214,* 242, *266*
Baudrillard, J., 59, *74*
Baym, N.K., 140, *162*
Beavin, J., 80, *108,* 174, *186*
Becker, F.D., 77, *105*
Becker, K., 6, *25*
Belkin, N., 80, *105*
Bellah, R.N., 50, *51*
Ben-Ari, E., 57, *74*

Benedict, R., 9, *25*
Bennett, S.E., 37, *51*
Berger, P.L., 8, *25,* 33, *51,* 58, *74,* 81,
  82, *105*
Best, S., 82, *105*
Blumer, H., 38, *51,* 81, *106,* 168, *185*
Bolan, R.S., 78, 88, *106*
Bolger, N., 112, *135*
Bordo, S., 188, *214*
Bounds, W., 61, *74*
Bourdieu, P., 9, 10, *25,* 34, *51,* 188,
  190, *214*
Brashers, D.E., 116, 127, *135*
Brown, P., 118, *135*
Bruckman, A., 140, 141, 156, 158,
  162, *162*
Buber, M., 118, 121, 122, 123, *135*
Budd, R., 78, *106*
Burlson, B.R., 112, *135*
Burton, J., 61, *74*
Butler, J., 10, *26,* 188, *214*

C

Caplan, G., 112, *135*
Carbaugh, D., 4, *26,* 243, 249, *266*

279

Subject Index